REBEL

A Memoir

by

Anita Bohbot

REBEL

A Memoir

by

Anita Bohbot

Cover art by Michel Bohbot

This book is dedicated to my parents Elias and Ryta Benaim, to my sister Glad Levy, and to my husband Charlie, who was my partner in so many adventures

Acknowledgements

This book would not have been possible without the tireless efforts of my son Dominic Bohbot, who put in hundreds and hundreds of hours as the principal editor, layout person, and chief (constructive) critic. Many thanks go to my other son Michel Bohbot, who created the cover art, helped sort through hundreds of photographs and formatted the chosen ones for printing, and was a great source of encouragement. I also want to thank Kamila Kaminska Palarczyk and Robert Castellano, who provided invaluable help in proofing and correcting large portions of the manuscript. Finally, many thanks to Anna Kaminska, and to all my friends who encouraged and supported me throughout the long process of bringing this book to completion.

Prologue

Journey to the unknown

The big thermometer outside the main entrance of the Gare de Lyon read eighteen below. Paris appeared frozen on that December early evening, the snow drowning street lamps and moving cars in patterns of diffuse light. My little sister Gladys and I ran through the doors of the cavernous train station, laden with gifts and flowers. Our parents were ahead of us, keeping a fast pace. We were late, and the platform gates were at the other end of the hall's vast expanse. Maman turned around several times motioning us to hurry. Glad – she hated the name Gladys, and everyone called her Glad – dragged behind me, looking pitiful, crying "Wait for me, wait for me."

At last we reached the turnstile. A tall controller in a spotless black uniform studded with silver buttons took our tickets. He caressed Glad's little head and smiled.

"Do not cry little girl, you will not miss your train."

Clouds of steam billowed out of the huge locomotive like a great black animal breathing heavily. Porters were taking our luggage – dozens of suitcases and two large trunks – far down the platform,. It was cold on the open platform, and whirling snow was hitting us from all sides. Glad and I huddled together, looking at each other in desperation, refusing to say goodbye to the city we had grown to love so much. Father, wrapped in a big gray overcoat, was trying to be jolly, joking with the good friends that had accompanied them to the station, but his eyes betrayed him - his heart was not there. Maman, tall and beautiful in her silver fox coat, was crying. So were her two best friends.

There was so much sadness in this departure. A passerby would probably be fooled by our appearance, thinking, 'rich people, must be traveling to the Riviera'. Especially looking at us, two little girls dressed like princesses in expensive light blue wool coats trimmed in white fur with matching hats, our little feet warm in black patent leather shoes, half hidden by immaculate white leggings. Two wealthy kids holding golden boxes and bouquets in gloved little hands.

How wrong could you be, passerby.

The year was 1933, the heart of the depression, and we were leaving Paris in semi-poverty. Father had lost everything in the Wall Street crash of 1929, and with the little he had salvaged we had been able to meagerly survive. In the late twenties Father, impressed by his in-laws' great fortune, had invested all his money in their reknowned art and antique business, which consisted mostly of fabulous tapestries and precious antique rugs. Their headquarters at the time was in New York City, with branches in London and Paris. Before the crash, they had invested heavily in Deutsch Marks with a promise of great gain, but instead the stocks went down to nothing. In a few instants the whole family was ruined.

To survive, my grandfather Leopold and his brothers had to sell their priceless tapestries and rare rugs for practically nothing at a Parke and Bernet auction in New York. Father also had to sell paintings he treasured, among them a Corot, a John Sargent, and a Monticelli. The beautiful flat we owned in Auteuil, an elegant Paris district, was also sold for a song. Other kids, I thought, would sleep in our cozy bedroom with its glowing and reassuring fireplace.

A year earlier, Glad and I had been dropped off at an elite boarding school, not far from our home. It was actually our regular school, but until now we had not been boarding there. Our parents explained that they would be traveling and couldn't take us with them. About two months passed without any word from them.

One morning, the school principal summoned me to her office. She was an old and strict lady always dressed in black, turn-of-the-century fashion. Father had not paid the tuition or board for our stay, she said, and he wasn't responding to any communications.

"I have a good heart," the old lady said, "but without payment I cannot keep you here."

Despite that, she let us stay, but she daily threatened to expel us if

Father didn't come forth with the money owed. And our plight wasn't kept secret – everyone in the school knew.

As the months stretched on, I began to feel real fear. What was happening with our parents? Why hadn't they come, or even written? We didn't know if they were alive or dead. I lived in terror of Glad and I being thrown in the streets of Paris, alone. Glad was too young to understand what was happening, but I was already nine years old.

I felt diminished in the eyes of my schoolmates, and to counter their taunts, I tried to surpass them in all the games we played. At the parallel bars I performed daring somersaults and all kinds of contortions to get their admiration. I was also envious of the girls whose parents came every week to visit with arms full of presents. The pressure was intense for a little girl my age. It translated into stomachaches and vomiting spells, plus bad grades, but also I gained a new toughness, a will to survive it all.

Only years later did I learn why my parents had disappeared that dreadful year. To their friends in Paris, they had pretended to be on vacation in the south of France. In reality they had stayed in Paris, hiding in my grandparents' apartment, a luxury dwelling on the Champs Elysée. They had no money to buy food, and starved on bread and coffee for long months. There was no way they could have supported two growing girls, hence the scheme to leave us at the boarding school and trust to the good heart of the principal. I can now imagine the torture they endured, knowing that their children were a few streets away and they could not approach the place. A whole year of searching for work passed before Father was finally hired by an Italian insurance company to represent them in North Africa, Father's birthplace.

I think the principal was as astonished as we were to see Father and Maman arrive at the school one day, with the money for the entire year – an advance from father's new employer. We were in ecstasy to see them, and though at the moment we were just happy, that year of abandonment changed me at a deep level and for the rest of my life. From then on I was tougher, but I also constantly needed to be the center of attention, craving recognition.

Just a week later, here we were on the train platform. What would the future hold? Up to now Glad and I had been protected in a world of riches. It was difficult for us two to imagine a different life. For as long as I could remember we had grown up like princesses. We went to one of the top schools in Paris, the Lycée Molière, and at home Glad and I enjoyed the life of rich kids. Most of our vacations were spent in my grandparents' palaces. The one in Florence was a thirteenth century masterpiece, only rivaled by the one in Nice, an eighteenth century beauty that was originally the palace of the Duke of Savoy. In Paris we had been chauffeured in a long black Rolls Royce, and often on weekends my uncle Salvador, mother's oldest brother, would come to take us out for a ride in his latest Bugatti. This type of life was the only one we knew.

Since our earliest childhood we had had governesses to care for us. They taught us how to read, write, and behave, but as good as they were they could not replace our mother and father. We rarely saw our parents, and ate with them only on rare occasions. They were not there either to help us with our schoolwork. I resented that, feeling abandoned.

In the evenings mother would appear at our bedroom door to say good night in a flurry of silk, jewels and perfume, all dressed up for the opera or some other function. It only lasted instants and she was gone. There was a sort of sadness that stayed with me for the rest of the evening. I was always wondering if she really loved us? This was the unwilling price my sister and I had to pay for having been born into Paris society.

Would we get closer to our parents now that we were poor, now that they were away from the fancy friends and the Paris glitter? The train would take us far away from that life, first to the southern coast of France. Then, in Marseilles, we would board a ship bound for Africa.

Africa! The black continent. I had only a vague idea of where it was from what I had learned at school. Pretending my father was a big game hunter, I boasted in front of my friends the reasons for our sudden departure, falsely showing how excited I was at the prospect of a trip to such a mysterious land. In reality I was afraid of the unknown and psyched myself up by telling lies. On the train I couldn't help thinking of the wheels turning under us, and how in some mysterious way they were connected to our fates. We were rolling away from our previous lives toward new and uncharted experiences.

Marseilles' harbor was swarming with working men. Various languages were spoken here, filling the air with shouts and commands. I had never seen so many ships, from fishing boats to huge cruisers. Maman was worried about our luggage.

"There are so many thieves," she said.

Glad and I looked around imagining the worst and clutched at our little handbags with fierce determination.

At last we boarded a long white ship from the Holland line. I was impressed by the rich wood paneling, the chandeliers and mirrors, and also with the steward's spotless white livery. As we started to move out of the harbor, I felt how deep the sea was and how powerful the tide. The ship had a strange indefinable odor. Was it food, disinfectant, floor polish, or the three together? I did not know, but suddenly my stomach felt queasy.

Later, feeling better, I roamed the various decks. I felt a sense of freedom I had never experienced before. The queasy discomfort was gone. I was drinking the wind, filling my lungs with the invigorating sea breeze. I understood now how exciting it was to travel, especially to cross a sea. My fear of the unknown had magically disappeared. From that day on deck and in the years to come, I would always seek adventure in many different forms.

The same evening the sea became violent as we approached the Golfe du Lion at the very southwest corner of France. The pitching was rough and sudden. Diners were taken by surprise, their meals upset when they had to make a dash outside to the nearest rail. I could see them bending overboard, pale and distressed. Strangely enough I was not affected by the ship's strong rolling, and continued to gorge myself with the delicious food on the table.

Two days later in the early morning the ship's motors stopped. It woke me up. I could hear the sailor's voices outside and the noise the anchor made as it was lowered. Running to the porthole I opened my eyes wide. Here she was, Tangier rising out of the mist, crowned by the morning sun. In no time we were all on deck peering into the indigo water and looking up at a perfectly blue sky. The ship could not anchor in the harbor, as it was too shallow. We had anchored out in the bay. Launches were already loading passengers and their luggage.

For the first time I was hearing the rough sounding Moroccan Arabic being spoken by the men manning the boats. I was fascinated. They wore robes and turbans. It was so exciting, so exotic. As we approached the pier, Tangier appeared all white, as if a jug of milk had been spilt from the highest hill, dripping in trickles and splashes, surrounding gardens and narrow winding streets until it reached the windy beach and the sea.

Father's mood had improved during the trip and now he was beaming. After all, he was coming back home to his beloved Tangier, where he had grown up. For Mother it was different. She had traveled to Tangier only once when she was seventeen years old, and it was there she had met Father at a wedding. That was a strange coincidence, because at the time he was living in Scotland and she was living in Paris. Father had fallen in love with her and did not waste any time in asking for her hand in marriage.

Mother, on the other hand, had no feeling at all for the man she was supposed to marry. She was madly in love with a poor Spanish pianist she had met in Paris. Alas, her parents refused to have anything to do with a penniless artist and she was obliged to comply with her father's wishes. They were married in Nice, a sumptuous affair that took place in the palace the family owned.

There were other ties to Tangier: Grandmother Nejma, Maman's mother, had also been born here. She came from a poor family and had twenty brothers and sisters. I always thought she was telling us kids a tall tale, but found out later it was all true.

So started our new life in an archaic land, where for us kids it was like entering a storybook, a place of wonders and surprises. We stayed a year in this exotic town, then we moved further south to Casablanca, to what became our new home. At the time I could not fathom how these first steps of my voyage to the unknown would play out, or how all the frightening and exciting moments that were to come would change my life forever.

Chapter One: 1939

A Wedding and a War in French Morocco

I still see myself on that terrace in Fez, Morocco. It is funny how little things stay imprinted in your mind for the rest of your life. I was wrapped in a warm chestnut-brown coat, hair flying in the cool September wind, and my life was about to change forever.

At the end the summer of 1939 we – my father, mother and younger sister – had all been invited to a big family wedding in Fez, the ancient capital of Morocco. Father said he could not go. He seemed very preoccupied, and would not explain why. Mother decided she would stay also. That was strange. She liked all the glitter of such parties so much. It was decided that we girls would go alone. I did not ask any questions for fear they could change their minds. I was then sixteen years old, and thought it grand to be traveling alone with my younger sister Glad. At the time she was fourteen and very shy. We would be free, with no parents on our backs to tell us what we should do and what was forbidden. Glad didn't have an opinion on the matter – she always followed my parent's wishes.

We departed Casablanca, where we lived, full of joyous anticipation, and arrived in Fez, that ancient and mysterious city, a week before the wedding. In Morocco, a wedding was an elaborate affair, including several days of festivities before the main ceremony.

Our cousin's house was already full of guests. It was customary for the host to lodge the family at home, as sending relatives to a hotel was considered shameful. The house already looked like a marketplace, with so many people milling around. We were given a small room at the end of a hallway, but with a beautiful view. Through the window we could see the old city, the Medina. It seemed to be nestled in the palm of a hand like a treasure, cupped by mauve mountains.

Glad was tired and wanted to take a nap. I wanted to go out and explore. Opening the window wide, I felt the crisp autumn air. The sky was very blue with small clouds floating by.

"Come on Glad, let's get out of here and get some fresh air," I said. "You'll have plenty of time to sleep later. There's so much confusion in the house, nobody is going to notice we're gone."

Glad was sweet and said OK, but she followed me reluctantly. I was always the boss. I think that at times she was afraid to displease me.

Stepping into the street reminded me that our father had been born here in Fez. This was a place of great beauty, of palaces, lush gardens and ancient history. Weeping willows trailed in the rushing waters of the Sebou river. The waters meandered in and around the walls of the eight hundred year old city.

The Medina was reached through ornate arches and gates. Its narrow streets were roofed in latticed bamboo. It created shafts of light that fell at random in uneven patterns on passers-by. The Medina was divided in sections of universities, guilds, and mosques. We passed through one of the entrance gates, and stepped into another world, another time. Here were coppersmiths hammering brilliant trays in intricate designs. Nearby, the goldsmiths illuminated the street with dazzling jewels of gold and precious stones. Water vendors in multi-colored costumes had an ornate brass cup hanging on a chain with several tiny bells. They went on jingling as they walked about shouting their wares.

"*Ma, el ma.*" 'Water, the water'. I had always wanted to buy some of that water spilling from their leather jug, but I was afraid.

"Typhoid!" Mother always warned. That was enough to frighten anybody. I took Glad further and further into the heart of the Medina.

"Lets go back Anit. "I am afraid," she kept saying.

"Oh leave me alone!" I replied "I know what I'm doing. Just follow me, and stop complaining."

The truth was it was a dangerous place for two girls alone. We could have been kidnapped very easily; young girls had been abducted more than once before. Adrenaline was running high in my veins. To be in a forbidden place was very exhilarating, but getting lost in dark crooked streets under towering Mosques made my heart beat faster. We peeked through heavily sculpted doors. We glanced at pink marble courtyards, enchanted by the sound of rippling fountains. Many generations of students had studied in the renowned universities here. How many times had they looked at those green tiled roofs reflecting the sun in thousands of facets? So much had happened here in this ancient city. Feasts and wars and sometimes pogroms against the local Jews, depending on which Sultan was reigning at the time.

As we went by the tanner's quarter, the foul smell of Moroccan leather being treated assaulted our nostrils. I dragged Glad inside the open tannery. It was suffocating. Half naked men standing in vats of red, green, yellow and violet dyes looked at us with frightening eyes. Funny how they stuffed their noses with sprigs of fresh mint leaves. It was the only thing the poor fellows had to endure the stink of their slave-like jobs. We scrambled out of there in a hurry. Glad was panicking again. I told her to shut up, but for the first time I felt uneasy myself. I could not remember my way out of this place, toward the European part of the city where our cousins lived.

The Medina was a real maze. One could wander for days without ever finding the way out. We started running through dark, narrow streets and arched alleys. At times, we had to stop abruptly and plaster ourselves against humid walls. Cavaliers burst in from nowhere on fierce stallions, galloping as if they were in open country. We discovered a little plaza around a corner. I was thankful to get out of those dark passageways. There, an old blue mosaic fountain spilled its singing waters into the jugs of veiled women. I remembered that fountain. I had been here before with my father. From here, I knew the way out. I was proud of my daring, but very happy to be out of that bewitching but dangerous place.

That day on the terrace there was not a cloud in the sky. We were so totally carefree, just enjoying the moment. Through the years, it would be that very moment that would stay stamped forever in my memory. A feeling of great joy, but also a strange sensation of desolation. Why? I could not explain it.

In the house, mountains of food were being prepared. Cooks had been at work for almost a month. The smell of spiced and honeyed pastries and meats made my mouth water. It was a time of great rejoicing. It would be a regal wedding. Maids were scurrying around in their tinkling ankle bracelets. Errand boys brought down from the mountains wore a single gold earring. They seemed naïve, but they knew how to peep at us girls through

9

keyholes. There were receptions upon receptions given in the house before the actual wedding.

Old rabbis came to read the Ketouba, the Jewish marriage contract, a drag that lasted for hours. The showing of the trousseau was another occasion for a feast. A mother was always very proud to amass a trousseau for her daughter-to-be, which included household objects like embroidered sheets, tea services, and satin and lace underwear. To me it was a little disgusting to see these personal objects touched and criticized by the guests. And oh! the horror of seeing an old bearded lecherous man, lifting one of these lace panties and fantasizing upon it.

Food and drinks were being served at all times during the festivities. Musicians could be heard late into the night. We were having the time of our lives. Our only thoughts were dresses, coiffures, and boys.

Simha, father's first cousin, was the mother of the bride. After marrying her oldest daughter she would still have seven children left to wed. Six girls, and one boy. She was a Berber beauty with high cheekbones and sensuous eyes. Her jet-black hair made a contrast with a pearly white skin, a feature that was highly praised by Moroccan men. Simha, as the majority of women in our country, was the queen mistress of her household. Running everything smoothly, but with an iron fist. She could be as hard on the servants as she was sweet with her husband.

We called him Mr. Danan. He came from an illustrious family. His father was the Chief Rabbi of Fez. He was a very rich man, owning impressive vineyards that yielded a very potent red wine. From his olive groves came tons of unctuous green oil, and he also raised horses, savage Arabian beauties.

Mr. Danan in his tweeds really looked the part of a gentlemen farmer, even to his red face and his big black mustache. On his ample well-fed stomach, a gold chain rested lazily, reflecting wealth and contentment. He was still very much in love with his wife, even after fathering eight children. She knew it, always appearing to him bejeweled and enticing in her superb silk caftans. Like other women of her generation she had been married at thirteen, while he was at least twenty years older.

Finally the wedding day was upon us. The bride was married at home, as was customary in Moroccan Jewish families. She stood under a canopy of white satin tulle and fresh white roses. Around her stood her father, the rabbis and the groom, all forming a tight circle. I saw a tear rolling down her cheek. What were her thoughts at that moment? Was it sentimentality or was it a premonition?

As soon as the glass was broken the party began. Two hundred guests were crowded in the immense Moorish salon. Some were spilling onto the balconies, others sitting tightly on damask velvet couches that went all around the room. Then the doors to the dining room were opened. The crowd of guests rushed in to feast on innumerable delicacies. The food was displayed on lavishly dressed long tables. Some of the women belly-danced, swaying their lush hips to the sound of a Moroccan orchestra.

All the musicians were sitting on the floor at one end of the ballroom. They were dressed in the traditional Jewish costume. On top they wore a black djelaba, a long robe. Underneath could be seen a very white shirt covered by a fancy colored velvet vest. On their heads a black tarboosh, a felt cap that they wore at a jaunty angle on their heads to be more attractive. They looked like a bunch of happy crows. Their music was exhilarating. Drums were beating, violas crying love songs, melodies from lute strings cascading like shining waterfalls.

Ornate mirrors around the room reflected lights, jewels, shimmering caftans, moving heads, dancing hips in a series of moving images. The bride was dancing, cuddling in her new husband's arms. Laughter like fireworks burst from every corner of the room, coloring the party with joy. Some of the guests were already drunk on Mr. Danan's good wine and his homemade Mahia, a potent alcohol made of figs and dates. On the open balconies the moon and some stars had appeared. It was like the Thousand and One Nights. It seemed like it would never end. We would dance forever, eat forever, abandon ourselves to the pleasures of life forever.

Suddenly a disheveled man appeared at the ballroom door, yelling.

"Stop, stop everything."

There was too much noise for him to be heard. Pushing people on the dance floor, he looked like a mad dervish whirling around.

"Stop, I tell you stop!" he shouted again, frantic. "France has declared war on Germany. All lights must be dimmed. There is a curfew as of this moment. All eligible males are to report to the nearest military post."

We were stunned. The silence that followed was like the aftermath of a bomb exploding, scattering all our hopes, all our dreams of happiness.

I felt an icy cold wind sweep the ballroom. The music had stopped abruptly. We looked at each other in disbelief. The disarray was total and tragic. All the beautiful women in their scintillating jewels and fineries now looked like so many clowns in a sad masquerade. Tears were rolling down their painted cheeks. Men gathered in small groups whispering. Some couples left in a hurry, not even saying goodbye.

Glad and I stood dumbfounded in the middle of the room, not really understanding the urgency of the moment. I heard somebody cry. Turning around I saw the bride sobbing. Her new husband was saying goodbye to the family. The young couple would be denied even that first night. Heads were lowered and shoulders hunched as family and friends went downstairs. Each heavy slow step meant, "Will I ever see you again, will we ever enjoy such a beautiful feast again?"

I went down with the guests. Glad was following behind, her little face white with fear. Looking outside, the night had turned pitch black. Big clouds had rolled in, hiding the moon and the stars. The street was empty and dark. A few dead leaves fell in circles to the ground.

Tonight was the end of the merry party our lives had been. It had been shattered like so many pieces of glass. All that was left were the silent shadows filing past the door and disappearing into the void.

Hastily we made plans to return home the next morning, haphazardly stuffing our suitcases. It was not easy to buy bus tickets, as so many people seemed to be traveling somewhere in a hurry. Glad and I slept during the four-hour trek, a heavy sleep full of nightmares. Father was waiting for us at the bus station in Casablanca.

"Darlings, you don't know how happy I am you are back," he exclaimed. Father was trying to be jolly, but his face betrayed his words. He looked tired and worried. Things must be really bad, I thought. He blessed us both right there on the sidewalk. He mumbled his blessings in English first, than he switched to Hebrew and Spanish, and finally he said in French, "Let's hurry up home."

In the parking lot he looked for the attendant to whom he spoke in Arabic. In Morocco It was a common thing to speak several languages, but rarely all at the same time the way he was doing now. We climbed and slumped into the black Citroen.

At home Mother was at the balcony waiting. I saw her disappear and emerge at the door just in time to see us come out of the car. How lovely she was, svelte, elegant and so full of life. I was a little jealous of her, she always attracted all the looks and all the compliments.

"*Oh mes petits poulets, venez que je vous embrasse.*"

"Oh my little chicks, come that I may kiss you."

She hugged and kissed us again and again. Mother had grown up in France and always addressed us in French. I pulled away. It was not to my liking to be smothered with kisses. Glad stayed in her arms like a kitten in search of warmth.

"The news is horrible," Mother said. "I was worried sick about you two." She pulled us aside, and whispered, "Your father didn't want to tell you, but he was very worried about his job with that Italian company. That's why we didn't go. Our little secret, mes cheries."

The four of us went into the house. How strange the rooms looked, dark, unfamiliar. I noticed that all the windowpanes had been covered in dark blue paper, the same one we used to cover our text books.

"There is a curfew, mes cheries," Mother said. "We had to do this in case of air raids."

"It will not be for long. Do not worry," was Father's answer. "This war is going to be over just like that." He snapped his fingers. "You'll see."

I was wondering how close that war would come? I knew that Germany had swallowed Czechoslovakia and invaded Poland, but that was so far away. Even the fighting in France seemed remote to us in North Africa.

Glad and I went back to school in October at the French Lycee de Jeunes-filles. Clans had formed, and there seemed to be a rise in anti-semitism. It had always existed, with flare ups here and there, but now it was flagrant. This year the teachers were nasty and harsh to us Jewish girls. We had to swallow their insults without being able to answer. It made me boil inside. Ancient curses would form on my lips – 'May your luck sink down to the wavelets at the very bottom of the sea' – but were never uttered.

We were immediately accused of stealing, if any object went missing. I had fights with Christian girls who accused me of having crucified Christ, as if I had personally driven the nails into the cross. They tried to beat me up three or four at a time, but I would defend myself so well that they ended up being the defeated. For that, I was often summoned to the principal's office, disheveled, my clothes in shreds. I was always the one punished for something I had not started. The punishments were to the tune of four hours of math on Sundays. If I did not show up, the punishment was doubled. It became impossible to concentrate. I started losing all interest in my studies.

13

There was a sort of gloom enveloping us. Something I could not touch, but felt as an opaque, dark viscous matter into which we were sinking little by little. I went to school with a heavy heart. Everyday I had to confront the enemy. Glad became very quiet and more studious than ever. Some of our best friends, Algerian Jews with French nationality, had been drafted. They suddenly looked foreign, with shaved heads and horrible uniforms. I could not even imagine the horrors of war, in spite of books I had read on the subject. At home the days dragged. Father had lost his lucrative job as an inspector at the Italian company. It was very unsettling for us, but mainly for him, to know that the fascists would dig so far and deep to find and expel their Jewish victims.

Mother had a strange reaction to all this. Instead of showing her fear, she decided to redecorate the entrance hall. Two enormous armchairs covered in a pale almond green wool were made to order. It was really the wrong time said father, but she thought the change would cheer us up. It certainly brightened the dark hall and strangely enough, it did not detract from all the antiques in that room. From then on I spent most of my free time curled up in one of the big green armchairs, reading Daphne Dumaurier's latest books. This warm and cuddly corner became my refuge during the bad war years. Today that green almond color still reminds me of the war.

Father owned a few parcels of land here and there that he was forced to sell. Disposing of them one by one at a loss, to survive, was sad. There were no opportunities to start another business now, it was too dangerous. We were going down a steep decline like in a bad dream, where no matter how much you try, there is no way to reach the top again.

Day and night, regiment upon regiment of soldiers pounded the streets with their heavy boots, on their way to the harbor. There, troop carriers were waiting like huge gray fish hiding in the fog, ready to swallow all that youth and regurgitate them onto the battlefields of France.

The city was full of rough soldiers in ill-fitting heavy wool uniforms, sailors on leave, and troops of Legionnaires coming in from the Sahara. They congregated on the cafe terraces, and it was a concert of whistles and obscenities each time a woman ventured past. Occasionally a group of Spahi officers, an elite corps of the French army in North Africa, would cross town. Riding on superb horses, dressed to the hilt in their exotic Arabian costumes, they dazzled the pedestrians. The streets belonged to the armies.

We could no longer wander around town or go for a stroll in the afternoon. Everything and everywhere spelled war. Sundown brought the strident curfew siren, pouring panic into the population every evening. People had to drop whatever they were doing, and go running home fast lest they were caught by patrols. There were no excuses for being out after hours. One could be dragged to the nearest police precinct and be interrogated for hours. Often these sessions would include cruel beatings. By the end of 1939, we were already feeling the effects of war, deprivation, and oppression. We could not know just how much worse it would get.

Chapter Two: 1940

The war comes home

The news from France was very bad. At the end of May 1940, Dunkirk in the north of France had been the scene of a terrible battle. 200,000 British soldiers from the 1939 expeditionary force, plus 150,000 French troops, had been pushed to the edge of the Channel by the Germans. With the aid of hundreds of small fishing boats and other craft launched from Dover and other ports in Operation Dynamo, most of those brave soldiers had been rescued, but many lives were still lost.

The school year ended unexpectedly early in mid June. For once I was not looking forward to the summer vacation. I had nowhere to go, no money to spend. There were restrictions everywhere, and I was almost cloistered at home. One evening at dusk, I was reading curled up in the big green armchair. Through the open living room window, I was half watching a flame red sun descending slowly into the ocean. The maid was setting the dinner table. I could hear Mother playing Chopin at the piano. There was no sign of Glad, she must have been reading in our bedroom. I heard the heavy entrance door bang violently. Father appeared with a newspaper in his hand, his face was decomposed, his hair mussed.

"Those bastards," he said (meaning the French) "signed an armistice with the Germans! God of Abraham, what is going to become of us?"

It was the twenty second of June 1940. In July worse news reached us. A new French government had been constituted in Vichy France, headed by an old illustrious army man, Marechal Petain. His fame came from World War I, but he was certainly not the right man to free the French nation from the hated invading Germans. On the contrary, he was siding with them. How could such a senile old man be chosen for such an important task?

It would be a tremendous job to push back the German advance. The devils were already cracking the French defenses in the east. These fortifications, called the Ligne Maginot, were supposedly impregnable. Marechal Petain was deliberately betraying his countrymen. His second-in-command was Pierre Laval, a conniving peasant from the Auvergne, a central province of France. Laval was highly anti-semitic, which suited the Germans perfectly. Laval announced new restrictive laws for the Jews in France and in the french colonies. The Masons and other fraternal organizations were outlawed.

We were trapped. At home we started making plans to hide valuables. The paintings were taken down from the walls. We looked at them with tears in our eyes, touching the canvases to say goodbey to landscapes and portraits that had graced our everyday life for so long. Replacing them with engravings of lesser value was a must. It proved difficult to cover the exact areas that had faded behind the original canvases. Then Mother's jewels were put into a strong box. Before the lid came down, we all peered at the marvelous emeralds she had inherited from Grandmother Nejma, her mother. Father had a bag of gold coins to hide, and most important of all his Freemason objects. Those were dangerous items if found in the house.

Every night after dinner, when the maids had gone, father would open the large coat closet in the entrance hall. There he would remove a few coats and jackets to reveal the back wall. This was to be the hiding place for all the treasures we owned. He was trying hard to dislodge enough bricks to create a reasonably big space. We all helped, with Mother on the lookout in case somebody came to close to the front door. Glad and I were very proud to be useful and to be taken into the secrecy of the project. We had been asked to swear not to say a thing to anyone. For me it was going to be hard. I loved telling stories. Our job was to hand dad any tool he needed from a big box on the floor. We also had to sing loudly, to drown the noise our sweating father was making banging at the wall.

It was a good week before the whole thing was finished. It was done, sealed, and concealed, and even the new paint matched, only to discover the next day that father had forgotten to put in his bag of gold coins. A lot of cursing went on that day. He was tapping walls, opening closets. He even looked behind furniture for a possible hideaway. Then inspiration came suddenly. He was going to pry open the window frame in the living room, align his coins inside and replace the whole thing. This time Mother was watching the street from a little tear in the blue paper lining the window. Glad and I resumed our job as tool handlers. Both of us felt very professional, but inside we felt a sort of turbulence, of fear. The secrecy of it all made us girls uneasy. Looking around, it seemed we were living in another house. Everything had been changed, from the papered-over windows to the almost-bare walls, and our mood was grim and somber.

With the fall of France, it became very risky to get information from the Allied side. Nevertheless, our ears were glued to the the B.B.C. in secret late at night on Father's short-wave radio. Ironically, the B.B.C. broadcast always began with the opening notes of Beethoven's Fifth Symphony. The radio was then carefully concealed until the next evening. We lived with anxiety, but also with hope, for that was the only good thing remaining.

On a Sunday morning towards the end of July, we were all having a leisurely, if meager, breakfast. Suddenly we heard a big crash in the direction of the front door. We all got up, very frightened. Father opened the dining room door, Mother, Glad and I huddled behind him. The heavy door had been smashed. Horrified, we stood confronting four men in trench coats. Their faces were concealed under black felt hats. There was one instant of silence as we looked at each other. Then with a deluge of insults, they violently pushed us aside and proceeded to demolish everything in the house. Opening cupboards, throwing china and glasses on the floor. Ripping through wardrobes, wrenching clothes from hangers, banging the walls, turning beds upside down and ripping up the mattresses. What fury! The four of us stood absolutely still, our eyes wide open, our mouths agape, paralyzed with fear.

Who were these men? What blind hatred motivated them? I wanted to beat the hell out of them, to spit on them, to reduce them to cinders, but I could not do a thing. I just stood there like a dumb ox. What could I really have done against such rage, such savagery? They pulled Father into a corner of the room, and shoved him against a wall.

"Where did you hide the stuff?" one man screamed at him.

"What stuff?" he asked.

"You know very well what!"

"I have nothing to hide, you can see that for yourselves."

"Shut up!" the man replied.

They slapped his face and threw him to the floor. Then abruptly they walked to the door and disappeared, leaving chaos and desecration in the house, but also in the very core of our souls. One by one we sat on chairs, stunned. Father dragged himself to the sofa, his mouth was bleeding. For a moment we were turned into weeping stones, silently grieving, while outside birds were singing in the palm trees as they did every day. The sun was splashing gold on the sidewalk where people were walking leisurely, unaware of the tragedy around them.

Why us, why always us? Was it some kind of eternal punishment by the Almighty for having presumed to be the chosen people? I was confused, pained. I had always thought of myself as equal to anybody else, with a head, arms, legs, a heart, a brain and all the rest. What was so different about us? Since my first time in school I had been reminded almost every day that I was a Jew, which for the Christians in Morocco meant something low and dirty, almost untouchable. Little by little I had to build a carapace, scale by scale, to be able to withstand the blows. My heart though, would still stay soft and vulnerable through all the sorrows to come.

After that terrible visitation by the forces of evil, as father called them, the presages were alarming. A week passed, but we could not dismiss a foreboding feeling, a chilling expectation for the near future. What was it going to be? The summons came soon enough. Dad was to present himself to the police headquarters in Casablanca, alone.

Dad came back late that evening accompanied by a policeman wearing a black trench coat. Father was told he had fifteen minutes to get ready. He managed to tell us in a low voice that they were sending him to a prison camp. In particular, one for Moroccan-born citizens that had adopted a second nationality. Father had acquired a British passport when he was a young man living in England, before his wedding. He had always thought that having two nationalities would protect him, but this time it proved to be his undoing. He packed a small suitcase in a few minutes. We were all very silent. Mother was trying hard to keep herself together, but her face was drenched in tears.

We hugged him, Glad hanging by his jacket weeping, and me holding his hand tight in mine, telling him without words how much I loved him. The fellow in the trench coat grabbed him by the sleeve.

"That's enough let's go."

The front door banged shut. We just had the time to run to the balcony to see him being shoved into the back of a truck. It was all over – he was gone.

The next day dragged, empty. Mother stayed closeted in her room as she always did when things went wrong. Glad and I went round and round the house, like two lost souls. The servants arrived early as usual. I could hear them talking in low voices in the kitchen, but they did not ask any questions.

A few days later, we received a postcard from Dad, bearing a Censor's red stamp. Our hearts leapt. Until that moment we didn't even know if he was still alive. Dad wrote that he was imprisoned somewhere near Settat, a dusty small town in the middle of nowhere between Casablanca and Marrakech. Father wrote that we would be allowed to see him once every four months for two hours. Mother sighed heavily when she read the message. What kind of prison was it, in that God-forsaken place? Settat was an area where one could freeze in winter and suffocate from heat in summer. The speculations were endless. Would father have enough to cover himself? What kind of food if any, would he and the other prisoners have? We were powerless to help the father and husband who had done so much for us. We were finding out how indispensable he was, and how much of what he did and who he was that we had always taken for granted.

By now the summer was almost gone. Mother spent her time preparing packages of food and mailing them, in hope they would arrive safely at their destination. Some were for father, but she was also sending parcels to her mother in Nice, France, where she lived. Our grandmother Nejma had been caught by the war. She could have taken the last ship for Casablanca, but she intentionally missed it to attend the grand openng of the Casino de la Jetee. Later in the war, that foolish passion for gambling and her refusal to leave France would bring her a lot of suffering.

Preparing parcels was tricky. Mother had to build false bottoms in the boxes to conceal the items that were forbidden. There were many restrictions on what we could send, so we had to cheat. Glad and I were usually sent to the post office. Mother said there would be less suspicion from the inspectors if two young girls brought the parcels to be mailed. One day Glad and I were both standing in line at the post office, in a long queue of mixed people. Most were French, with a sprinkling of Moroccans, both Moslems and Jews. The line went almost around the block. It was very hot. The street was dusty and still gritty from a recent sandstorm. We were blinded by the reflection of the shiny green tiles on the building walls. Each of us carried two big boxes that we held close to our chest. It looked like we would be there for a while. We were chatting, hoping to have enough time to go rollerskating before dinner. A fellow in a postman uniform was walking up and down the line with a bored, disgusted, and nasty look on his face. He stopped in front of us. We froze.

"You two get out of the line."

"Us?" I asked, pointing to myself and Glad. He grabbed us both by the arms, and dragged us up the steps into the post office. People were staring, but nobody came to our rescue. We held our parcels tight, afraid to drop them. I felt weak and wanted to disappear under the floor. What was the man going to do to us? Panic took a hold of me inside, but I was strong enough not to show it. My body tensed and I stood perfectly still. I did not want to look at Glad, knowing already how she must appear, like a frightened gazelle with eyes and mouth wide open. The postman asked my name. It was like having a deadly snake staring at me. I hesitated for a second, but there was no way out.

"My...my name is Anita Benaim."

"So, you are a Jew! I knew it the moment I saw you both."

He roughly grabbed me by the shoulder, tearing my sleeve. The parcels fell to the floor.

"Open your parcels now! Who is the other girl with you"?

"My little sister, sir."

As I bent down to pick up the parcels, he kicked me to make me fall. I sprawled on the marble ground. Glad was trying to pull me up, crying. Slowly we opened the packages. We were not going fast enough. The man pounced on them and tore them apart with rage. All the forbidden goods spilled in every direction.

We were trembling with fear. The blows came down as fast as the insults. My cheeks were burning. Glad was bleeding from the side of her head. I was viciously kicked in the groin and fell again, almost fainting from the pain. The people in line were still watching. Some turned into stone, but others joined in the insults. A rain of maledictions fell upon us. I did not know where I was anymore. My head was spinning fast, but I couldn't take anymore. I took Glad by the waist and started walking out, but two hands hauled me up from behind. I was thrown into the street like a bag of dirty laundry. Glad landed on top of me screaming.

From that terrible day I understood we were in constant danger. Our life became more and more somber. Mother had stopped playing piano. No more laughter. For lack of money, there were no more servants. Food ration cards were issued. Jews and Moslems were given half the amount that was given to the French colonists. Often the evaporated milk that was distributed to Jewish families was tainted. There were several cases of food poisoning, babies died. If we complained, the French authorities canceled our cards. Bread became unpalatable, containing pieces of plaster to make up the weight. To top it all off, it also contained a variety of dangerous oddities like nails and dead bugs. From eating the bread we developed scabies on our hands and between our fingers. I kept scratching all day long and felt like a mangy dog. I was ashamed to show my hands, trying to hide them behind my back or in my pockets. But the worst was yet to come.

September was closing fast. We went shopping for school items. It was difficult to find new books. Glad and I spent most of our time in second hand bookstores climbing up and down ladders. Finally we had everything ready. Books and exercise books were neatly covered in dark blue paper, the same sort that was covering all our windows. Our pen boxes had been shined and filled with new pencils, pens and brushes.

The first day of school was the third of October. We were eager for a change of pace, anticipating perhaps a better school year because the subjects would be more challenging. Early morning that October day, we gulped our imitation café-au-lait, the real coffee replaced by ill tasting roasted barley. It was important be on time for that first day of school. We felt good in our brand new uniforms, consisting of a beige cotton pleated pinafore with long sleeves. Walking fast, we crossed town and the Parc Lyautey, a vast expense of green lawns, flowering bushes, and tall palm trees. We were running now, our feet noisily crushing leaves on the ground. I was sweating. Glad was dragging behind as usual.

At last we were in front of the school's massive bronze door. A crowd of girls were gossiping with high-pitched voices, sounding like an aviary of colorful birds. The big door opened. There was a sudden silence. At the entrance stood a woman, the assistant principal. We all feared that old spinster and kept quiet. She was calling out and checking off names on her register as the girls went in. When our turn came, she looked at us for a second with a cold stare.

"Your names."

"Anit and Glad Benaim."

I tried to smile while she went down her list. She stopped reading and with her crooked lips said,

"You and your sister cannot come in. Jews are now barred from this school."

My jaw fell. I tried very hard to suppress tears that were coming down my face in spite of my efforts. Glad came into my arms for protection. We were shaken. Other Jewish girls were treated in the same manner. It was pitiful to see the bunch of us being ridiculed by the rest of the students. We lifted our heads proud, turned around rigidly and walked away in the bright morning sun.

Little did we know how much this blow would affect our entire lives. At the moment we were stunned. Later we spent days in a kind of stupor, not knowing where to turn, what to read, what to study. Mother was more practical, and sought out an older friend of ours to tutor us in math and literature. It was definitely not the same as going to school. I tried my best, but was constantly distracted by all the little things happening in a household. A cat meowing, The swaying of the big palm tree in the courtyard, my mother talking to a neighbor. I just could not concentrate.

My thoughts drifted toward father with anguish. We had not received any news from him since that postcard after his arrest. We went to the police headquarters. There we inquired about the possibility of visiting him sooner. They answered that the four months had not yet elapsed, and there was nothing they could do. We had to wait until the end of October and receive a written permission to go. Glad immersed herself in books. She became very silent and looked as sad as I had ever seen her.

Every night we still listened to the BBC on the clandestine radio, And what we heard was frightening. Germans were raining bombs on England since the sixth of September, destroying the land and the people. The toll was heavy, and there was no stopping, but the British people showed a toughness that gave us courage. In East Africa, Italy had invaded Somalia, Sudan and Kenya. What was in store for us? What next?

We could not go out of the house without being followed. Two men in trench coats seemed to be glued to the corner of our street day and night. The moment we stepped out, we could feel them at our backs. It was frightening. We never knew what their intentions were, or if we were going to make it home that day.

To make things worse, food was getting scarcer by the day. At home we were starting to feel the pangs of hunger. Rations were so small that we had to split a can of sardines in three portions, and that had to last for the whole week. Mother became very inventive in the kitchen. Fortunately our ration of eggs was not too small, Morocco being one of the big exporters of this commodity. With a few sweet potatoes, two eggs, plus a little sugar and a sliver of a piece of chocolate, she prepared a wonderful dessert. It tasted so good to our deprived palates that it tasted like an expensive cake. She really outdid herself for us, working often into the night to mend our socks and our clothes – items that could no longer be found in stores.

It was so lonely for a woman her age. The last day in September, we had meagerly feasted her thirty-six birthday. Such a young and beautiful woman with her husband gone must have been so hard for her. These kinds of thoughts never entered our minds then. For Glad and I Mother was just a mother with no other function. One day, while I was foraging in her room, looking for God knows what, I discovered a bottle of cognac hidden under her bed. When I asked her why, she answered.

"Cherie, it is very cold at night in that big bed and anyway, I just sip a tiny bit to help me fall asleep."

Glad and I giggled. In secret we made fun of her. Silly us, we could not at the time understand her distress.

The waiting to see our father was almost unbearable. We had no news whatsoever since that first postcard. Were the authorities going to honor their promise? His forced silence weighed heavily on our everyday life. We could very well imagine how he felt, his sorrow to be unable to answer our daily letters. Was he even getting our mail? Our minds were filled with nightmarish thoughts. The weather did not help our situation. Casablanca in late autumn was cold and humid. The nights were blanketed with a heavy sea mist. We had no more wood for the stove. At night in our beds we shivered, listening to the mournful foghorn.

November had arrived with furious rains and gale force winds. It was difficult to walk the streets without being drenched to the bone. Our shoes had holes. We had to stuff them with newspaper. Our clothes were mended and not warm enough. We had outgrown our old coats, so we used them on top of our beds for warmth instead of on our backs. Days went by almost without food. Our constant thoughts were how to fill our stomachs. Fortunately we had books, and they were, in a way, our only real

24

nourishment. Everyday we anxiously waited for the mail, hoping for another letter from father. When it came one morning, I burst into Mother's room brandishing the envelope.

"Maman! A letter from dad, open it fast!"

Music was in my ears. I jumped all around the house dragging Glad after me. Mother was crying from joy.

"We are going to Settat at last!" she said.

Father wrote that we would receive the official notice any day now. We were to meet him in the center of town, on the market plaza. The exact date would be revealed in the letter from the authorities.

A real whirlpool of frenzy took over the three of us. We had to look our best. I needed a haircut. Maman was fishing in our closets to find the best clothes we owned for the occasion. Glad tried to fit into one of her old pairs of patent leather shoes that had no holes, but they were too small. The house looked upside down, with so many old dresses, shoes, ribbons, thrown all over the place. Feverishly we filled boxes with all the food we could find. Wrapping the parcels in old newspapers, and cursing when the string snapped. It was so wonderful, we were going to see Dad!

We left early in the morning. The sky was still dark outside. Streets were silent and empty, making it feel even more like an adventure. Even the two guys who spied on us everyday were not at their post. We felt like robbers escaping. We walked to the station as fast as we could without actually running, and got there just in time to climb into an old jalopy of a bus. The seats were filled with smelly peasants returning home. Traveling was an ordeal during the war. Buses were running on ersatz fuel called gazogene. The fumes came out of an exhaust built on the roof of the cabin, but somehow filtered inside. We were all enveloped in a black stinking smoke.

I could not believe the cold when we stepped off the bus in Settat. We were much too early for our appointment, and Glad and I were ravenously hungry. After inquiring here and there, we were told that a market was open a few streets away. To our great surprise, there was still food to be had in Settat. The stalls were full of stuff we had not seen for a long time, even if by normal standards it was meager. Thin strips of meat were hanging on large hooks, inviting flies to a feast. Peasants were arranging some vegetables on wooden tables. We walked for a little while. our eyes wide open in anticipation. Maman found an old woman selling sewing threads. I discovered, of all things, a French charcuterie opposite the Arab market.

Mother gave us a little money, and I bought a slab of pork fatback. It looked so appetizing. Solid food, shiny with salt crystals. It was not kosher, but what the hell – we were starving! A little further, I purchased two hot whole wheat breads from a vendor and a few green onions from another guy. What a meal we had, Glad and I. Sinking our teeth into the fatback would have seemed disgusting in normal times, but here we were devouring the stuff eagerly, licking our lips in delight. It was still a little early for our appointment, but already we were pacing the plaza, sharing the space with a bunch of dromedaries being loaded with merchandise.

At eleven o'clock sharp, coming out of a side street, we saw him. Dad! The three of us were running and waving. Next thing we were in his arms kissing, hugging, crying. The emotion of that moment was so strong that when I think of it today I sob uncontrollably. Suddenly the sky grew brighter, the breeze became softer, I was floating on pink clouds. For an instant I thought everything would be all right, until I lifted my head and saw an armed soldier standing just behind father. Why was he there, I asked?

"Remember, I am a prisoner, my darling," my father explained. "As a matter of fact, I'm one of the lucky ones. Because I am the oldest in camp, I am allowed to get out of the prison when you come to visit. But as you can see I am accompanied!"

Dad made a slight gesture which said, it can't be helped. I felt frightened to have a soldier follow us in this manner. The passers-by turned around to look at us. I just stuck out my tongue at them. Too bad I could not do more. I whispered curses at them. As we walked around I heard little cries coming from dad's coat pocket. What could it be? Smiling, father produced a tiny dog out of his pocket. He was barely four weeks old and looked so fragile. He was so funny with one black ear and the other all white.

"His name is Jock," Dad said. "He is going to be my everyday companion. Jock was given to me by Pastor Green, a British fellow and a friend of mine in the prison."

It would be good for dad to have something so soft, so gentle to care for, making him forget the lonesome days and troubled nights. Maman was hanging on his arm, her head leaning on his shoulder. Glad and I were hanging on his coat. He was telling us that the prisoners had to work in the compound gardens everyday from dawn to sundown. I remarked how much weight he had lost. He told us that the food was minimal but edible. With a smile he said,

"Beans a la Ritz everyday, my loves, and at night we even have guests! Beautiful enormous rats. They crawl all over us, not to mention the roaches and all the rest. But as you can see, I am holding up well." He patted his chest. "Have patience all of you, I am sure it's not going to be for long."

We knew very well father was not telling the truth. It probably was much worse than that. He had lost a lot of weight. Mother was trying to put on a good face, but I could see how shaken she was. Dad took us through narrow, dirty streets to a small park. There, the branches of bare trees twisted into the gray sky. We tried to sit on the ground, but it was half frozen. Our shoes were all wet. We were cold. The guard was constantly looking at his watch, just to make us nervous. Time was passing too fast. Maman was clinging to dad's shoulder. She looked so distraught. I refused to be sad, there was so little time. What could I do to brighten the day, to make us warm, to erase the gloom that was hanging on our heads? The idea came in a flash.

"Dad, can we go to that restaurant I saw on the Plaza, the one that says Hotel Restaurant. It looks inexpensive."

"What a wonderful idea darling," he replied. We were all hungry again by this time.

Father turned around to speak to the guard. I saw him nodding. It was the only restaurant in town and the only hotel. No luxury there. The place was in bad need of repair and the owner, a Frenchman, looked as decrepit as the building. We all sat at a round table covered in a red and white checkerboard tablecloth. It had holes in it. We pulled our chairs together to be closer to each other. A young Moroccan waiter in a dirty apron came to take the orders. Meanwhile, the owner was looking at us with suspicion, because of the armed guard at the entrance door. There was only one dish on the menu that day, cervelle au beurre noir, sauteed brains in blackened butter. It was a delicacy for us, as we had not seen a piece of meat for so long, let alone butter. The platter arrived with a bottle of cheap red wine. I could not believe the size of that brain, it filled the whole platter to the very edge. We all looked at it with sudden disgust. What could it be?

"Camel brain," said the waiter. "Very tasty!" Almost closing our eyes, we tasted a piece, hesitantly at first, but then we plunged into the dish with relish. It was delicious. No camel would ever know how wonderful his brains could be. The mood was jolly after a glass of wine and a hot meal. It was almost like being home, and all together again.

27

A short dream though, that had only lasted moments. The guard gave us a sign. It was time to go. Our hearts sank, the joy vanished from our faces. We had to say goodbye. Father was brief as he kissed us all. 'No tears', he said, and he was gone. We saw him round the corner with his guard, and disappear into one of Settat's dreary streets. The three of us stood hunched together, not believing it was over. Another four long months would pass without father. Nobody spoke a word. Silently, we left in the late afternoon with heavy thoughts, and our hearts tight with emotion.

Returning home, we restarted our daily routine. Study every morning. Mother was on us at all times, to see that our homework was done. Our teacher, Rene, who came three times a week to tutor us, was captivated by Glad. Later on, he would fall in love with her. He would also become the head of our group of friends. I did not take him very seriously, because I thought he was too young to teach. He must have been around twenty.

The afternoons were a little more fun. Sometimes I would ride my old black bicycle to the Municipal pool. I swam furiously. When I returned home, before the curfew, I was so tired, that I did not care what I ate. I just wanted to slump in my bed and disappear under the covers, to forget that stupid war and the trail of tragedies it created.

Other days I would meet my friends. They were more or less in the same predicament we were. Often we decided to go hunting for empty bottles, to sell them, even though that was illegal. The difficulty was to lug all these bottles without being noticed. We discovered alleyways and back streets to get to a local grocer who would buy them from us on the sly. This little money would pay for an occasional movie, or a trinket if we could find it. What a pleasure it was to feel money in my hand.

Stella Benzaquen was my most trusted friend in these adventures. She was a statuesque girl with long jet-black hair, falling past her shoulders, about a year older than me. She had pale green eyes and a sensuous body. Even with all that beauty, she was always miserable. Often she had fits of depression because of her impoverished, impossibly shrewish mother. Her ugly, dimwitted brother Henry fell madly in love with me, begging me for kisses. I would have rather died than kiss that guy.

The days passed. We were entrenched in our miseries. It became normal to be hungry and cold, to have mended, ragged clothes, to devise all kinds of schemes to make a little money. It also tightened our bonds with our friends. We suffered together.

Chapter Three: 1941

Despair and Determination

January was upon us, 1941. As usual we listened to the B.B.C every night to hear the news of that day. The local radio was pro-German and directed by the Nazi controlled French Vichy government. Hearing what they broadcast made us sick. On the other hand, British radio was giving us some real news, both good and bad. The good news was that British troops were taking back Somalia. They had also reinstated Haïle Sélassie, the Emperor of Ethiopia, on his throne. The Free French were also on the move. Starting from Lake Chad in Africa, they were joining General De Gaulle's forces. They took Koofra, a group of oases in the Libyan desert, under the command of General Leclerc.

We understood that this African war was mainly fought to maintain British supremacy in the Mediterranean. They were masters of that sea from Gibraltar in southern Spain to Alexandria in Egypt, and were fighting like the devil to keep it. The bad news this January was that Mussolini was asking Hitler for help to regain his lost African territories. Hitler was preparing his Russian campaign. Nevertheless, he sent General Rommel and the Afrika corps to Libya. No, the war would not be over soon, as father had predicted. As a matter of fact it was getting worse by the day.

About that time something new appeared on the market in Casablanca. Mother came back one day with a bag of what she called Japanese mushrooms. Where had she gotten them? She did not say. It seemed these dried-up, unappetizing brown things were a cure-all. They had to be soaked in water for several days before they were ready to be consumed. We were supposed to drink the water. It smelled and looked like rot. Maman had put the concoction on the fireplace mantel in a huge antique Chinese bowl. She started drinking a small glass a day and asked us to do the same. Reluctantly we put our lips to it and tasted. It really tasted better than it looked or smelled. So we drank of the potion not knowing what to expect. We suddenly felt great. We were happier than before, laughing, dancing around the house. It was wonderful. We were not even hungry anymore. Alas, the supply did not last very long. Mother had told her friends about it, and the friends had told their friends. Every one in the know was mushrooming. For a time we almost forgot there was a war. I never found out what these mushrooms contained. It will stay a mystery that brightened a few months of that year of sadness, hunger, and fear.

We were without news from father. Our next visiting time would be sometime in March. Already we were getting impatient and sadly wondering what his fate was at the moment. At home, we had less and less of everyday items like soap, toothpaste, cigarettes, and lots of little things that we all had taken for granted before the war. Mother was not a big smoker, but she enjoyed a good cigarette, especially to compensate for the bad meals. One of our everyday chores was to pick up butts in the street. I hated to do it, I felt diminished, but she was good to us. It was normal to do something nice for her in return. Late afternoons, we would sit together at the dining room table with all the cigarette butts Glad and I had collected that day. A nasty burnt smell pervaded the room as we were cutting both ends of the ugly little things. Once we had discarded the paper, the tobacco that was left was intact. In another big Chinese bowl it went to keep company with the Japanese mushrooms on the mantelpiece. I called them war ornaments.

In February a strange animal appeared in Casablanca - the black marketer. One by one they came to our door, two or three times a week. They mostly were young Moroccan Moslems with a keen sense of opportunity, and absolutely no remorse for what they were doing. If one was caught selling, or one was caught buying from black marketers, the authorities would send the culprits to a little village in the Sahara desert called Bou-Dnib. There they could rot for a long, long time.

Few of them were caught though. Some of the black marketers even became rich. After the war, they bought cattle or land, or both. We anticipated their coming, knowing they carried meat, butter, sugar, sometimes chocolate. Often we could not buy, it was too expensive, but we would make them open their packages to smell the wonderful forgotten aromas.

Just when we had gotten a bit of good news – we were given permission to go and see Father for our March visit – more bad news came. The newspaper headlines said, 'Hitler to invade Russia.' My God. Europe was crumbling to pieces. Hitler was swallowing the whole world with a vengeance. We started hearing about the concentration camps through our faithful B.B.C. It was horrifying, but we were very far from knowing the whole truth.

The newspapers headlines said Rommel and the Afrika corps had taken back the cities lost in Libya, except Tobruk. We were asking ourselves if America was ever going to come to the rescue. They knew very well what was going on. When would President Roosevelt act?

I just learned to put all the bad news in a little corner of my brain. It was not forgotten, but it was not bothering me everyday anymore. Besides, we were going to see Dad once more. This alone filled us with joy. This time, all our friends decided to come along for the trip to Settat. They had a genuine affection for Father, to whom they would confide their little miseries, knowing that he would listen and try to help. It would be a great surprise for him to see all this youth coming to cheer him, when we all stepped out of the bus.

Lison, our beautiful, coquettish and sometimes fickle friend stepped down from the bus first, with a bright smile and a flourish - a would-be actress. Then came Rene our teacher friend, who was holding Glad's hand. We all knew they had become an item. We were all hanging around father trying to hug him, Stella sumptuous as ever, Dede and his brother Robert who were on leave from the army. Lagging behind came Stella's brother, whom I could not get rid of. After all the embraces, father took us to the same park we had gone to the first time. It was different now, the trees were greening and the ground was covered with soft grass and hundreds of yellow and white flowers. The mood was happy, what with all the chatting and laughter. Nobody among us wanted to let father know how much he had changed in these few months. His hair had thinned and grayed. His face was emaciated and full of deep new lines, from lack of sleep, hunger, and forced labor. It was hard to look at Mother pretending to be jolly, when we all knew that she was ready to crack, seeing him in such a state. My friends all chipped in, and insisted to invite Father for a good lunch. We ended up in that same restaurant we had gone to before. Dad told us that Jock the little dog had died of malnutrition, even though he had given it some of his own food to survive.

"I miss Jock terribly," he said. "That little dog was such a companion. I am left with only Pastor Green as a friend. He is a nice chap and we help each other."

We ate a lunch of 'roasted rabbits' – we knew for certain it had actually been roasted cats, but we were so hungry that we were happy to pretend otherwise. Father lead Mother, Glad and I away from our friends for a moment, to tell us that he was being transferred to a maximum security army fort. He did not know where, when, or why. It was very alarming, because he was not sure we would get his letters. We felt like crying, but we tried to cheer him up. Then we departed with a stone in our hearts, not knowing if we would ever see him again. This time our friends were the ones to console us all the way back to Casablanca. They forced us to sing with them, saying that Dad would not like to see us with such long and sad faces.

Back home, on Sundays, all our group of friends would get together. If the weather was good, like now in spring, we usually took our bikes for long rides along the seashore. Finding new or used tires was impossible. We all had numerous rubber patches of every conceivable color on them. It was a challenge to keep our bicycles running. At the end of the morning, after several sweaty miles, we would pile our bikes on the beach, strip to our bathing suits and run into the cold Atlantic waves.

Often, we chose a forest of Mimosa trees just across the road from the beach to stop for a meager picnic. It consisted of that awful bread and whatever we could find to put in it. The reward was to lie down on the soft emerald green grass, and to peek at the intense blue sky through masses of bright yellow flowers hanging from the branches. There we could forget the war, forget that Germany was invading Russia and forget the trail of miseries the world was enduring. We filled our nostrils with the intense perfume pervading the woods. This was our secret place of peace. The wind was salty and brought us the roar of nearby waves. It lulled us into a tranquil afternoon sleep.

Things got worse for us that summer, and July 1941 would be remembered with horror for a very long time. The German command in Casablanca poisoned the wells in the Jewish neighborhoods with typhoid. Jews were dying by the dozen. The younger generation was the most affected. We lost a lot of our friends that fateful summer. Week after week, we went to funerals, as one friend after another disappeared. There was no end to our sadness and our fear of being the next victim.

There was absolutely no news from Father. We had no idea where he was. Nothing also from our grandmother in France. Mother was crying very often and there was nothing Glad or I could do to console her. She had always been very sentimental, but now she looked like a shy flower folding her petals and slowly withering. Glad was not doing well either. She was so thin she was frightening to look at. To kid her, I would call her 'black olive on a string bean'. Black olive for her straight black hair.

As for myself, I had lost a lot of weight also. I could see the bones of my hips protruding when I undressed. Still we had to go on. The voice of Winston Churchill late in the night, coming out of the concealed radio under the covers of my bed, gave me the courage of a lion. He represented the father figure we needed. Many things were happening in rapid succession between the United States and Japan. Americans were tightening their economic policies toward the Japanese. In October in Japan General Tojo became all-powerful. He decided on the quick conquest of the rest of Asia, while America was still unprepared.

After a long dusty summer without one piece of good news, we were once more experiencing the cold of fall and winter. Mother had cut the lining of the heavy curtains in the living room, to sew one good dress for each of us girls. The color was strange, a faded blue-green that had once been a beautiful teal hue. Nevertheless, we were proud as peacocks wearing the dresses. None of our friends were as lucky as we were. Our mother was a genius of invention and skills. Naturally we only realized this fact much later.

What we heard on the eighth of December was blood-curdling. The American fleet in Pearl Harbor had been destroyed by Japanese kamikazes the day before. It was a real disaster – only three carriers were left to the US navy. America immediately declared war on Japan, Germany, and Italy. To us that declaration was like a victory. We had an immense admiration for Americans. They were, in our eyes, the knights in shining armor coming to the rescue.

Chapter Four: 1942

A Narrow Escape

It was a long hard winter, cold and humid. We had to ration on wood
for the stove and for our hot bath, which we reduced to once a week. The
other days it was cold water only. Now that it was winter, there was no
more riding up the coast, but we still met our friends on Sunday afternoons.
Dancing was one of the few things we could still do, each week we met at a
different house. Only Stella's mother never invited anybody. It was difficult
if not impossible to find new records. We had to enjoy the ones we had, and
played them again and again. Dancing on Blue Moon and Caravan, and the
Cuban tune Babalou. We finally got bored of the music and of each other.

It was Rene who had the initial idea to start an amateur theater
company. All of us were well-read in the French classics. At school we had
had to learn sixteen verses a day, whether it was poetry or classical plays
from Racine, Corneille and Moliere. At the end of each school year most of
us had acted in a production. We all thought the project exciting. Finally
our lives would be meaningful in some way. Finding plays was a challenge,
but the new group was persistent.

After weeks of rummaging dusty second-hand bookstores, we came
up with a few plays. Some Comedia Del Arte, some light French comedies
like Courteline, and some American plays as well. The Israelite Alliance
in Casablanca had a large theater. They let us use it for rehearsals and
production, on condition that we would put on plays for their charitable
organization. This was perfect. We started working right away. Each of us
had an assignment besides acting. I was to design the costumes and assist

my cousin Chewing with the sets. His real name was Salomon, but he was constantly with a piece of gum in his mouth, hence the nickname, which stuck for the rest of his life. My sister Glad and Lison, our very pretty friend, were the make-up girls. I have to admit that a lot of the beauty stuff was disappearing from our mother's meager supplies. I am sure she knew about our little larcenies, but closed her eyes and said nothing. Rehearsals went on every day under our director, Rene. It was really very serious.

Our plays were great successes. The performances were always packed. It gave people a way to forget their sorrows, at least for a little while. It also captivated us completely, and left little time to grieve on the fact that Americans in the Pacific were losing island after island. That early spring of 1942 was also the time where the Axis powers were at their apogee.

Naval battles were still raging in the Atlantic, but starting in May 1942, America started to slowly make progress in the Pacific. In June, the American victory at Midway marked the turning point of that terrible war. Now more than ever we were glued to our radios.

That summer I met Roland at a friend's house. He was a young man of medium height, built like an athlete, strong as an ox, but his eyes were soft and honey-colored. He fell in love with me at first sight and I decided to let myself be loved. For me it was more desire than anything else. I was at an age where my body was craving for something new. His arms encircling my tiny waist made me gasp. I loved it. His kisses were tender but insistent, and I did not resist for very long.

As the weeks passed, he introduced me to his parents and later to his room, when his parents were out of the house. It was difficult for me to go out without telling Mother where I was going. I learned the art of lying, but 1 sensed that she knew something. I would tiptoe into her room to look for a piece of jewelry or to douse myself in perfume to be more desirable. What I did not know was how sensuous I looked to men. I really did not need any artifices to lure them. In Roland's room we would pretend to make love in strange little ways, but never the real thing. I was afraid to go any further.

He was going crazy with desire. He told me often that my green eyes were pools of fire, my round hips drove him to madness, and my auburn hair touching his body made him crazy. All this was new to me, I became self-assured, turning fast from a girl into a woman and savoring every minute of it.

Had my father been home, I could never have gotten away with it. I would have had to marry Roland first. Still, I would have given anything to have Dad around.

While we were sweating through the sweltering month of August, more good news came to us through the sound waves. Another victory for the Americans at Guadalcanal, and that was not all. A letter came from the authorities telling us that father was being moved to a fort near Fez. We had permission to go and visit him near the end of October. That is all the letter said, but that was enough. We had not seen or heard from our father in a year and a half. Mother, Glad and I sobbed in each other's arms. We still had about a month to go before that wonderful day, where we could hug him and embrace him. The three of us got busy mending clothes, and searching for ingredients to make palatable cookies and whatever we could concoct to bring him.

In the beginning of October, some strange writing appeared on the street walls all over Casablanca and in other cities in Morocco. Everybody was intrigued by the words 15th NOVEMBER in capital letters. What did this mean? There were so many speculations as to what it could be. A date, nothing more? Was it good news or bad news, nobody knew. To me it spelled trouble and more.

The day we left for Fez was the twenty-second of October. Our hearts were swelling with joy. In a few hours we would be in father's arms. Before we took the train in the early afternoon, our faithful B.B.C had given us some very good news. General Montgomery and his British troops were beating Rommel and the Afrika corps near El Alamein in Libya. I forgot completely about the writing on the walls. We were to meet Father in the city itself. He had obtained permission to see us at his cousin Simha's house. While we were climbing the steps four by four, leaving Mother behind, I could not help remembering the last time I had been here for the wedding. The stairs still had echoes of that fateful day.

Father was there waiting at the entrance door, so completely changed that I gasped. His hair had turned completely white. He was as skinny as a scarecrow, his old clothes floating around him. Mother closed her eyes for an instant, to hold to this new image. Then it was an explosion of cries, laughter, and embraces all at once. Dad was here, here with us. We still could not believe it. This time he had two guards around him, but they looked a little more human than the previous one in Settat.

Simha had gone out of her way to create a decent dinner. Mr Danan came up with three bottles of his best wine. We were all talking together. We had so much to say. Glad was describing her new passion for classical dance. I talked about the success of our new theater company. Maman, not so talkative, looked at dad with so much love and longing.

That night Father had to return to the fort. We were blessed to see him once more the next day for two wonderful hours. Then it was goodbye again – until when we did not know. The way things were going with the allies gave us hope. Soon Father would be back with us for good.

After father left, Simha begged us to stay a few more days in Fez. We accepted her offer with gratitude, knowing that we would be better fed in her house than in ours. The next morning I was strolling the main avenue in Fez' European part of town. Benjamin, my cousin was walking by my side. Suddenly, I said,

"Stop. Listen."

Near us was a group of the French Vichy militia. They were talking loud, discussing something about the fifteenth of November. We stopped, pretending to look at the Seville orange trees growing on the sidewalk. We listened to their conversation.

"Yeah, this will be a great day. Imagine, no more dirty Jews. A clean sweep," one of them said.

"You mean the fifteenth of November?" another asked.

"That's right. We are starting by killing the old farts first and immediately after, all the younger males, Hallelujah."

Benjamin and I stood glued to the spot, unable to move. Our feet were made of lead. Blood curdled in our veins. From the deepest place within me, I summoned all the strength I had left.

"Run! Run as fast as you can," I yelled. "They are going to kill our fathers."

Out of breath, we reached the house and found Mr. Danan. When he heard what we told him, he stood up slowly, his face red with anger.

"So that's what they are going to do? Well, let me tell you kids, we are not going to let them!" He banged heavily on the table.

"Tonight, I'll have some of my fieldhands rescue your father. I am powerful enough to pull it off, Anit. I'll hide him where the bastards will never find him! Then I am going to alert all our people. After that, I shall disappear with my son."

He put his hand on my shoulder and Benjamin's.

"Not a word to your mothers, or to your brothers and sisters. This is a matter of life and death."

Imagine me with such a heavy secret to bear. As we were traveling back to Casablanca, I was mentally imagining the rescue. I could not stay put on my train seat. Mother said I was probably coming down with something. She put her palm to my forehead to see if I had any fever. If only she knew!

After this, days had no end for me at home. Roland could not understand what was going on with me. Even while rehearsing the latest play our group was preparing for the new year, I was jumpy and nervous.

Then, on the very early morning of November 8th, 1942 our whole world changed. It was still night outside. I woke up suddenly hearing a loud rumbling. It seemed to come from everywhere. I ran to the window and what I saw filled me with awe. Hundreds of planes filled the slowly lightening morning sky and thousands of pieces of paper were floating down to the streets in eddies. I yelled at the top of my lungs,

"Maman, Glad, come and see what's happening!"

The three of us tumbled toward the balcony and grabbed as many pieces of the flying papers as we could. The planes made a tremendous noise that made the whole building tremble. The three of us were shaking with emotion. As we read the words on the flyers, we could not believe our own eyes. The Americans were landing in Casablanca! Here they were. Our princes in shining armor that we had prayed for for so long had finally arrived.

Chapter Five: 1942

The Americans

We read and reread the flyer, unable to believe it. When the planes had gone, Maman, Glad, and I sat down, stunned. Was it really true, were the Americans landing in Morocco, in our town of Casablanca? Or was it a hoax? No, it was really true. We could already hear the cannons belching fire. The glass in the windows trembled and we trembled with it. A frightening roar filled the air.

"We have to gather our things," Mother said. "Go down to a shelter, the way the flyer says. Come on, hurry, girls! There's no time left."

"But Maman," I said, "if we go to that shelter I am going to miss all the fighting."

I was so excited – it was all too wonderful. The minute Mother left the living room with Glad in tow, I started jumping up on the couch, down to the floor, up again, down again. I could not stop. I felt possessed, like a mad goat. The blasting sirens outside made me jump higher. I started yelling or singing, I didn't know anymore. Maman's voice sobered me up.

"I have everything, lets go. We will have to go outside and cross the street to Mrs. Bessis' basement. Your aunt and your cousins will meet us there. But we have to hurry! No one is to be on the streets."

It was a bright cool morning, with a piercing blue sky. A few stragglers were running to take cover. The noise was appalling. Windows were exploding, sending glass flying through the air. We covered our heads with our arms and dashed across the street. My aunt and uncle were already there with all their kids, Jimol the oldest daughter, Rachel, Semtob, Lycie,

Chewing, and Soly, the youngest. They were all huddled together, waiting for the elevator to take them down to the safety of the basement shelter. My cousin Chewing stayed clear from his brothers and sisters. The minute I saw him, I gave him a sign to join me behind the others.

"Listen" I said, "I want to see the fight. You want to join me? We can slip out. Everyone's facing the other way. Are you game?"

"Anit, you're totally crazy!" Chewing said. "We could get killed."

He was four years older than me, but I certainly had more courage.

"I'm going now." I said. "We're wasting time."

As I was inching back up to the entrance, I saw him from the corner of one eye. He was moving back too, he was coming. I was relieved. It was a good thing to have a companion for such an adventure. We raced across the street and climbed the three stories to the roof terrace, four steps at a time, almost without breathing. We were panting hard as I opened the door.

A giant clamor greeted us as we stepped out on the terrace. We looked toward the harbor, and stood frozen by the sight. The horizon was lined with warships as far as the eye could see.

The shelling was relentless. The American cruisers were firing on the Jean Bart, the largest and newest French carrier anchored in the harbor. In turn the huge ship was firing its guns on the American fleet. We were mesmerized by the power of the cannons, the smell, the smoke. The whole town was shaking from the barrage. Planes circled over the carrier, dropping bombs that exploded in gouts of flame.

Pieces of shrapnel and glass were flying everywhere, criss-crossing above and around us. We suddenly realized the danger we were in. We ran to take cover, but there was no cover to be found. Finally we ducked under the short vents that dotted the terrace. It was frightening, but still we did not leave. We felt part of that big battle. Our hearts were beating in unison with the warships' cannon. Our heroes had to win. The wind was strong, swirling. Huge pieces of metal were blown in all directions, I screamed.

"Chewing, Chewing! Something cut my arm. I'm bleeding."

He could not hear me, the noise was so intense. I crawled on the tiles toward him, inching my way on my left hip and my left arm. He was crouching under the balcony ledge. I grabbed him.

"Look at all that blood, what am I going to do?"

"OK, lets not panic. You must have a laundry room up here, maybe we'll find a rag or something."

The battle was getting worse. As we peeked above the ledge, we saw the carrier Jean Bart explode with a titanic roar, vomiting its entrails into the blackened sky. Chewing and I were terrified, our bodies shaking uncontrollably. The building shook for several seconds as if it were made of cardboard. We huddled together, thinking this was the end. We were going to die. Then for a few moments there was a deadly silence. It did not last long. The cannons were belching their fire again. We inched our heads up just above the ledge, to witness the horror of this gigantic battle.

The line of cruisers was firing non-stop. The burst of blinding white lights at the end of each cannon, and the enormous white crown of smoke it produced left us dumbfounded.

I had totally forgotten about my arm, but now it started to hurt. We crawled across the terrace to the laundry room. Inside the room, we scurried around like two rats looking for food. The place smelled of boiled soap and bleach. Inside the big granite washbasin, we found what we were looking for, an old half-wet cotton dress. Chewing tore some uneven strips to make a ragged bandage for my arm. I felt like a hero.

During all the time we were up there, in that other world, we never thought for an instant that our parents might be frantically looking for us. We had no idea how long we had been up on the terrace. I figured it was past six in the evening from the position of the sun.

Both of us felt exhausted. We could barely stand. Slowly we came down the three flights of stairs, our heads full of what had been the most extraordinary day in our lives. What our eyes had seen, our ears had heard, and our minds had registered would never be forgotten as long as we lived.

Downstairs we sat on the last marble step. My head felt heavy, pounding. Chewing was half deafened. He kept banging at his ears to make his hearing come back. We stayed there for a long while, pondering the meaning of the terrible battle we had witnessed. How many of those brave Americans had already died? How about civilians? It was too much for me. I was really very, very tired and just wanted to sleep.

We went back to the shelter across the street. When we reached the elevator, we realized how hungry and thirsty we were. I had no idea what I looked like. My tattered dress was covered with bloodstains, my arm was bandaged, my legs blackened. I could imagine the reception I would get when I reached the basement.

We braced ourselves for the blows to come, and went down. Uncle Joseph, Mother, and behind her aunt Mazaltob fell on us like a band of hyenas, ready to tear us apart. There was no end to the yelling. On the other hand the younger cousins cheered us. To them we were heroes. We had dared to be under fire. They all sat in a round to hear the fantastic story we had to tell, though it did not last very long. In a matter of minutes both of us were sound asleep.

The day after, Chewing and I snuck out again against our parent's wishes. Up there on the terrace, there was more of the same. The Casablanca harbor batteries did not stop firing their guns for one minute. Fortunately the carrier Jean Bart was totally out of commission.

Other battery guns were situated a little further out, near the lighthouse in El Hank. They were pounding the American fleet. We were all very anxious without news. In the harbor, American cruisers were blasting at some French ships that were trying to escape under cover of smoke screens.

Coming from the north, we could also hear the sound of big guns. So far, there was no sign of American soldiers on the ground. Where could they be? From the terrace ledge, I could scan the whole street. It was totally deserted and strewn with debris. The cannons pounded constantly. Fire and explosions followed, and billows of black smoke surrounded us. When was this madness going to stop?

That evening, when Chewing and I came back to the basement we were beaten without mercy by my uncle Joseph for sneaking out again. I yelled like a pig being slaughtered.

Chewing looked pitiful in his mother's arms. He was my aunt's favorite boy. She always defended him against his father's rages and severity. As for me, my father being absent gave my uncle the 'right' to punish me. I hated him. I decided I would do as I pleased, no matter the cost.

Two days under fire and it was far from being over. Today was the tenth of November. Not a drop of rain, almost no clouds. God was with us, even though the French – most of them – were resisting with savage obstinacy. On the one hand were the pro-German pro-Vichy officers. On the other, there were those French officers that were for the allies. These were waiting for a propitious moment to surrender to the Americans.

The French radio was silent, after having blathered for forty eight hours, advising citizens to resist the invaders. As for us civilians, we were still in the dark, not knowing how things were really going to turn out.

The third day, I escaped the basement prison while everybody was napping rolled in heavy blankets. Up there on the terrace I could see some action to the north, but it was too far away. I stayed for a while, but could not stand the thunderous sound anymore. My ears were ringing and my eyes were smarting from so much debris in the air. I could barely keep them open. I was also extremely fatigued, both mentally and physically. Chewing appeared at the terrace door.

"Anything sign of the Americans, Anit?"

"No, not really."

As I was saying these words, I finally saw what looked like black ants or pinheads, thousands of them running in our direction. In the first instant I did not realize what it could be. But suddenly my eyes opened wide and I screamed.

"The Americans, Chewing, Chewing, they are coming, they are coming, the Americans!"

I started jumping again, all my fatigue gone. I was torn between a desire to see the soldiers come closer and the urge to run back to the basement, to give everyone the good news.

We entered the basement triumphant. I yelled.

"They are here, they are here, Maman!"

We fell into each other's arms, Glad, Mother and I, all pressed together shedding tears of joy and relief. Uncle Joseph was praying aloud, thanking God for his grace, while all my cousins were nestled around their ample mother, laughing and crying at the same time.

At three o'clock the next morning I woke up. The noises had stopped. The cannons were silent. Throwing my covers off, I ran to Mother's corner. She was sound asleep, her beautiful black hair fanning out on her pillow.

"Maman! Maman, wake up. The battle is over."

I shook her awake. I was screaming so loud that Aunt Mazaltob and everybody else in the basement woke up with a start.

"What's going on?!"

They all were up in minutes and ready to go, but where? It was much too early, it was still night. We could not go back to bed with all the excitement.

Mother boiled some water, to make some erzatz coffee with no sugar and no milk, accompanied with a rancid and hard piece of bread. Never mind the awful food, our thoughts were elsewhere.

At seven o'clock we could not stand it in that basement anymore. We all clambered up to the street. There, we saw a pale blue morning emerging behind the buildings. We felt a strong rumbling that made the whole street tremble. It seemed to come from the north of town. I broke off from the group and started running like mad. I could hear Mother yelling.

"Anit come back, let's stay together."

But I could not stop, like a horse at a gallop I was devouring the street. I was going as fast as the wind. The tremor had intensified to a level where I had to block my ears, pressing hard with my hands. At the end of our street, Rue Guynemer, I turned left on Boulevard de Marseilles, and stopped dead in my tracks.

Like huge monsters, the tanks appeared, rank upon rank, the rising sun bathing them in light. Awesome in their heavy carapace, they rolled forward with the noise of clanking chain mail. My mouth was wide open, my eyes not believing what they were seeing. A crowd had gathered and was getting bigger by the minute. Shouts of welcome were springing from everywhere.

"Hourra! Vive les Americains."

Some French people were silent and stood still, with a nasty look on their faces. They did not have to tell us who they were, it was written all over them, Vichy!

I was trying desperately to get closer to the tanks and the soldiers perched in glory on top of their machines. The crowd was dense. Not a single inch of the street or the sidewalks could be seen anymore. But still we were all running in sync with the huge iron monsters, as a river flows, passing over and around any obstacle we encountered, heading toward the center of town. Exhilaration was in the air, arms were raised, hands waving, fingers showing the V sign for victory.

Finally after much effort, I elbowed my way close to one of the tanks. Lifting my arms waving, I said in English.

"God bless you, God bless you."

I found myself being hoisted way up in the air by two powerful arms. All of a sudden I was sitting on one of the big monsters, surrounded by friendly faces, my American heroes. They looked awfully tired, mud and dirt caked on their pants, boots and faces. But they looked happy, a hard-won victory. Soon my hands were filled with chocolate bars, chewing gum, cigarettes. So much that it was spilling over. I had not seen such bounty for many years. It seemed impossible to own such treasures.

I wondered about Mother and all the others. Too bad they couldn't see me up there riding with my heroes. Pretty soon they had to set me down from my perch. It wasn't permitted for a civilian to ride a military vehicle. Other youngsters were doing the same, coming down from the tanks loaded with goodies. Our American friends were also throwing cigarettes and chocolates to the delighted crowd. It took more than an hour to get to the center of town, the Place de France. There the French high command for Casablanca was assembled. A few civilian dignitaries were standing in front of stiff troops, perfectly lined up. I had decided to climb to the Hotel Excelcior terrace to witness the big ceremony, the formal surrender of Casablanca to the Americans.

Getting off the street was a challenge. I entered the Excelsior. In the lobby, Mr. Levy, the owner, and his three sons, Jacques, David, and Albert, were greeting guests at the door. The Levy brothers were longtime friends. They were also the most glamorous bachelors in town. Every girl in Casablanca, including me, was in love with at least one of them. Albert saw me.

"Anit how did you get here?" he asked, clearly astonished. "My God you are courageous. The crowd is like a wild sea. Are you alone?"

I confess I stared at him while he was talking. So much beauty. He was resplendent, like a sun, a Greek god. I remembered how, a few years ago at school, a photograph of Albert Levy would disrupt a whole class.

He took me by the arm. We went up to the hotel terrace. Up there, I found myself among a small crowd of people I knew. It was the best place to witness the whole show. Roland my boyfriend was up there too. I had not seen him for several days. When he saw me with Albert, his expression changed – jealous no doubt! He pulled me aside, angry, asking why I had not tried to contact him during the three days of battle. Frankly, I simply had totally forgotten that he even existed. The battle had been my sole concern. I did not feel one iota of guilt. I saw pain on his face, but I said nothing, turning my attention to what was going on below, in the Place de France. The ceremony was awe-inspiring. For us all, it was a very emotional moment. We were all silent, some of us crying.

The American troops were very impressive on their huge tanks, filling half of the plaza and all the adjacent streets. There were a few shouted commands on both sides, arms were presented, echoes of trumpets and drums filled the sky, and people cheered. From up on the terrace, we were too high up to see who exactly was down below. The only person I knew was there, because I had seen him enter the city, was General Patton. It was a glorious moment. For all of us, a moment never to be forgotten. The air was vibrating with joy. It was almost palpable.

A sort of contented peace enveloped me, as if I were in a shiny silk cocoon floating on a cloud. Unfortunately, there was an ugly side to this otherwise fantastic day. Some Moroccan Moslems were pro-German. What we saw was frightening. They were pulling Jewish kids by the hair, dragging them on the cobblestones and beating them. We could hear their screams, but nobody was coming to their rescue. People were in such a state of excitement, that they did not pay attention. We were afraid that if we went down to help, we would get the same treatment. It was so sad to see that wonderful, unforgettable day marred by such fanatics.

That same night we were back home. How good it felt to sleep in my own bed and not on the floor of some basement. Even in normal times, no matter what happened during the day, I always had a friend waiting for me at night, that bed to whom I confided my most secret thoughts.

I was wondering where my father could be. The telephones had been cut almost immediately after the battle had started that first day, the 8th of November. Mother had tried to call Fez, to tell Mr. Danan the good news about the American landing, but the phones were still dead this morning.

We had no idea where dad's hiding place was, except that it was somewhere in the Atlas mountains. Did Father even know of the battle, of the American victory? I had difficulties falling asleep at night. Swirls of soldiers in the shape of tanks rolled behind my lids. At the same time, blinding lights were exploding in my head. Smoke was choking me. I sat up coughing, realizing I had had a nightmare. In reality I was safely in bed, too tired to sort the events of the past days.

Years later, I learned a few important things about Operation Torch, the American name for the landings in North Africa, and all the political intricacies and the disasters that occurred during the landings in Morocco.

On the eleventh of November, while the fighting was fierce, at two o'clock in the morning, an American army vehicle flying a white flag had passed the American forces north of Casablanca. They were speeding to reach the city before daybreak to ask the French for their surrender. At the same time, in Casablanca, a daring special civilian commando unit had gathered in secret. They were local people and Americans living in

Morocco. They had been briefed secretly, months ago, by the American high command to carry out sabotage missions, spying, and more. That night, they had reached the elegant neighborhood of Anfa, situated on a large hill overlooking the ocean.

In the wee hours of morning, the civilian commandos had penetrated into the Anfa Hotel, the headquarters of the German Command. They blocked all exits, and cornered the Nazi officers stationed there, caught in their pajamas, like rats, while they were asleep. They never thought for a moment the American advance would be so rapid. Their luggage was already packed for escape, but they were not fast enough. At the same time, the Americans were seizing important Vichy officers and holding them prisoner.

I also found out how difficult the landings themselves had been, and the intrigues that had split the French command. Under the orders of General Eisenhower, Commander-in-Chief of Operation Torch, General Patton and Admiral Hewitt were assigned to the landing in Morocco. Casablanca was the main goal of the landing, but it was not tactically possible to land there. The port defenses were too strong and there was a frightening wall of surf. Three sites were ultimately chosen for simultaneous landings; Fédala, a small fishing port eighteen miles north of Casablanca, Port-Lyautey, another eighty-eight miles further north, and lastly Safi, one hundred and forty miles to the south. These forces had come directly from the States. At the same time, American and British forces coming from Britain via Gibraltar at the tip of Spain were landing in Algeria on the Mediterranean sea, at Oran and Algiers.

Early in the morning of November eighth, General Emile Béthouart, commander of the French army division in Casablanca, and friendly to the allies, sent messages to General Nogués, the governor of French Morocco, and to Admiral Michelier, who was in command of the French fleet. Both were staunch Vichyites. The messages said that the Americans were landing, to give no resistance to the Americans, and that he, Béthouart, was taking command of French North Africa.

General Nogués threw the note away. Admiral Michelier thought the message was a hoax. But Nogués was suspicious, something was going on. He got in touch with other generals in Méknés and Marrakech, two inland cities. They too, had received messages and had ignored them. Nogués took action. General Béthouart was arrested for high treason.

The Safi and Port-Lyautey landings were plagued with problems. High surf, resistance from French batteries on the coast, and a sudden squall caused heavy damage. Many men were lost.

By five o'clock on the morning of November eighth, the first men were ashore, despite landing craft crushed on rocks, or turned over in the surf. Men were overloaded with equipment, and many brave soldiers sank in the cold Atlantic waters. The tragic events did not deter their courage, and by six AM they had taken Fedala. General Patton landed that same afternoon. There were several battles on the way to Casablanca.

During the three days of battle, the French forces had been overwhelmed by the American task force. Thirty-three thousand troops had landed. In the end, the French lost their confidence and surrendered.

Two days after the surrender, the phone rang. It was very early in the morning. Startled, I jumped out of bed and yelled.

"The phone is working, Maman, Glad." I ran like mad across the rooms and grabbed the receiver.

"Hello, hello?"

The voice was faint, covered by static, but then I heard it full force. It was Dad. He was free, free! Father asked us to come and pick him up in Fez. It proved to be impossible. No trains were running, and bus lines had also been disrupted.

A week passed in preparations for his return. Mother wanted the house to look like a palace and put us to work. Windows and tiled floors were shined to a sparkle. We bought flowers for every room. The house had a festive look we had not seen for a very long time, like a beautiful woman dressed for a ball. After a few conversations on the phone, it was decided Mr. Danan would drive Father back.

Hastily, we looked for a black marketer who could get us a leg of lamb for the occasion. Food was scarcer than ever, and it would prove difficult to put a decent meal together.

Then we waited anxiously, all the time preparing and fretting. Finally, we heard a car horn, three short blasts and a long one. Dad was here! The three of us ran to the street. 'Father, Father', we cried. We embraced him again and again, almost choking him. He had lost most of his hair and looked very thin, but had a healthy tan on his face.

Father told us all about his escape. He was working outside the prison fort that day, in the potato fields. Several other prisoners were laboring at various tasks. Some were pulling potatoes from the ground, while others were carting them away in primitive large wheelbarrows. Toward dusk, Father had almost finished his back-breaking work when two men approached and whispered his name. They looked like mountaineer peasants. He thought they were helpers at the fort, but they mentioned Mr. Danan, and told him to be silent and do exactly as they told him without question. They threw a large blanket over him, wrapped him in a bundle and shoved him on top of a wheelbarrow.

It was almost dark by now. The two peasants told him not to move, they would come back later in the night to get him. They gave him a password. Father remembered being very cold and frightened to death. Where were those two men taking him? Were they telling him the truth? What if he was discovered by one of the guards? The thought made him shiver. Hours passed before he heard the password again. They traveled for a long time. He felt the rough ground rolling under him. They stopped. Father had no idea where he was. The night was very black, windy and cold.

"You are a free man, sir. We're taking you to a hiding place," one of the men said. He unwrapped the blanket and helped Father out of the wheelbarrow. "We have to climb a lot and be swift, to put as much distance as we can between us and the fort before daylight."

They went hour after hour in single file. The men had given him a dark wool burnoose, asking him to pull the hood down over his face. It was very rough going, tripping on rocks, ankle deep in snow, cold wind lashing. Father was crushed with fatigue, but still went on climbing. As dawn colored the sky a pale milky blue, they stopped and sat down on the frozen ground.

"We're very near the farm where you are going to hide," the men told him, "but we cannot tell you where you are. Those are Mr. Danan's orders."

Father was short of breath. They must be very high up, he thought. He could see the majestic summits around him, emerging from the night, their snow shimmering in the rising sun. He felt like an eagle free to soar. Alas, he was confined in a donkey's stable, without showing his face outside, for fear of being discovered. A peasant from a nearby village brought him food and milk every day. He suspected that the fellow was also making sure that he had not escaped. None of us ever found out the exact place where Father was hidden during those troubled days. After two months of isolation, one day the peasant didn't show up. Father became worried, but finally he heard something – a familiar voice. It was Mr. Danan!

"The Americans have landed, Elias!" They embraced. "Let's get you home," he said.

In Casablanca, the streets were dense with American commandos patrolling the various neighborhoods. Glad and I were forbidden to go out unaccompanied. Now that Father was back, we did not dare. After a few days I could not stand it anymore. Dragging a reluctant Glad, we simply walked out of the house without permission.

Adventure was in the air. I had convinced Glad that it was important to seek out an American soldier. We had to touch a real American, I told her. We had to try to converse with one, to test our English. We did not have to go very far. Around the corner from our street was the Rue Gallieny, a large thoroughfare. On the other side of the street we found our soldier.

Here was our hero in full camouflage uniform, armed with rifle, knife, and all the paraphernalia. He was looking at a furniture store window. Standing behind the soldier, I dared to touch him first, Glad stood behind me - she was too shy. The man turned abruptly, and grabbed my arm. I felt all the blood drain from my face, and stood there speechless. Then his expression mellowed, and he smiled.

I gave him our names and told him that we only wanted to talk to and actually touch a real American. I also asked him if he wanted to come home, that we lived just around the corner.

Of course he wanted to! His face was beaming as he took both of us by the arm. I was proud as a peacock, walking with an American. When we entered the house he seemed surprised, looking around with suspicious eyes. I took him to the living room and asked him to sit and make himself comfortable. Slowly his manner changed, he pulled me toward him and tried to kiss me. Glad brought her hand to her mouth in horror. I wrenched myself from his grasp, opened the window and ran to the balcony.

I was shocked and realized how naive I had been. The soldier followed me to the balcony where he tried again, grabbing me by the waist this time, pulling me violently against him. I could feel his hot breath. His face was crimson red. I yelled,

"No, no!"

A figure appeared at the living room door. Father.

"What's going on in here?"

The soldier let go of me, startled.

"Nothing, Dad. I just brought a guest to talk to in English."

Father looked at me with a somber face, but said nothing. He went to the bewildered soldier, greeted him and asked him, in perfect english,

"Can I help you with anything?"

The soldier, still a bit in shock, shook his head.

Father walked him toward the door.

"Please excuse my silly daughters," he said. The soldier nodded and quickly left.

I was not punished for my foolishness. Father deemed that my fright had been enough punishment, and that I had had a good warning. In the days that followed, newspapers were full of terrible stories. Soldiers breaking into households and raping women at bayonet point. This was war, and that type of behavior was as old as the world. We had been very lucky.

The thirteenth of December was my 19th birthday. Mother went out of her way to give a wonderful feast in my honor, and in honor of father's return. For the occasion, I had a dress made by a seamstress. I had no idea where Maman had gotten the fabric, probably from a black marketeer. It was a rich blue-gray heavy silk crepe, made into the latest fashion. This was incredible luxury for the time. I was planning on making all my girlfriends very jealous.

The day was a success. Most of my friends came. Stella wore a light green dress matching her eyes, the same one she had worn since the start of the war. Poor thing, she had outgrown it and was bursting at the seams. Lison, always elegant and more coquette then ever, was trying to steal every boy in the room. My cousins Chewing, Lycie and Soly were there too. The rest of the family would come later. Some friends were far away in German work camps, like Dédé and Robert. I missed them.

Roland came with an enormous bouquet of flowers and a bottle of very expensive perfume, Guerlain's Shalimar. I saw the look Father gave me when Roland kissed me as he was giving me the flowers and the bottle of perfume. I had not told father about Roland. I was afraid of his reaction, but we would have to talk at some point soon. Roland was very much in love and wanted to marry me. I was the right age to get married. In Morocco, a girl past twenty had much less chance of getting get a husband.

Roland was a nice guy, and I was trying, without too much conviction, to believe I would be happy if we got married. Frankly, I did not want to get married. There were too many things to discover in this world yet, before becoming a wife.

Two weeks later, I still had not talked to Dad about Roland. Imagine father's surprise when Mr. and Mrs. Laskar, Roland parents, called for an appointment to ask for my hand.

"Who are these people? I don't know them," Father said.

"Dad," I explained, "Roland wants to marry me."

"What do you mean 'marry me'? What is there between you two? It seems I'm the last one to know!" His face hardened. "In any event, it is no. Never! I shall never give my daughter in marriage to an Algerian."

And that was that. He even refused to see them. I felt so embarrassed, not only with Roland, but also with his parents, who had been so nice to me. In a way, at the bottom of my heart I felt relieved, but still I was piqued by his refusal, and I wanted revenge for Father's snobbishness. I wanted him to be hurt, the way he had hurt these poor people. Father was trying to justify his refusal, telling me that I was still young, that I could get a much better husband, and so on and so forth.

"Well, Dad," I replied tartly, "I don't care about all the things you are telling me, because I am already his mistress."

It was not true, but this was my torture tool. Father's jaw fell, and his face closed into a gray mask. He looked at me, and there was so much pain in his eyes, but I did not budge. It was open war. He turned around and left the room. As soon as he had gone, I realized the enormity of what I had told him. I felt sick and disgusted with myself, but the harm had been done. Nothing I could say now would make him believe me. When Mother found out she also turned against me. She was not going to talk to me anymore.

Inside me a big machine was churning. Anger, at my parents' narrow views on marriage. Desperation, knowing that I was stuck there with nowhere to go. I made a decision to be more secretive, to live my life the way I wanted, without telling anyone.

At home Mother and Father would communicate with me through Glad. I was forbidden to see Roland again. I felt like an outcast, diminished, like an Untouchable. Only a few weeks had passed since Father had returned. Where had all the love we had for each other gone?

Chapter Six: 1943

Far from over

A big brouhaha was going on in the city. President Roosevelt and Winston Churchill arrived in Casablanca on the 14th of January. They stayed at the Anfa hotel, the same place where officers of the German commission had lived and had been captured two months ago. The American and British leaders were here to plan the strategy for the next phase of the war. The conference produced the Casablanca Declaration, which called for the Germans' unconditional surrender. We rushed to see the arrival of these two very famous men. We knew their voices, especially Churchill's. He had given us so much courage in the darkest hours of this dreadful war.

There was a dense crowd on hand to greet them as they entered the city. We pushed and we shoved, but in the end we just could barely glimpse two smiling faces as their car rushed by. Nevertheless we were happy and impressed that Churchill and Roosevelt had chosen our city for their conference. Glad and I went back home elated, and this event was the talk of the town for months.

Other things that were not so pretty were happening in our town. The American camps were located at various points at the outskirts of Casablanca. MPs were guarding the compounds twenty-four hours a day, armed to the teeth. We knew the Americans had all the food they needed and more, but it was not available to us civilians. There was an enormous amount of waste in the food they threw away every day: Whole white breads, half turkeys, jars of peanut butter barely consumed. For us civilians, food had never been so scarce. We were hungry and desperate for a piece of white bread, let alone butter. The goodies the soldiers had given us when they had entered Casablanca had been consumed in no time.

Driven by terrible hunger, some youngsters, probably sent by their parents, milled around the bins where American soldiers threw what they considered trash. The temptation was too strong. Under the cover of night, the kids would steal from the bins, then run like mad for safety. Several kids were shot by MPs. We were in shock. The whole city was in an uproar. How could they shoot hungry kids for stealing food from garbage cans?

Two or three days later, early in the morning, passers-by found two American soldiers hanging from trees in a small park right in the middle of town. Notes had been left pinned to the unfortunate soldiers. "We have avenged our children. Each time a hungry child is shot, you will find an American soldier hanging." We had been saved from the Germans, but war was still all around us. The North African campaign was far from over.

It was an unusually cold winter, and it had snowed briefly on Christmas night. We had never seen snow in Casablanca before and did not know what to make of it. Was it a good omen or a bad one?

The badly wounded American soldiers were housed in a vast mansion that had been loaned by a generous Moroccan citizen for that purpose. My friends and I had been busy preparing a show to cheer them up. It was an exciting project, making costumes for two ballets with nothing but scraps of fabric, colored crepe paper, and bits of tinsel. We also rummaged our Mother's closets for old evening dresses and discarded laces.

We girls would dance the opening ballet to Paderewski's music – barefoot, as ballet shoes were impossible to find. For that dance, the costumes were classic Greek with veils of pastel hues. The second portion of the evening would be more fun. We came up with the idea of a French Cancan to the music of Offenbach, and danced by the boys. During the rehearsals, we had a lot of fun seeing those hairy guys in garters and stockings, waving muscled arms out of corsets and ribbons. We almost forgot the war was still on. The entertainment was an enormous success. We made those poor wounded guys happy for a little while. Some of them, though, could not even smile, they were in so much pain. I also had made little Moroccan dolls, representing men and women from different regions of Morocco. After the show, we distributed them to all the soldiers as souvenirs.

It was eleven at night when we left the mansion. We were walking slowly, loaded with costumes, make up cases, and decor. The sky was pitch black and so was everything else around us. The Americans had given us a safe conduct pass in case we were stopped for trespassing the curfew. We were tired and very cold, and had about two miles to walk to get to our respective houses. A flash of fierce light suddenly blinded us. Sirens wailing stopped us dead in our tracks. "Get down!", I heard somebody yell. We threw ourselves in the ditch, covering our heads with our arms. German bombers! They were flying so low it seemed impossible they had not seen us. The sky turned from black to a riot of crisscrossing anti-aircraft tracers. In the distance I heard a few explosions. My God! I was trembling, praying for the bombers to go away.

"Anit where are you?"

Glad's little voice was imploring.

"It's OK, Glad, it will soon be over. Don't panic."

Once again the sirens wailed, but this time it was a comforting sound, signaling the end of the air raid. Slowly we picked ourselves up from the cold ground, exhausted. As we walked single file, we started singing to give ourselves courage on the way home.

'Stalingrad Retaken by the Russians!' Those were the big headlines in the newspapers that morning, the second of February. With unbelievable courage, the Russians were regaining their country, city by city, from the Nazis' cruel grip. Here in Casablanca, people were standing in groups outside cafes, sitting in living rooms, discussing the Russian campaign with fervor. That same week Roland was called as a reservist into the army. We saw each other briefly, against Father's wishes, to say goodbye. We exchanged promises to write to each other, and shared a last kiss. I did not know if my feelings were of sadness or of relief, but I suddenly had a wonderful sensation of freedom.

Father came back one evening with four soldiers he had met at a café. All of them were Army photographers stationed in Casablanca. They were delighted to be invited into a home, and Glad, Mother and I were agreeably surprised. It was decided they would come every Wednesday for dinner, if they could make it. But what were we going to feed these four hungry men? We had no idea, but we were counting on Maman's imagination. In the back of our minds we anticipated the wonderful goodies the soldiers would certainly bring.

On Wednesday evenings, the conversation around the table was animated. We were as hungry to know about their country as they were to know about ours. John Vergis came from Brooklyn, New York, and was of Greek descent. Among the four, he was the scholar, studying to become a history professor. Bill Murray was a wiry, funny guy, always clowning around, his very blue eyes sparkling. In later years he would work for the Atomic Energy Commission as a photographer. Leon Chooluck had Russian origins. He was Jewish and was a ballet dancer in Los Angeles, CA. When we met him again several years later, he had become a successful producer in Hollywood. The fourth fellow was also a New Yorker, and was studying to become a concert pianist. They were so different from each other, but their love of photography bound them together in friendship.

These evenings changed our lives at home. We had something to look forward to. Often after dinner, our pianist would give us a concert. We were fortunate to own a beautiful citrus wood Steinway grand piano. While he was playing, chocolates and cookies our friends had brought were passed around. Listening to a Beethoven sonata while a piece of chocolate was melting in my mouth was the equivalent of being in heaven.

That spring, I decided to take sculpture lessons with an excellent teacher. Madame Berbudeau had been one of Rodin's last students before his death. There were several of her monuments and art all over France and Russia. At her age, she was still a very talented sculptress. She seemed to survive solely on red wine and cigarettes. Her students worked in her immense warehouse studio that was forever filled with billows of cigarette smoke. Often she stood behind us students to correct our mistakes. We had to endure her foul, wine-soaked breath and listen to her croaking voice, as she uttered vulgar curses. I really did not care, as I learned a lot with her and soon was able to sculpt my first bust. Besides, the lessons were very cheap. Father, I realized, would do anything I wanted to make me forget Roland.

At the same time my friends and I continued putting on plays. The taste of success was in the air. Our presentation for the wounded American soldiers had given our confidence a boost. People were desperate for anything to distract them from the war. Sewing costumes, learning lines, helping for the decors and going to my sculpture lessons, took up all my time. It helped me forget our troubles.

During the spring of 1943 two French generals, General De Gaulle and General Giraud, mended their dislike for each other. De Gaulle had been discarded by the Americans before the landing in North Africa. President Roosevelt did not trust him. The Americans placed Giraud at the head of the North African Free French army after the landings in November 1942, which created bad blood between the two generals. Now reconciled, they rallied their troups under Giraud's command. With the participation of General Montgomery, who had battled in Libya for years against the notorious German general Rommel, they finally routed the Nazis out of North Africa.

At home, it was cause for jubilation on that day of May 12th, 1943. We feasted with our American friends. All four of them came back from the fight for a well-deserved rest.

But Glad was not well. She looked like a wilted flower. The years of deprivation had left their mark on her frail seventeen-year-old body. That constant little cough was alarming.

"Maman I am tired. Why do I feel like sleeping all the time," she said.

Mother took her to see a doctor. X-rays were taken of her lungs, and the results were shocking, our little Glad had a pre-tubercular condition. Father, Mother and I were beside ourselves with worry. The doctor's orders were for Glad to leave for the mountains immediately to take advantage of the fresh, cold mountain air. It was decided I would accompany Glad, administer the drugs she had to take everyday, and make sure she rested completely.

"Why me?" I asked. It was an enormous responsibility. Would I be capable? Frankly, I was scared. I did not see myself in the role of a nurse; this was not a play, it was for real. We took the train for Fez where we boarded a local bus for Ifrane, a known vacation and ski village in the Atlas Mountains. Mother came with us for a few days, to see that everything went according to the doctor's orders. As we traveled, Maman was overwhelming me with a list of chores I needed to attend to in my new role. She entrusted me completely with Glad's recovery. We arrived at the entrance of the mountain resort that was going to be our home for quite a while. I was apprehensive, but nothing had prepared me for what was to come.

Chapter 7: 1943

Jack

The village of Ifrane was a surprise. Nestled in the Atlas mountains of Morocco, the ancient Berber village was dwarfed by what looked like a European mountain valley resort. French colonists had built summer houses in this unusual place, where they found rest, shade and pure cool air. The place reminded them of faraway France. Pink-tiled roofs gleamed through lush oaks, ashes and pines all along the meandering streets. In the spring, a multitude of flowers spilled from garden fences.

Ifrane was also a choice ski resort. Winters here were extremely cold, and the village was routinely blanketed in heavy snow. For Glad and I, it was the first time in this ideal place. It was the beginning of June, so vacationers had still not arrived. Summer houses were still closed. The silence was eerie. We could hear the wind playing in the tall cedar trees, giants reaching one hundred and sixty feet in height, which towered above and around us. July would bring an avalanche of families with their broods, and hordes of campers would follow. People would fill every house, every meadow and all the hotels. The charm would largely be lost, but in a way it would be good to hear voices again and to mingle with people.

At this point Glad and I were almost the only guests at the Balima Hotel. In regular times, this was an exclusive and expensive place, but during the war years the price of a stay was much lower. The first week, I was so involved in my new role as a nurse to Glad that I didn't have time to admire the landscape. Glad was really quite sick. I had to check her temperature twice a day, and make sure she slept enough and ate enough.

Besides, administering her medicines was complicated, each one at a different time of day, and each one with a different dose. I took my job very seriously, always liking to be in command. Here at the hotel, feeling all-important, I would order the help around, not noticing the smiles on their faces. My appearance – the way I dressed and did my hair – certainly belied the seriousness of my behavior.

By the end of June the hotel looked like an enormous beehive. Children were everywhere, screaming in corridors, laughing and running noisily in the gardens around the property, while mothers tried in vain to round up their reluctant kids for a much-needed bath before dinner. Glad was happy when I took her down to the enormous dining room. She ate better, even though the food had not improved after the Americans had landed. We still ate donkey disguised as beef, and cat or worse in sauces made for rabbits.

People looked at us with curiosity. Two unaccompanied teenagers was an oddity. Both of us were the same size or almost, but we certainly did not look like sisters. Glad was very thin. Because of her sickness her skin was transparent, which contrasted with her straight jet-black hair. She also dressed in subdued conservative clothes that gave her a sad romantic look. I, on the other hand, looked wild. I emphasized the look with the avant-garde clothes I wore. It showed the sense of freedom that was the real me, but did not fit my new role as a nurse.

Accenting the auburn color of my hair with a concoction of henna and red wine gave my head a burgundy aura of curls. I wore men's suspenders, pulled on each side of the chest to let my breasts protrude. I also wore tight skirts and men's shirts, mostly father's old silk shirts that I had dyed in fierce colors of ruby, emerald, or amethyst. I realized in later years how strange we must have looked to the conservative families gathered in the hotel.

It was time to make friends. I was bored alone with my sister. Every day was the same routine. I resented the fact that being in Ifrane was an imposed vacation, that I had had to drop my sculpture classes and the theater rehearsals. None of my friends were coming to visit this summer. I never thought of the money sacrifices my parents were going through to send us to this mountain resort.

Meeting people here was more difficult than I had expected. I decided to smile here and there when passing guests in the hotel, it proved to be the right thing to do. Soon I made friends with a little French woman. She was here with her two children, ages five and seven. At first what attracted me to her was her round face and ready smile. I found out she was a recent widow. Her husband had been sent to France at the beginning of the war, after the debacle of 1940. He had joined the French resistance, and later had been captured by the Germans and executed. My new friend sometimes looked distracted, as if she was somewhere else. Perhaps it was her way of grieving for her lost husband.

We often came to sit at each other's table at dinnertime. The meals were not good, but our new friendship was. She came from an entirely different background, French and Christian. Arlette was her name, and to my surprise she had no ill feelings against Jews. I was delighted to have at last found a French Christian person that was not anti-Semitic. Days went by lazily. We went for long hikes in the afternoons while Glad was asleep. Sometimes we took our bathing suits and went splashing in the icy cold waters of a waterfall. Other times we climbed a few hundred feet to rest where the tall cedar trees grew, and there we sat breathing their superb fragrance.

Up here the war seemed nonexistent. What a feeling of peace there was in that immense forest. With a breeze always weaving through and bending the heavy branches, only the thump of a cone falling to the ground or a bird call would disturb the silence. I felt rinsed clean from all the ugliness of the past years. My friend Arlette was also benefiting from all that beauty, and her mood was improving. She now thought that perhaps soon she could remake her life with another man. Her children needed a new father.

One afternoon at the beginning of July, coming back from a hike tired and dirty, we found the hotel personnel running around in a frenzy. I asked the barman what was all the fuss about.

"Haven't you seen the military cars outside? We are getting a large group of American Air Force officers taking their vacations here. Can you imagine? I have to organize some kind of cocktail party and dance for them tonight! I hope we have enough liquor in the cellar. By the way, all the ladies are invited, eight PM."

Arlette and I looked at each other. It was like we were given a super adrenaline shot. My immediate thoughts were what was I going to wear and how fast I could feed and put Glad to bed. Arlette had the same thoughts about her children. We parted in a hurry all excited, agreeing to meet at eight at the bottom of the grand staircase.

The hotel hall was full of guests milling around, most of them young

French officer's wives without their husbands. They were notorious for their loose conduct while their husbands were away at war. Loud music was pouring out of an old phonograph. I came a few minutes after eight, Glad would not fall asleep, probably on purpose, jealous of my going out. Arlette was already there, all dressed up and waiting. Both of us were now facing the grand staircase looking at the stream of these gorgeous American officers coming down the steps. Arlette pulled on my sleeve.

"Anit, look at these two at the top of the stairs. Aren't they magnificent?"

They were both very tall, resplendent in their well cut beige uniforms, with an array of decorations on their chests.

"I'll take the one on the right, " I said laughing. "He looks very much like Gary Cooper."

"OK, I'll take the other one," said Arlette. "He's also very good looking, don't you think?"

How confident we were that these two men would come to us. We looked at them with faked innocence and the contact was made. The strangest thing was that the one I had chosen came directly to me and the other went automatically to Arlette. Without knowing it, our fates were being sealed at that very moment, for better or worse.

After we introduced ourselves, the four of us. Their names were Jack and Ralph. Arlette and Ralph, Jack and I sat at the hotel bar. I had never sat at a bar before and felt uneasy for a while. The two men offered us cigarettes and drinks. At the time the only available drink was bad cognac. The effect of cheap alcohol was almost immediate. I was in a sort of euphoria that was not a bad feeling at all. Jack asked me for a dance. He was so tall, my head only reached his chest. Very correct, he kept me at a distance, but looked at me intensely. His eyes were blue and hard, his face lean and determined. Little by little he was drawing me closer to him. I was floating in bliss, his body was hard against me now. I was trying to pull back, a little frightened, but his arms were powerful. A moment later he took me by the hand.

"Lets go and sit down, otherwise I am going to make a fool of myself."

We sat on a sofa away from the crowd. Jack was looking straight at me.

"Your eyes are so green a man could drown in their waters. You are bewitching. I must admit that you drew my attention as soon as I saw you standing at the foot of the stairs earlier tonight. You could damn any man with your looks." He smiled, perhaps to erase the crudeness of his words.

So he had noticed me also while he was coming down the stairs. I was flattered, especially coming from a man much older than I, figuring he was at least thirty years old. In a brief moment of clarity, I thought of what I was getting into with this total stranger, it could be a dangerous game, but how dangerous I had no idea. The thought dissipated almost instantly. Why was I worrying? Here I was with the handsomest man in the room, who thought me beautiful, who had rapturously danced with me, and was now holding my hand.

"Would you like to go for a walk, Miss Anit?" he asked. "It's getting too noisy in here, don't you think?"

We slowly descended toward a patch of dark woods not far from the hotel. As we walked, our shoes crushed little stones on the trail. To me they seemed to say 'don't go'. Lightheaded from the two cognac and waters I had drank earlier, I dismissed the thought. We could hear muffled voices around us, but could not see who the people were. The night was pitch black.

Against the trunk of a huge pine he pulled me to him, his arms tightening around my waist, his lips looking for mine, I could not move, his grip was so strong. The kiss was soft at first. I felt a wave of pleasure rippling from my fast-beating heart all the way to my toes. Then his tongue tried to part my lips. I was shocked. I had never been kissed like that before, not even by Roland. I tried to back away, but it made him angry. Holding the back of my head with his large hand he forced his tongue into my mouth. I felt like biting him, but I didn't. Roughly he pulled me down to the ground, ripping my pretty lace blouse, and feeling my breast.

"No, no please don't!" I cried. Already, he was urgently opening his fly while pinning me down with his other arm. I panicked and started screaming. Caught short, Jack released his grip for an instant. Wrenching myself from him I was up in an instant, gathering the shreds of my torn blouse I started running. Behind me I heard him yell at me.

"You little idiot! I'll see you tomorrow."

I was shaking all over. So that's all the man wanted. I should have known better. The whole thing was humiliating. Fixing my mussed hair with one hand while covering my chest with the other, I came into the hotel's back door hoping nobody would see me in that pitiful state. Our room was dark when I entered, save for a tiny light on Glad's nightstand. Hopefully Glad would be asleep. I didn't want her to see my disarray.

Later, lying awake, my thoughts were in a turmoil. Jack had appeared so proper when he had met me. He looked neat, serious and very handsome.

Why did he act like that? Why so much violence? Was it my fault? Had I done something to trigger it? I was still very naive when it came to men. I realized that I had much to learn. The love with Roland now seemed to be a childish game, not much more.

Something was blinding me. Opening my eyes I realized it was morning. The sun was pouring on the rug, on my bed, God! what time was it? Turning around I saw Glad was still asleep. Somebody was knocking at the door.

"Who is it?"

"It's me, Ralph. We'd like you to have breakfast with us. I think Jack wants to apologize. Please come, we'll be waiting on the terrace in about an hour."

I'm not going. That was my first thought, but under the shower's cold water I changed my mind. I was curious to see a man like Jack making amends. Also, I had to admit I was attracted to him. His rough ways excited my senses. Last night I had panicked, it had been too fast, no prelude. I made sure not to wear extravagant clothes, tying my hair in a ponytail and putting on plain sandals, a white shirt, and a straight brown skirt.

They were sitting at a large round table, deep in conversation. A large blue umbrella flapping in the breeze protected them from the biting morning sun.

"Hello," I said, trying to seem nonchalant.

Ralph and Jack stood up in a flash, while Arlette gave me a little wink of the eye. We sat, called the waiter and ordered. There was a sudden silence. From the corner of my eye I was observing Jack. He really looked like Gary Cooper, and he probably knew it too. While we were eating, I could feel his eyes on me. We talked about the war, about the recent invasion of Sicily by the Americans and the hardships the troops were enduring. I found out Jack was in the Air Force supply and Ralph was in his outfit. Jack told us he came from Cincinnati, Ohio, and Ralph said he was from Iowa. Arlette and I could not imagine places with such strange names. Arlette stood up.

"I have to find my kids. Would you accompany me, Ralph?"

Jack and I were left alone, leftovers still on the table and cold coffee in our cups. The moment was awkward. I could feel the sun burning my back, but I felt unable to move, glued to my chair. Tiny birds had jumped on the table and were pecking crumbs. Jack was trying to compose himself. Obviously it was difficult for him to apologize. I did not say a word, enjoying every minute of his embarrassment. After ten deadly minutes of this game, seeing that he was not speaking, I stood up.

"I have to go. Will you excuse me, my sister is waiting for me upstairs."

Jack suddenly said, "Please sit down for a moment. I want to apologize for what happened last night, I was overwhelmed by your body, the perfume in your hair, and I had too many drinks. I'd like to know you better, Anit. I promise I will be gentle and conduct myself properly."

The whole speech had come rushing out of his mouth like a torrent flooding a gorge. I could see how relieved he was, but I wasn't ready to forgive.

"I have to think about it," I said, smiling, and left.

In the days that followed, Jack seemed to know all my moves. I could not go anywhere alone. He always appeared on my path. I suspected Arlette gave him the information. She was very happy with Ralph. Both looked very much in love. She wanted me to be as happy as she was. Then one day around the middle of July Jack stopped me when I was entering the dining room with Glad.

"We are leaving in a few days, I see you everyday, I talk to you but you are cold. Why this punishment? You drive me nuts! I want you more than anything. Could we meet alone?"

Frankly I felt the same about him. I was torturing myself not giving in, but I also was a little afraid of him. Something in him made me think of the devil, so suave, so elegant, but with a hardness about him that said a lot.

I gave in. Jack invited me to his room one very hot afternoon. The hotel was silent, guests having succumbed to the extreme heat of the day. Tiptoeing, I entered the room, a little apprehensive. The windows were open and the light curtains were drawn, waving in the hot breeze. It gave the room a sort of intimacy. Jack was standing up in mid-shadow.

"Here you are at last. Anit, you have no idea how much I longed for this moment. I thought it would never come. My desire for you was becoming intolerable. I believe you bewitched me."

As I stood undecided near the door, I looked around the room, noticing open magazines on the floor, clothes and papers strewn on the desk, and among all of that a large opened can of peanut butter. It made me smile. Jack came to me and held me so tightly I gasped. We kissed, slowly at first, his hands moving all over my body.

"I want to undress you so slowly, and savor every moment. I want you to undress me too, from the top button of my shirt all the way down."

I unbuttoned his shirt and was surprised at the whiteness of his skin. He threw my blouse across the room and looked at me. Now there was urgency in his gestures to see more. I hesitated when I reached the fly of his pants. His hands joined mine to help me and there we were all naked. I saw how excited he was. We sank to the floor where Jack had hastily thrown two pillows. A searing flame entered my body, taking my breath away. Sweat was running down our bodies. I was panting. Little by little that flame transformed itself into extraordinary pleasure, an explosion of ecstasy.

Exhausted, Jack rolled to the side. Looking at the blood spot on the pillows under us he said,

"You were a virgin, I had no idea."

He seemed surprised. A vague worried look crossed his face. I, on the other hand, had a feeling of power, leaving behind my girlhood and all the taboos it encompassed. In a few minutes I had shattered something my parents held dear—my virginity—that commodity without which they could never make a 'good' marriage for their daughter.

For the few remaining days I saw Jack every afternoon, sliding noiselessly in his room at siesta time. There in the darkened room we made love with the utmost passion, drinking of each other to the last drop.

The last Friday of the month Jack's whole outfit left Ifrane. Jack had told me he was temporarily stationed in Rabat, the capital of Morocco. He gave me the address of a French couple he had befriended. They were on vacation for two weeks, Jack had the key to their house.

"Will you come next weekend?" he asked.

"I don't know, Jack," I replied. "I'm responsible for my little sister, and I really should not leave her."

"I'm sure you will find a way. You must come."

In a billow of dust and noise the troop transports started up the road, with men yelling goodbyes while waving handkerchiefs. Jack hugged me tight before jumping in a jeep with Ralph and two other guys. Around the bend they stood up and turned around to wave a last time.

The scene on the hotel steps looked tragic, but also comical, like on a stage. All of us women, young and not so young, were suddenly left like discarded goods, sad and teary. God only knew what would follow. For French officers' wives it had meant having a good time, something to add to their numerous adventures and to classify in a mental little black book. For us young girls it meant much more. We were still at the age of dreams.

As soon as they had left, I started concocting a way to go to Rabat. Glad was much better. She had gained a little weight, her eyes were bright and her cheeks rosy. She knew about Jack and me, though I had not told her everything. Getting away without Glad finding out was impossible. For a few days I did everything she wanted without questioning, then I told her I was going to Rabat for the weekend.

"Anit, you just can't do that! What if mom and dad find out? You're crazy." She started crying. "Anyway, you can't leave me alone here. I'm still convalescing and you have no money for the bus and train."

"Well I am going," I said, maybe a bit too harshly. "I have stashed away a little money from what father gave me for our needs here. Don't worry so much, you won't die and I won't get lost."

Glad was still crying, but I was losing patience, even though I knew she was right.

"Come on don't be such a sissy," I said. "Besides, I've arranged for Arlette to take care of you. I'll bring you back a present. Its only two days. As soon as I get there I shall call you. Anyway, here is the address where I am going to stay."

Friday noon I left poor Glad, still in tears. She just could not understand why I was doing that to her. How could she know? She had never experienced a man. She could not understand the feeling, the pull, the tide of desire invading the body as fast as a poison, the twisting of the soul, a thirst that had to be quenched.

The bus arrived late. It was already full. The new passengers, including me, had to climb onto the roof up a narrow ladder at the bus's rear side. I had to find a place squeezed between peasants and their voluminous bags. I was the only person dressed as a European and got nasty looks from hardened Berbers. Little did they know that I was part Berber on my father's side. I made myself as small as I could.

After a noisy departure, we were now descending the mountain at a frightening pace. The driver was taking curves like a madman, raising billows of dust. Up there on the bus roof it was pandemonium. We were thrown from one side to the other crashing into each other, chickens spilled out of baskets squawking, barley and oats were flying out of punctured bags, women were wailing.

At last we came to a flatter terrain. As we settled once more, I noticed a white louse on a man's wool djellaba robe. They were the most dangerous, they brought typhus. Recoiling into my corner I made a gesture toward the man and showed him the louse. He laughed, took the insect between thumb and forefinger, and threw it in the middle of the passengers. Horror! I started scratching, even though I didn't know where the louse had landed, and couldn't stop all the way to the train station in Fez.

Fortunately the train ride was uneventful, even though I had to travel in third class for lack of money. It would be evening before the train reached Rabat. Only now did a troubling thought come to my mind. What if Jack was not at the station or at the address he had given me? There were no trains back until the next morning. Where would I sleep? I dismissed the thought immediately – it was not possible – but in the back of my mind I was uneasy.

The station was dark, only a few yellow lamps that faded into the fog. I saw shadows of people waiting on the platform. Frantically my eyes were trying to pierce the dark, and still I could not see him. My heart was beating hard. What if he did not show up? The train stopped, and I gathered my bag and walked to the door. As I was stepping out looking right and left, I saw him running along the train. A sigh of relief came to my lips. I waved with my bag, and in a minute he was there lifting and holding me up in the air.

"Anit, I could not see you in the fog. For a moment I thought you were not coming."

I didn't tell him that I had had the same thought.

It was hot and sticky in Rabat. Later in the evening a breeze from the sea would give us a little comfort. I felt slightly uncomfortable when we entered Jack's friends' house, not knowing who lived here, and feeling like an intruder. The place was neat, tidy. From the type of furniture and the images on the wall I deduced that the people who owned the house must be civil servants.

Jack wanted to take me to a fancy French restaurant and could not understand why I declined his tempting offer. The simple truth was that I was scared stiff to be recognized, perhaps by friends of my parents. We settled for a little bistro around the corner and still I was fidgety, looking right and left with apprehension. I was not even hungry and had to pretend the dishes were to my liking. Jack was caressing my hand, kissing the inside of my arm, giving me more wine. All this mellowed my fears for a while.

I let go and enjoyed the moment, but still was on the alert, realizing the enormity of what I had done. I was overwhelmed by guilt. To ease my mind, Jack was asking questions about my life in Casablanca, and in turn I was curious to know more about him and that faraway city of Cincinnati. The conversation turned to war news. Jack was concerned with the turn of events in Italy after the American invasion of Sicily. He had friends at the front there. Toward the end of July, Mussolini had been made prisoner. The king, Victor Emmanuel, had been reinstated on the throne. Rumors were that he was secretly negotiating with the allies. Jack hoped all would be well for the troops.

When we finished our meal, I had calmed down to a degree, reflecting on how silly my little worries were when compared to what was going on in Europe. Once we were back in the house with all the doors closed I let go completely. We played like kids at hide and seek and made love on every bed in the house, oblivious of the outside world and its troubles.

Saturday, we stayed mostly indoors. We could not get enough of each other. We made love, ran into the shower, and fixed a meal with whatever was in the house. I was literally transported into another world that I could never have imagined before this weekend.

I asked Jack not to take me back to the train station, for fear somebody would see us together. I called a cab. If I was seen alone I could always invent a story. Jack said he would write, and told me he was going to ask for a transfer to Casablanca.

"I would like to meet your parents, Anit." He smiled and kissed me. "I am happier with you than I've ever been in my life."

So it was really serious.

During the whole trip back, I had time to ponder the events of the past few days. How had I ever had the courage to do such a thing? What if my parents had called the hotel, as they often did? Would Glad betray me? The thought made my insides knot with pain. The train was not fast enough, and I still had that awful bus ride back to the mountains. Gathering my things around me I tried to sleep, but in vain. The flames of remorse were eating me up. As it turned out, Arlette had taken good care of Glad. All was well, though Glad was still upset.

The summer was over but not the heat, as was often the case in September. We had returned home at the very beginning of the month. Glad was totally well now, and had forgiven me. Casablanca seemed noisier than ever after the relatively quiet summer in the mountains, and once again the war was part of our everyday life. As a matter of fact Italy had just capitulated, on September 3rd. At the same time General Montgomery had landed in Calabria and General Clark and his American troops were landing in Salerno, south of Naples. To retaliate, German troops had invaded the north of Italy and had liberated Mussolini. What a mess! Things were happening everyday now. From the Nouasseur air base north of Casablanca B-29 bombers were leaving for Europe every night at dusk. They passed in enormous formations over our house, shaking the china and crystal on the dinner table, thundering black birds loaded with lethal eggs.

I got a letter from Jack that was intercepted by father. Fortunately he had not opened it.

"Who is that letter from?" he asked. "I see a military address."

"I was just about to tell you father. I met this officer in Ifrane."

I then proceeded to explain who Jack was, where he came from, and how serious he was about me.

"An American! Ahem! Well, we will see, we will see."

Another letter from Jack came soon after, but this time it was not for me. It was addressed to father, asking him permission to come and visit and to have the pleasure of meeting the father of such a delightful daughter. Father was impressed and immediately answered, welcoming Jack to our home. Mother, always romantic, thought it marvelous.

"An American – Oh darling, how wonderful!"

Jack came to the house in mid-October, but he wasn't alone. Was he scared to meet father? He brought three of his friends. Ralph, whom I already knew, Bill, another tall guy with a good-natured face, and Charlie, the youngest of the four. Jack had loads of presents for the family, mostly for me.

I had not seen him since the episode in Rabat. We had written each other, but love words in letters cannot replace being together in the flesh. I could see by his looks how much he wanted to hold me. The feeling was mutual, but of course we had to go through the ritual introductions. Mother insisted on showing them around the house. Tea and pastries were served. Father's face was beaming, presiding over the dining room table. I could almost read his mind. 'At last, Anit has found a decent man. I could consider a marriage'.

"Fellows," he said, "consider this house as yours. You will always be welcome here."

No doubt father had been impressed by their perfect manners and also by their spotless uniforms and their shiny medals.

"Sir," Jack said, "we have made new friends. You are quite a man, and your lady and daughters are most charming. We thank you for your hospitality."

While this polite talk was going on, Jacks thigh was touching mine under the table, the sensation burning through my body. I hoped it did not show. At the same time, I was observing the game with interest. Again watching Jack I thought of the devil, why I could not say.

Father had been mesmerized by Jack's suave manner. He gave me permission to go out dancing with him and his friends.

"Jack, I see that you are a perfect gentlemen," father said. "I am sure Anit is in good hands with you, but bring her back no later than midnight, please."

As soon as we were outside Ralph excused himself. He was going back to Rabat where Arlette was waiting for him.

"By the way," he said, "Arlette and I are engaged to be married."

I congratulated him, and was really very happy about it, because it gave me hope for my own future with Jack. Bill and Charlie had dates and disappeared soon after. At last we were left alone. We went for a drive along the coast, and made plans for the future.

Jack's whole outfit was transferred from Rabat to Casablanca at the end of November. It was also a time of great hope for the free world. Churchill, Roosevelt, and Stalin were meeting for a conference in Teheran. On Stalin's insistence, the three leaders decided to open a new front in Europe, larger than the one in Italy. Naturally we did not know the details of that meeting, for it was top secret, but we anticipated great things soon in favor of the allies.

I saw Jack almost every day now. At least once a week the four of them, Jack, Bill, Ralph, and Charlie would have supper with us. They brought Scotch, Johnnie Walker, my father's favorite. Also loaves of white bread, butter, candy, cigarettes, and chocolate. Those were still unbelievable luxuries that we could only get on the black market. On top of all the goodies, Jack always brought silk stockings for the ladies of the house, or shoes and dresses from the PX, items that we had not seen for such a long time. In return Father and Mother made them feel very much at home. After a time Jack and his friends were treated like members of the family.

At these gatherings, Bill would get steadily drunk, which dismayed both my parents. They thought it very upsetting, especially in front of young girls like Glad and me, but we did not really care. Bill needed a bottle of booze for him alone, and on occasions became violent and started breaking things. Jack, always cool and composed, even though he too consumed enormous quantities of alcohol, would take charge and take Bill outside to cool off. Bill must have been a very troubled man. He was a good man, and we would have liked to help, but he never did reveal any of his private life.

Ralph on the other hand was very open. He often talked about his farm in Iowa, his face radiating cheerfulness. He usually left early to go back to Arlette who still lived in Rabat and could not leave her children. Charlie was the sweetest of all, telling us stories of his beloved Brooklyn where he had grown up, a Jewish boy in a tight-knit family. He called my mother Mama and took her into his arms saying,

"I feel good here, I feel at home."

Chapter 8: 1944

The End of the Beginning

In January of 1944 Jack and I were engaged, with my parents' blessing. What happiness! I was so much in love it hurt. I felt so lucky to have a man like Jack as my future husband. On the day of our engagement, Jack gave me a beautiful opal ring to put on my finger. He was really part of the family now.

Still, there were some things that did not seem quite right with him. Each time I asked about his family I got vague answers. I found out after a lot of questioning that his father was dead, his mother still alive, and that he was a Protestant of German origin. I could never find out what kind of work he was involved in back home, or if he had brothers and sisters. All this annoyed me, but I kept quiet. I did not want to 'spoil the pudding', which was one of father's favorite expressions.

Little by little I saw less of my old pals, except the handsome Levy brothers, who mingled very well with our new American friends. In some circles, I was criticized for being engaged to an American. Jealousy, perhaps – there were always people out to destroy one's reputation. I was an easy target, but I could not care less what people said. I was the happiest girl in town.

Toward the end of January, American troops opened a beachhead at Anzio a few miles south of Rome. Three days later Leningrad in Russia was liberated after nine hundred days of siege, famine, and death. At home we celebrated with our friends. Little did we know what fierce battles were still to come in the fight for Italy during that terrible winter and spring. Night and day we listened to the news and praised the courage of these soldiers. The casualties were enormous and we knew there would much more bloodshed before the final victory over the Axis powers.

During the spring I attended a few charity balls. The most difficult thing for us ladies was to find cloth to make ball gowns. It seemed incongruous that we would even have thoughts of dressing up while so many battles were going on, but we were avid for pleasure in any form, to make us forget the terrible things that were going on in this war. For one of these balls, Mother and I put together a magnificent dress, made from a length of pale apple-green chiffon that she had found in a forgotten box belonging to my grandmother Nejma. With it was a piece of antique velvet the same pale green color. Mother made a tight-fitting top with a generous décolletage. On it I painted flowers copied from a Chinese vase. I was a sensation when I entered the ballroom with Jack at my side. As we danced, I could feel a hundred eyes on me. Nothing could have have pleased me more, but Jack got jealous. He accused me of having roving eyes.

From that night on he became very possessive and would not allow me to look right or left. I was afraid to displease him, and complied. Then one day he asked me to dye my hair black. When I refused he got very angry and threatened to leave me. No, no, I could not lose him and so I dyed my hair black. The man was controlling me more and more, and I couldn't or wouldn't see it.

As spring became summer, I fell deeper under Jack's influence. But there were important things happening in the outside world. The allies had entered Rome on the fourth of June, lead by General Juin and his French troops. On June sixth the greatest surprise of all was announced on the radio. D-Day, the formidable landing of thousands of American and British men on the beaches of Normandy. We called our friends, we danced, we jumped around like banshees. Bottles of liquor were opened. "In case we lose" was the toast our American friends repeated again and again, drinking themselves silly all day.

Together we planned a trip. As usual Jack was the organizer. Being a supply officer it was easy enough for him to get hold of an army truck. Fez was our destination. Father, Mother and of course Glad were coming with us. Three of my friends, David and Albert Levy, and his fiancee Isabelle joined the party. On the morning of departure we were in a joyful mood. We were dressed in fatigues that Jack had brought for us. It was a measure of security, as civilians were not allowed to travel on military vehicles. This gave a little piquant to the trip. Father was acting like a kid, dancing around so happy. Our American friends had given him a nickname, Kingfisher. Perhaps seeing him carry fishing poles that morning had triggered the name. The inside of the truck was loaded with cases of beer, food, and blankets. We had reserved rooms at the famous Palais Jamaï, an antique Moorish palace that had become a luxury hotel. It was set on a hill overlooking Fez' old city, the Medina. During the war the hotel was deserted, as very few families went on vacations. So we had the best of prices and we had almost the whole place to ourselves.

Up there, in that magnificent palace, a sort of madness took hold of us. We saw very little of our parents – most of the time they went their own way. They were here to rest, they said, occasionally coming with us for a picnic. Glad and I shared a superb room fit for a princess. The other rooms were even grander with high sculpted ceilings, intricate paintings on the walls, and ornate columns. There was something erotic about the whole palace, the smell of sandalwood drifting through opened doors, attendants sliding noiselessly through long plush corridors in their sumptuous Moorish costumes. For Jack and his friends who had never seen such a place it was like a drug. We went out of our minds drinking, singing, yelling, spraying those magnificent walls with beer. Jack and I disappeared two or more times a day. His room served as witness to our sensuous lovemaking. We wanted more and more pleasure, more extravagances, and let loose our passions. We acted as if this was the end of the world, like today was the last. All our pent up stress from the war needed to be released.

Coming back to Casablanca was like an antidote. Jack went back to his base, and we went home to our everyday routine. News that we had not heard while on that fantastic journey reached us now. Germans were sending robot bombs over England, the Russians had started their great summer offensive, and Hitler had escaped a bomb attempt on his life. Our minds were again full of war.

On the 15th of August the Allies invaded the south of France. Mother was hoping at last to have news from Grandma Nejma, but deep inside she was fearing for the worst. Would she ever see her mother again? We were also following very closely the Allies' progress from Normandy into the heart of France. We trembled during the battle for Paris. And then suddenly Paris was free! In Casablanca it was pandemonium. The French, Moroccan

Jews, and many foreigners were dancing in the middle of the streets, cars were honking madly, bells were ringing from the great white cathedral and soon joined by other churches. Father was overwhelmed, he had tears in his eyes, holding Mother tight in his arms. He kept repeating,

"These bastards," meaning the Germans, "are going to pay. They are going to pay for all the carnage they have caused."

On the day of my twentieth birthday, December 13th, Jack said we would marry very soon. Bill and Charlie were there. I was floating in bliss. Jack was particularly sweet that day. We embraced and toasted with champagne. Later in the day, while Jack was deep in conversation with father, Bill came to me to talk. He held me by the shoulders and looked straight into my face.

"Anit," he said, "I don't know how to tell you this, but stay away from Jack. Dump him. He's a no good man."

My eyes widened in disbelief.

"What are you saying, Bill? What do you mean? Leave Jack? You must be crazy."

"Believe me, I'm sincere when I tell you to get away from him. I've discovered things about him that I cannot tell you."

"What things?" I replied, my heart racing. "Please Bill, tell me!"

I was getting frantic, but I couldn't get one more word out of Bill. I was angry with him – how dare he spoil my day in that manner! He must be drunk as usual was my immediate thought. But the threads of that conversation lingered in my mind for days. Should I tell Jack what his friend had told me? No, I would not peep a word. I had to dismiss that thought once and for all. Jack seemed so amorous, so attentive. I was not going to spoil my happiness because of a drunkard.

Chapter 9: 1945

Two Endings

The new year 1945 was full of promises. The Russians were fighting hard against the Nazis, and had just retaken Kharkov. To honor that valiant army, Mother gave a Russian-themed costume party. We made costumes with what was available at the time, which wasn't much. Nevertheless we had a lot of fun. Jack and his friends brought the vodka and Mother, Glad and I prepared a very decent buffet *à la Russe*.

During the spring, Jack left the country several times, always returning with an armful of presents. I was curious about these trips. Where was he going? The reply was always the same. He could not tell me, it was classified. Each time he came back, his desire for me seemed stronger. We made love often in his remote and well hidden apartment, an off-base lair that he and his friends had acquired in secret.

In March I missed a period. Jack said to wait, not to be rash, and he was sure everything would be all right, but he looked annoyed. I couldn't sleep anymore. What if I was pregnant? Father would kill me, of that I was sure. Days went by and the period did not come. Jack wanted me to have an abortion. In those days, that was not easy or safe – or legal, and I was deadly afraid. I told him we could get married now. Jack's answers were vague. He said we could not get married without certain papers that were difficult to obtain. I didn't understand why would it be so difficult? A month passed and nothing, no period. Now I was sure I was going to have a baby. We had to do something. I was starting to have nausea, and was afraid Mother would find out. Jack was urging me again to have an abortion. He looked very troubled and said he would pay for everything. By now I was two months pregnant. I was desperately waiting for those papers to arrive so we could get married, and kept postponing the abortion. Two weeks later Jack told me there would be more delays, and the papers wouldn't arrive for at least another month. We had to find a doctor now, that was his final decision. For me it was a nightmare. Why couldn't we get married, why?

I called our family doctor for an appointment, telling my parents I had a bad stomachache. In mid-afternoon, the day after, I crossed the street from our house to the other side, where Dr C. had his office. Jack had promised to come and get me, not wanting to be seen entering the doctor's office with me in broad daylight. I hesitated on the threshold. What was going to happen? I felt so totally alone, terrorized. Dr C. was a young doctor, a nice fellow I could confide in.

"Well, Miss Anit," he asked, "what is wrong today? Can you tell me about your symptoms?"

When I told him that I was two and a half months pregnant and I wanted an abortion, his jaw dropped.

"I cannot do that!" he replied. "It is illegal. I can go to prison, you know. Who is the man?"

Head down, tears rolling down my cheeks, I replied,

"An American officer."

"Hm! This is a nasty affair. I would not like your parents to be involved, it would be a disgrace for them. Let me think for a moment."

He clasped his hands together and looked at me intently for what seemed like forever. Finally, he whispered to me,

"I'll do it, but it's going to be extremely painful. I cannot put you to sleep or even give you a sedative, it would take too long. If my secretary does not see me within an hour or so, she will become suspicious. You see, once I have started the procedure I cannot stop. You could hemorrhage and die." He paused, letting that sink in. "Do you still want to do it?"

"Yes." My answer was barely audible.

It took two hours of the most indescribable pain. Dr C. had given me a handkerchief to stuff in my mouth. He did not want any screaming, but how could I avoid it when he was scraping at the core of my being. I screamed and he kept hushing me, saying.

"Shush, shush, the neighbors can hear us. Contain yourself."

Jack did not show up as he had promised. I was very weak, run down and aching. In the staircase leading to the street, I had to stop a few times. Taking a little comb from my pocket, I fixed my sweaty hair the best I could. Under my arm was a package wrapped in newspaper, Dr. C. had told me to throw it in the garbage. He could not do it himself, he told me, it was too dangerous. I did not want to think of what was in that crumpled newspaper. It was still warm. When I opened the door to the street a cool wind hit my face. I shivered, standing there at the edge of the sidewalk. A wave of disgust invaded me. At the same time a feeling of love for that little thing I was holding in my hands overwhelmed me. Slowly bending down I deposited the little package in the street and without turning around I started running.

Nobody was home when I returned. I was very fortunate. Had the family seen me they would have known something was terribly wrong. I went straight to bed, exhausted, and fell into the deepest sleep. When I opened my eyes I saw faces bent over me. Father, Mother, and behind them, Glad. The light of day was hurting my eyes. How long had I slept? Mother said that I had a high fever, she had called our doctor, and he was coming right away. This woke me up completely. My God!

At the foot of my bed Dr. C. was smiling. In a whisper he said,

"Do not worry, they know nothing. I am keeping our little secret. I told them it was a bad intestinal fever. You will have to take sulfa for the infection and put a bag of ice on your stomach. I'll come back tomorrow."

Jack came to see me, finding excuses for not showing up the previous day. I gave him a weak smile. I could not even hold a conversation. A week went by in a daze. At the end of that Father came to tell me Jack had brought some papers relating to our marriage. Father had filled them up, and he seemed very happy. I could not believe it was true. So we were really going to get married.

Jack came only once the week after. He said he had to go out of the country for a week or so, and that when he came back, we would wed. He had brought me a bottle of champagne and some fresh oysters. It was a pick me up, he said, it would help get on my feet. I sat up on my bed, suddenly feeling better, all my fears gone.

We heard on the radio that President Roosevelt had died. It was sad news for the free world. For me it was a distraction to listen to the news every day and follow the progress the Allies made. Jack did not write. The week had passed and I had no news, but I waited patiently. He would be here any day now, no need to be nervous. The American First Army was meeting the Russians at Torgau on the Elbe river, what exciting news. What date were we? April the 25th. Jack had been gone fifteen days now. Not a word from him! Where was he? I tried to call the base, but could not get anyone who knew him. Where were his friends? The radio kept blasting news that I did not even hear anymore: Mussolini killed by partisans, Hitler commits suicide.

Father, Mother, and Glad were beaming with joy, while I was drowning in worry and pain. Berlin fell today, the 2nd of May. Bells were ringing again, cars were honking like mad, people were in the streets. I was alone in my room, crying. Seeing the distress I could not hide anymore, Father decided to go to the American Air force base and inquire.

"Darling, I am going to find out what's going on, do not worry, I'll find the bastard that makes you suffer so much. He is not worth the sole of your shoes. Do not cry, please darling."

When dad came back that evening, his head was down, and his jaw was so tight it made his face chalk-white. I knew it was over. Father took me in his arms.

"I went to see his Captain," father said. "I showed him the marriage papers, but the man looked flabbergasted. He asked me to please sit down. I sat."

"Sir," the Captain told me, "I am very sorry to tell you that supply officer Jack Huddleston has gone home with most of his outfit. He is a married man and he will never come back. My apologies, sir. You see, among so many good man we are bound to find one rotten apple."

I fell into a deep depression, crying day and night. I would not eat and could not sleep, accusing myself of stupidity, inflated with vanity and lust. I had fallen into Satan's arms with so much ease. I had lied, connived, concealed. The price I paid was very high. While half the world was rejoicing at the Germans' total surrender, perhaps the most beautiful day of their lives, all I wanted was to forget, forget, forget.

I was not the only one to grieve in our family. Mother had been worried about her own mother – since the Germans had invaded the south of France she had had no news. Now, after the German defeat and the liberation of France, Mother could at last contact the French Red Cross. She kept writing letters, but got no answers. Tension was mounting. Every passing day might cost Grandmother Nejma her life, if she was even still alive.

Summer days peeled away in heat and despair. Father, who had gone through so much during the war, consoled Maman.

"Darling Ryta, have more faith," he said. "Your mother is alive – I can feel it. Nejma is quite a woman. She has the endurance of ten men. You will get a letter soon."

But Mother couldn't stop worrying. Glad, who had regained her joy of living after that terrible illness, was a great comfort to her, but the fact that I was in a state of deep depression did not help.

In mid July we received a long envelope covered with red, black and blue French government official stamps. Mother could not open the letter, her hands were trembling. I came out of my room and seeing Maman in such a state, I forgot my miseries for an instant. Grabbing the letter from her hands I tore it open. Reading feverishly, I yelled.

"She is alive, she is alive!"

Taking her by the waist, I waltzed with her around the room. Glad joined us, the three of us whirling around like mad dervishes. I could not believe I was dancing. It came as a shock to realize that life was stronger than my sorrows. Father came back from his office quite early that day.

"I knew something good had happened," he said, beaming. "I had to rush home, it was as if somebody was pushing me."

For the first time in many months I thought of somebody other than myself. Grandmother Nejma would need all the love we could give.

Mother left for Nice, France. What would she find there? The Red Cross had told her that grandmother was in a pitiful state, that she would have to be transported home in an ambulance plane. Endurance and courage had kept her alive. What an extraordinary life Grandmother Nejma had had.

The third youngest in a family of twenty one children, her family was poor, but industrious. At fifteen, Nejma was already an accomplished seamstress. Besides sewing for a clientele of rich women, she also made the dresses and suits for her many brothers and sisters.

Tangier, where she was born and had lived, was a small but cosmopolitan trading center at the tip of North Africa. As a teenager, Nejma was considered a great beauty. She had a very white skin, thick shiny jet black hair reaching below her waist, and piercing eyes, two black diamonds. That was not all. She was exceptionally intelligent. She wrote poetry and played the lute like an angel.

Leopold, my grandfather, was a very rich young man from Turkey, trading in antiquities. When he met Nejma at a gathering in Tangier, he was mesmerized by her beauty and wit, and fell madly in love with this divine young girl. He decided not to leave Tangier without marrying this beauty. I do not think she was really in love with him when they married, but she went through with it more to help her family financially.

After their wedding they lived in France in the greatest of luxury. She became a grand dame of elegant Parisian society. Having more than one home, they traveled and spent time in the palaces he had bought for her. The one in Nice was a sumptuous palace resembling the White House in Washington, DC, and had been the palace of the dukes of Savoy. In Italy, Grandfather bought her the Palazzo Davanzati, a thirteenth century masterpiece in Florence. Leopold was also building a Moorish palace in Tangier for his treasured wife. With all this wealth, she never forgot her family and sustained them year after year. It was rumored that Grandfather's fortune was worth fourteen million dollars in gold just before World War I, and that was beside all his land holdings. After a few years of adulation, Leopold's insatiable lust turned him toward other women. All the money in the world did not make Grandma Nejma happy anymore. Her husband was cheating openly.

They had two sons, my future uncles, and my mother Ryta, who was spoiled. Her father adored her. Around 1925 Grandma Nejma and Grandpa Leopold separated. Nejma kept the palace in Nice. Leopold kept the other properties, constantly moving from London to Italy and to Morocco.

There was much less money left after the crash of 1929. They lost three-quarters of their fortune. At the onset of World War II Nejma still lived as a grand dame in her huge palace in Nice. Missing the last boat out of France, she was trapped.

We were all, Father, Glad and I bending over the balcony to witness her arrival. Mother, looking very tired, was walking behind the gurney where Grandmother Nejma was lying, carried by two solid men. A Red Cross nurse came out of the ambulance. We waved and shouted 'Welcome, Welcome.' Only maman looked up and smiled. Mother's big bedroom had been prepared for Nejma. We were asked not to go in until the next day. Grandmother was exhausted and needed to rest. When we tiptoed into her room the next morning what we saw disheartened us. Grandma Nejma, the beautiful and glamorous woman we remembered, was no more.

Paralyzed from the waist down, she was lying like a big lump on her white bed. She called us by name, her arms waving us near. We stood at the door unable to move forward. She called again to please come in, she wanted to hold us in her arms.

"*Anit, Glad, mis queridas, como crecieron, que bonitas se volvieron.*" 'my darlings, how you've grown, and how beautiful you've turned out!' In moments of great emotion she spoke Spanish, her native language. There we were now in her arms. The eyes that looked back at us had not changed, two pure black diamonds so powerful we could not look her in the eye. Her hair was white as snow, and her face, my God, her face bore all the suffering of these past years, in deep sad wrinkles.

Suddenly, she started screaming.

"Somebody come save me, save me! I cannot stand the pain!"

We ran out of the room in panic as Mother and the nurse went in. Before the day was over we found out what had happened to our beloved Grandma Nejma.

After the Nazis had invaded the south of France, the hated Gestapo were looking for Jews everywhere on the French Riviera. They had already taken some of her friends. She was desperate., and was afraid to confide in her neighbors for fear of being denounced. Rumors were that the Germans were closing in. She had to go fast, abandoning the beautiful things that had taken her a lifetime to collect, and leaving her beautiful home like a thief in the dead of night.

"I had to run," she told Mother, "each day hiding in another basement."

The only valuables she had carried with her were a few thousand francs and the twenty-two carat yellow diamond ring she treasured. She endured the cold winter and was still free when the summer came, but in rags and very hungry. All of her friends had disappeared, and she did not want to even think of what had happened to them. Another autumn came, and she could barely walk now. There was no more money, all of it had gone to buy pieces of dry unpalatable bread at astronomical prices. The precious diamond ring that once had belonged to the Queen of Portugal was gone too. Grandmother, more dead than alive, had had the courage to show herself in a jewelry store. The owner would not believe her story. He was certain the diamond was stolen property and gave her the measly sum of seven hundred and fifty old francs, the equivalent of thirty five dollars of the time.

At the onset of winter, a good soul had found her unconscious and half frozen in a shed, far away from Nice in a deserted farm at the foot of the Alps. He had loaded her on his cart after bringing her hot water to drink and covering her with torn blankets.

"Lady, I am taking you to the convent up there in the mountains," the man had told her. "The nuns will take good care of you in their hospital."

At first the place was peaceful, and little by little Grandmother recovered. The air was wonderful to breathe in the beginning of spring. Peasants would bring whatever food they could to the nuns and their patients. It wouldn't be long now. She was sure the war could not last much longer.

The region was being bombed by the Allies pursuing the Italian deserters. Part of the convent was destroyed, but still the nuns endured. Then the Nazis discovered the hospital, which had been kept a secret for so long by the nuns. The Gestapo interrogated all the patients, and all of them, Jews and Gentiles alike, were used as guinea pigs for the worst medical experiments, in the very hospital that had welcomed them. At the end of the war the Red Cross had taken over and had tended the mangled victims, those that were still alive.

We could not believe Grandmother had endured so much. What courage, what tenacity. In our eyes she was a miracle. How long would she last? We did not know. At times she was very calm and invited her friends to visit her. Her bedroom became a salon, where poetry was read and music was played. Propped up on pillows, she could still play the lute and sing beautiful sad ballads.

The war was really over. Still, for the rest of our lives we would drag little pieces of it with us.

Chapter 9: 1946

Glad's Wedding

Billows of blue tulle. Glad was getting married, and today was the big day. I had designed 18th century-inspired dresses full of flounces and frills for the bridesmaids at Glad's request. We were at her mother-in-law to be's house, and posing for the photographer. Glad sat in the middle of us, the flower's heart. A white gossamer veil framed her face, and her head was crowned with fresh orange blossom flowers, whose fragrance sent messages of purity. But unlike the bridesmaids, she was dressed in a simple, very elegant white satin gown by Dior.

Glad looked frightened. She could very well have been the doe in the hunting tapestry that hung on the wall just behind her. There was no escape anymore. The hunter was there next to her, relishing his prize. Gabriel, the groom, stood like a pillar, regally dressed in tails, his thick eyeglasses concealing the green of his eyes, his receding hair showing his age.

The display of wealth was oppressive in his mother's house. Rooms were panelled in precious woods. Heavy silk hangings were draped over the windows, and family portraits stared from every angle. Huge quantities of flowers filled every space. Two hundred baskets! somebody had whispered in my ear.

Gabriel's mother Henrietta was leaning on the bannister of the grand staircase. She was a woman in her sixties, of medium height, with sparse graying hair. She was dressed expensively in a gray sequined dress. Certainly she had been very beautiful in her day, there were portraits to attest to it, but it was a cold beauty, with slanted green eyes that Gabriel had inherited.

Today she was a snobby old harridan dressed in silks and bending under the weight of her diamonds. She oversaw the whole ceremony with a cold calculating eye. After inheriting her late husband's immense fortune, she was a lioness ruling everybody and everything in her sumptuous villa, feared by all and particularly by her three younger sons.

A few months before, Glad and Gabriel had met in one of the many parties given among our Jewish group of friends in this new year of 1946. In Morocco at the time, ethnic groups did not mix. Our group of Jewish youth was not welcomed by the French Christian party goers, and Moslems were rarely seen in either group unless they came from a rich family. Personally I found these practices intolerable and thought everybody was entitled to have fun and mix regardless of religion, race, or color. I was looked upon as a strange bird for these radical views and had to comply by the standards of the day to be accepted, which angered me to no end.

Glad and I, along with two of our best friends and our cousin Lycie were considered the most beautiful girls in our circle of Casablanca society. Eligible bachelors were plentiful and we could be choosy, which delighted us. We'd go dancing all night, our whole coterie, my sister and I always wanting to be the last ones to be taken home. It was a kind of endurance test to sit on the sidewalk at the entrance of our house, waiting for the first rays of sun to appear. We would then walk in silence through the entrance hall, trying not to wake our parents, a difficult task to achieve because of the heavy, creaky wrought iron door we had to open. Trying not to giggle, we'd take our shoes off and climb the marble steps three at a time. The real challenge was to open the door to the upstairs rooms without noise. Once we were inside, we stopped to listen, in case we had wakened our parents. Tiptoing to our room, feeling our way in the dark, we slipped under the covers all dressed up and listened again, with eyes wide open just above the sheets. Nothing alarming – Father was snoring loud as usual. He always left the door to his room ajar. Pure silence came from Mother's room. All was well, and we drifted into sleep.

All this frenzied amusement was the reaction to six years of war, of living in constant fear, dark nights, blackouts, the wail of sirens, and for all of us constant hunger. It took a long time to really feel that the war was over, as we were still on rations six months after it had ended. We were starved for everything. I remember standing in line with Mother from five AM to three PM, to get fabric at the Galleries Lafayette for the bridesmaids' dresses. The queue was four across and went all around the block. It was daring for two women to walk across the deserted city in the middle of the night to get there. Bands of thieves roamed the streets. But little by little we felt freer, we ate better, and tore off the dark blue paper that had lined all our windows for so long. Nights became a riot of lights, of loud music, of dancing until all hours.

As soon as the frontier with Spanish Morocco was opened in the north, Casablanca's residents as well as people from other cities in the center and the south of Morocco jammed all trains going to Tangier, which had stayed international and offered everything one could desire. There one could buy gold, diamonds, cashmere sweaters and nylons, Italian shoes, cheeses and butter from Holland. Much of the finery and delicacies for the wedding came from Tangier.

Gabriel was a very rich man. His parents owned one of the two big flour mills in Casablanca. During the war, gossip said they had had dealings with black marketeers, but because of their social standing it had been hushed up.

I never accepted Glad's infatuation for such an older man. The war had affected her in a strange way. She repeated constantly,

"I am not going to ever be hungry again, no matter what. I am not going to be sick or wear rags for dresses anymore. I don't care if I marry an older man!"

Gabriel certainly knew how to manipulate my little sister, flashing his white sports coupe, inviting her to the most expensive restaurants on the Ain Diab coast, and bringing her costly trinkets, like a little diamond tennis bracelet or a pearl choker.

"Little nothings," he said.

It didn't take long before it became very serious. Father was shocked at the news that his younger daughter might marry into that nouveau-riche family. Even though they were richer than us by far, Father's pride was not in money but in lineage. His family was of old stock, dating back centuries, to the times when the Moors were in Spain. His family, like many others in Tangier, considered themselves nobility.

At last father asked Glad for a talk. They sat facing each other, his face worried, hers timid but steady. Still, she was nervous and it showed.

"Glad," Father began, searching for the right words, "these people… these people are Algerians."

"But Dad, I see nothing wrong with Algerians," she replied. "Remember when Roland wanted to marry Anit ? You refused because he was Algerian, and his parents were in the meat business. 'Butchers!', you screamed, 'Never!' But it would have been a better match than that horrible Jack she fell in love with!"

"Perhaps," Father snorted, "but we simply do not mix with Algerians, and frankly I think you are too young to marry a man so much older than yourself."

"All I know is he loves me," Glad said, her voice gaining in confidence. "I am going to be spoiled and live in luxury. I want to marry Gabriel. Please, Dad."

She looked so lovely, so sincere in her desire for a pampered life. Father tightened his jaw and stared far away through the windows.

"These people are *nouveau-riches*, Glad. They have no breeding. All they have is money," he said dismissively. He turned back to her and shook his head. "Darling, you know that my assets are depleted because of the war. There is no way I can compete with them on that front, but there's more to life than money. Tell me the truth, do you really love him?"

There was a long silence. Glad looked pleadingly at father. It was her only weapon.

"I want to marry Gabriel," she said. Father lifted his eyes to the ceiling, perhaps asking counsel from above. He sighed.

"Come here my little daughter," he said. "Let me give you my blessings. I can see how much you want that marriage." He then put his right hand on her forehead and murmured a few Hebrew words.

Mother came into the living room.

"Oh, my little girl, I am going to lose you!"

She started crying. Tears came easy to her. Mother was the epitome of romanticism, always dreaming of beaus bringing her bouquets of violets. She would spend hours playing Chopin nocturnes on our beautiful Steinway piano, living in her own world of beauty. She was the youngest after two brothers. Mother as a little girl was often a witness to her parents' quarrels. Her older brothers were away at boarding school much of the time, but she was always at home and very much alone, retreating into her own make-believe paradise. Getting married didn't change things much for her. Father was a self-made, no nonsense businessman. He never remembered birthdays, for example. To Mother this lack of attention was a constant disappointment. Losing her favorite daughter to marriage would leave a big void in her life.

"But Mom, I'm so happy," Glad said. "Why are you crying?"

"Ryta, stop this," Father said curtly. "Compose yourself." He disliked shows of weakness. Father left the room without another word.

A week later Gabriel came to formally ask for Glad's hand. At home, Mother had overworked the maids for that special day. The brass and silver had been double polished, the furniture waxed to a shine. The huge copper urn in the entrance hall reflected a reddish gleam on the marble top of the massive Louis XIV chest. Above, an antique gilded mirror reflected the Moorish tiled floors. Flowers were everywhere. As this was spring, bouquets of sweet peas and anemonies competed with roses and carnations, their mixed scent giving life to the flowers on the Persian rugs.

It was almost three in the afternoon. Gabriel would be arriving in a few minutes. Everybody at home was running around like mad chickens.

"I have to go and comb my hair," Father said.

We started laughing, because he had lost most of his hair. He pointed to me with a frown.

"Go and make yourself presentable and stop laughing, all of you! "You should remember why I lost my hair."

We all disappeared to get ready. It was like rehearsing a play. Soon we would have to appear on stage and play our roles. It made me laugh again. I found all these preparations ridiculous.

The bell rang. Zora the maid went to open the door. She also had put on all her fineries, a long pink caftan covered with a yellow gauze tunic opened to the sides, and caught at the waist by a gold embroidered belt, her head covered with a fringed brocade kerchief. She felt beautiful and part of the family for that special day.

Gabriel walked in dressed in a light suit, perfectly cut. He looked stiff, as if he had been ironed with starch. His glasses glinted, giving him a cold air of superiority. It was obvious he was out of his element. Father, on the contrary, was very much at ease, and at the same time elegant in a navy sports jacket and gray flannel slacks. They greeted each other and walked toward the living room. The windows were wide open on the large balcony. Gabriel was eyeing the antiques, commenting on the precious Chinese vase full of roses, and about the many paintings on the walls. Finally, gathering courage, he turned around to face Father.

"Sir." He swallowed, intimidated by the steady look he encountered, "I, I have the honor of asking for the hand of your daughter Glad."

There was a minute of heavy silence.

Seeing father's stern face he added, "I want Glad for my wife. I promise to make her happy forever."

Mother came into the room chicly dressed in a navy and white silk outfit. She was always so elegant. Her smile illuminated the room. The atmosphere that had been tense was immediately relaxed in her presence. Gabriel stood up and kissed her hand. He sat again on the edge of his chair, impressed no doubt by such a beautiful woman.

I was listening behind the curtained glass doors, Glad was near me, shaking with fear in the pretty dress she wore for the occasion.

"Come on," I said, "go in."

I opened the door slightly and pushed her in. I heard father say that the wedding would be after Passover, and the engagement in a fortnight. Zora came in to announce tea was being served in the dining room. She opened the connecting doors and I joined the party, not wanting to miss anything, especially the good pastries that had been baked for the occasion.

Later on that afternoon, Gabriel asked Glad to go out for a ride along the coast. As soon as they had left, we returned to the living room. Zora was clearing the table, making an awful noise piling up dishes. Father walked heavily back and forth.

"I should never have accepted this marriage," he grumbled. "What got into me? Ah, my darling Glad, she looked at me so pleadingly. Now it is done."

Mother came over and held his arm.

"Elias, everything is going to be all right. Gabriel looks like a responsible man. I am sure they'll be happy, so stop torturing yourself. Don't you think I'm just as sad that she is leaving us. But after all it is her happiness. Did you see her face? She was radiant."

I sat near the piano listening to my parents' conversation with mixed feelings. I did not want to get married, remembering what I had gone through with Jack. But I was two years older than Glad. Sooner or later my fate was going to be the same, whether I wanted it or not. In the meanwhile, at least I was having fun. I did not take men seriously anymore. My escapades were an expression of freedom, while Glad, a pure white dove, was lured by money. To me, she was the doe being led to slaughter.

The wheel was being cranked, a big wedding was in the air. Gabriel's family and ours were supposed to work together and create a masterpiece, but things were not going smoothly. At home, lists of guests were being prepared. Family first – we counted fifty, and tried to find ways to eliminate a few, but that proved to be impossible. Friends? There was a selection to be made. We knew that no matter what, we could not invite them all. Some friendships would certainly turn sour as a result. We were trying for forty friends maximum to stay under one hundred guests as a whole for our side. Henrietta submitted her list of two hundred guests saying,

"Elias, you have invited too many people, you'll have to cut some out. The ceremony will be in my house remember."

As if we could forget. Father did not reply to "that lunatic", as he called her. All he knew was that he was paying for the wedding and he'd invite who he damn well pleased, although he did not know where he was going to find so much money for the reception.

Glad didn't know any of this. She was sailing on a golden vessel of bliss, and Father did not want her upset in any way. Mother was very excited, buying the most expensive fabrics for her dress and that of the bridesmaids. She did not realize that all this spending was way above our means. She was childish sometimes, and there were some tense moments with father.

"Ryta, for goodness sake," he fumed, "we cannot spend without counting! What is that bill for embroidered chiffon? Let me see."

Mother would look hurt and retreat to her room, her ivory tower as we called it, and things were left in the air. Dad was tortured by the fact that on top off all these expenses, Henrietta had given her consent only on the promise that Glad would come with a dowry. After a lot of thinking, some of Mother's heirloom jewels were sold for about thirty thousand dollars.

The day was approaching fast. Henrietta hired a woman of great talent, the most famous chef in Casablanca, Mamo. She came with all her retinue of cooks to prepare a feast, a sumptuous buffet for three hundred guests or more. Glad had chosen three cousins and me to be the bridesmaids. The days were flying by now.

Mother took us to countless fittings. It was tiring but oh, so exciting. I wanted my waist to be the smallest, even if it meant I couldn't breathe. I told the dressmaker to lower my décolletage to show some of my busom, to which mother replied, "Absolutely not!" Glad's dress was being made by Christian Dior, the famed French couturier. It was a present from Gabriel.

Perfumes, boxes of chocolates, and flowers arrived every day for the future bride.

Glad was floating on air, or so it seemed. I felt that at certain moments she had some reservations about the whole affair. I saw her silent and pensive many times. We were close to each other, but had never had a serious talk about ourselves. She was always jealous of my strength and my successes. I, in turn, was jealous of her goodness, her neatness, and the fact that she was Mother's favorite daughter. But this time I felt we had to talk.

"What are you thinking about?" I asked her. "You don't look so hot." Sometimes I was rather abrupt in my ways.

No answer. Glad looked at me as if to say 'this is too deep for you to understand'. That glance of hers pricked me.

"Oh, come on, Miss Princess," I said, testily. "You look like you fell off your high horse. Something must be brewing in that little brain of yours. Maybe you're thinking that with all his dough Gabriel is still an old kook and that he will be a flop in bed. Ha! ha! ha!"

She became red as a beet, looked at me with a hurt expression, and left the room. I was left without a real answer, and it was all my fault. I should have run after her, apologized and kissed her, but I didn't. I was too proud.

On the morning of the wedding father brought an envelope to Glad.

"This is your dowry darling, for you alone, in case you need it one day."

"Oh Dad," Glad said, "how wonderful it is to have you."

In Morocco, the custom was to give the dowry to the bride, and it was hers to keep or share as she saw fit. She put the envelope in her white satin purse. We were all ready to go, swishing in our gowns, feeling like queens. When we came out of our house we let the neighbors stare at us for a moment before stepping into the wedding cars, decorated with tulle and flowers. I was very involved with myself, with the way I looked, and the certainty that I would be turning every young man's head. Still, this did not prevent me from observing all that was happening with a keen eye.

We entered Henrietta's villa from a side door and went upstairs, where three rooms had been put aside for our family. One for the bride, where a hairdresser and a dressmaker were waiting to fix the last details on her hair and dress. The other two rooms were for mother and father and for us maids of honor. I could hear the noise downstairs. Through the windows I saw a long line of cars spilling out a continuous stream of women in brilliant gowns and stiff looking men in dark suits. The Moslem guests were resplendent in regal djellabas and brilliantly ornate caftans. I had to see who was already downstairs in the huge living room. Going to the landing I looked over the banister. The air was stifling and it was only April. I could see groups of people assembling and trying to get the closest possible to the canopy where the ceremony was going to take place. Waves of perfume floated up from below. The mixture of scents combined with the humid heat was sickening. I had to go back to finish my hairdo and put on my coif. In only a few minutes the bride would come down with Father at her side. I had to get ready fast.

As I was going back to my room, I heard voices coming from another room at the end of the corridor. Tiptoeing on the plush carpet, I reached the door and put my ear against it. I heard father's voice. A very angry voice, then it was Henrietta's high pitched voice answering.

"Elias the wedding will not take place if you do not remit to me Glad's dowry this instant, and that is final."

"That's outrageous. I'll do no such thing," I heard father reply.

Oh my God I couldn't believe what I was hearing. That bitch!, I whispered to myself. The argument continued as I rushed to the bride's room, hoping that their voices couldn't be heard that far. Glad was pacing, getting impatient.

"Where is Dad? The Rabbis are already downstairs waiting."

Father entered the bride's room, totally distraught.

"I'll be ready in five minutes darling," he said trying to keep his voice steady. He looked around and saw the white satin purse lying on the bed.

"Let me adjust your veil, it's a bit off," I said, turning Glad around so she couldn't see what Father was doing. Thank God the dressmaker and the hairdresser had already gone. Father glanced at me, took the white satin purse on the bed and the money inside. All this had taken less than a minute. He nodded at me, and mouthed "I'll explain later."

They came down the grand staircase, Father holding Glad's arm. He was white as a sheet, and she looked like an angel, so innocent of Henrietta's machinations and nastiness, and so unaware of the terrible family she was marrying into.

When Gabriel slipped the ring on her finger, Glad looked around. Her eyes seemed to seek approval, or was she scared? The circle of faces around her came closer and closer to congratulate, but it felt like a cage was closing in on her. I didn't want to look. Tears welled up in my eyes. Glad was really married, and a portion of our youth had flown away. I felt a funny lump in my throat as if I was being forced to swallow a pill.

I didn't want my sister to see me crying, so I ran to the bathroom to compose myself. The mirror did not lie – I looked terrible. Rummaging through my fancy beaded handbag, I fished out a little bit of rouge for my cheeks and some bright lipstick. I took the coif off and fixed my hair. Another glance at the mirror. Not too bad. My spirits were lifting. The hell with everybody else, let's have some fun!

Entering the ballroom with a big smile on my lips, sure of myself, I was aware that men eyes were devouring me. Nothing could have pleased me more. I had the power. If I ever married it would be with whom I pleased, and certainly not for money.

Chapter 10: 1946

A Taste of Freedom: Summer in Tangier

My sister Glad had gone now, married. Our shared yellow bedroom
became mine and it showed. We used to have the room divided without
a partition. Her side was always spotless, bed well made, clothes folded or
hanging neatly in the closet. She had her books, which I was not supposed
to touch. This made me so mad, I would call her all kinds of nasty names
beginning with 'G': "Garbage pail," "Gorgon's head," and many more. She
cried, but never gave up her precious books. Now I could throw my clothes
all over and wait for the maid to pick them up.

I sat on the floor, naked in the middle of the room, with paint tubes
and brushes all around me, an old mirror propped up against a chair
reflecting my body. I was painting nudes. For lack of opportunity and
money, I was my only model. None of my friends wanted to pose without
clothes; it was too much for their restricted minds. The walls were covered
with canvases and sheets of watercolor paper depicting naked women in
all kinds of postures. I even had painted one with dark green hair – it had
always been my dream to have hair tinted that color. The room was messy,
but it was my realm. Nobody ventured in to disturb me. One day, though,
Father opened the door unexpectedly.

"What is this, aren't you ashamed?" he said, furious. "I already told you
many times to take all these horrors off the wall. This looks like a bordello!
And get dressed this instant. What are the neighbors going to say?"

How the neighbors could ever find out stayed a mystery. In answer I
raised my shoulders, which was equivalent to an insult. Father became white

with fury as he banged the door shut; his voice was trembling:

"Wait until your mother finds out."

But mother knew, even though she did not approve. She kept quiet, realizing threats would not touch me, and she was right. What was I doing wrong anyway?

Besides painting, fashion also interested me. Father, seeing my interest, immediately enrolled me in a designing school.

"Better for you than staying naked all day in your room painting," he said. "Sewing may prove to be handy someday."

Father was always so practical; I wondered if he ever did anything spontaneously. So I started sewing, imagining dreamy or provocative ways to make dresses. 'Outrageous' was what my parents called them. To me they were creative. I liked beautiful fabrics and designs, and strong colors also appealed to me. Tango orange, apple green, turquoise and deep sea blue were some of my favorites, but I also had a foible for violets, forest greens and browns of all hues, while naturally black was always dramatic and white was so chic. I would drape a fabric around my body, no bra, so I could have a plunging back décolletage or liberate a shoulder. In my efforts to be different, I often tried to sew the whole garment with only one major seam, which proved to be difficult if not impossible.

It was unbearably hot that summer of 1946. All of July had hovered between 45 and 48 degrees centigrade. Every day I went to my favorite pool, La Piscine Municipale, the largest in Casablanca, an entire kilometer in length, which was really a walled off area of the Atlantic. I spent hours sitting on the pool's far wall, fighting the incoming waves from the ocean. It was dangerous to be there at high tide and even worse when the waves receded, making it easy to be swept over into the churning Atlantic. But it was one of the only distractions when it was that hot in Casablanca. My friends bored me. Always the same afternoon teas chaperoned by mothers or aunts.

I needed a change and a big one. An idea was germinating in my brain: to go on a vacation alone, far enough to be by myself for once, and do as I pleased. The more I thought about it, the more appealing the thought became. I approached mother first.

"Did you ever go on vacation alone when you were young?" I asked innocently.

"Well no, not really." She thought for a moment.

"As a matter of fact," she continued, "I did once, if I remember correctly. I went alone from Paris to Megeve in the French Alps, where I spent a vacation with friends of the family."

Aha! There was a precedent. Casually I ventured,

"I'd like to go to Tangier for a vacation, Maman. I'm not a kid anymore, I can very well take care of myself, and instead of bothering the family, I could go to a hotel on the beach."

That was it, I had said the words. There was silence for a few tense moments. Mother looked at me like she was seeing me for the first time, realizing that, yes, I was not a kid anymore, and that she saw nothing wrong in sending me to Tangier alone for the rest of the summer. I knew I had won when she said,

"I'll have to convince your father."

At last the date was set for my vacation. I'd be leaving in the middle of August. I went into a frenzy, sewing the most extravagant outfits. Fortunately, nature had given me a great body. I wanted to be a sensation for the summer of my dreams.

In previous years, before the war, I had gone to Tangier on family vacations several times. We had even lived there for a year, but then I was a kid; today I would be discovering that mecca of pleasures for myself. But I knew that I would have to sacrifice a few days and some evenings to the family. My grandfather Leopold, mother's father, lived alone in his Moorish palace, all the way up in the hills of 'El Marshan.'

I would have to also visit my grandmother Hola and my aunt Simi, father's mother and older sister, plus all the cousins on both sides of the family. I did not relish sitting at dinners that lasted for hours, being asked why I was not married, and having to endure prayers before and after dinner. I could already feel my male cousins' concupiscent looks, waiting to catch me in a dark corner, push me behind a door and plaster me with wet kisses, blech! There were also the looks of envy from my two spinster cousins Rachelle and Sete. Navigating all these obligations demanded careful planning, but for the moment too many things were whirling in my head to give these visits too much thought.

At last the day of departure had come. The trains in those days were less than adequate. There was an enormous difference between first and second class, and third and fourth class were the pits. At this point in time I could not afford the best; I had to settle for a second-class ticket. The train station near the harbor was damp and gloomy in the early morning hours. I climbed into first class to see and feel the luxury. As I passed through the cars with my suitcase in hand, I peeked into the half-curtained compartments with envy. How clean they were, the seats plush and blue, little white lace doilies in place for heads to rest. The people sitting there were not appealing at all, though. A skinny French woman, stiff as a broom, with an air that said "we own it all," sat there dressed in black, a large straw hat hiding her eyes. In the seats facing her sprawled an enormous man. A pasha no doubt, all dressed in white robes. He was dreamily picking his nose with his pinkie on which shone an enormous diamond. The situation was really comical. I started laughing; how ridiculous they looked together.

In the last of the first class cars I passed a weirdly dressed couple speaking loudly in English; British tourists, no doubt. I always wondered about English people; how strange were their ways. The trip was going to be interesting. 'I do not want to sit with such people' was my inner excuse for not being in first class. Reaching the second-class cars, I looked for my assigned number; fortunately it was near a window. The leather on the seats was dark and cracked – I hoped there were no bed bugs or fleas. I knew, though, that before the end of the trip I would be scratching somewhere. I sat wondering who my trip companions were going to be, hoping perhaps a handsome Romeo would appear.

I was disappointed to see a whole family come in; Casablanca Spaniards from the Maarif neighborhood. I could tell by the way they spoke and the way they dressed. All my dreams of seduction disappeared in two seconds. The two little girls were dressed in stiff Sunday clothes. The father (I presumed) was a slender olive-skinned man who looked like a raven; not very reassuring. He seemed ill at ease in his pointy patent leather shoes. I imagined they were all going to a wedding. He ordered the two girls to sit down and be quiet. The frightened kids went to hide in their mother's skirts. I got a big smile from the plump little lady while she tried to sit in her tight-fitting dress. I was fascinated by her bosoms, two formidable bumpers projecting her femininity way out.

Settling into my corner, I thought about the very long trip ahead. Two hundred and thirty five miles to reach Tangier; in Morocco it could prove to be a long day's adventure. I took a book out of my handbag and droppped it on the floor as a strident whistle made us all jump. A few people were running on the platform. The train started very slowly, there was a big jerk and we stopped again. The stationmaster was yelling insults in Arabic. After a few coughs the train started for good with a long wail. We passed slowly through Ain-Sebaa, a suburb with the strange name of 'the Lion's Eye', almost at the city limits, with little flowered villas and a long string of factories.

The train took on a little speed now. I really felt that I was on my way; I could start making plans. The Spaniards sitting in front of me were finally quiet. A while later we were slowing down again, reaching Fedala, a beach resort north of Casablanca, where General Patton had landed in November of 1942. This was also one of our preferred places for picnics on Sundays. The fun of those days came back to me. Getting there at seven in the morning, the sand still wet from high tide, we would plunge into the waves after a good game of volleyball, planting a big striped tent when the sun became too fierce. We then had lunch on cold Spanish omelets and watermelon and then succumbed to a siesta, but not for too long. Around three o'clock in the afternoon we were at it again. More games, more water, more sun until we were fried and refried by the implacable Moroccan sun, coming back home dead tired with our clothes full of sand and smelling of the ocean. What wonderful souvenirs I had from these outings.

We were back on our way north. With the train's regular vibrations, I almost fell asleep. As we passed Skrirat, another resort beach, the green line of the ocean and the crests of enormous waves crashing on very white sand could be seen from the train. This was another good place for weekends. More souvenirs of great times.

The Spanish lady started fumbling in various bags, producing a large salami, a liter of red wine and a big loaf of country bread. Already, greasy papers littered the floor. I smelled an orange being peeled. The little girls yelled they wanted to drink. I tried to divert myself by looking out the window. I had to admit that the smell of food made me hungry. I realized I had not brought a thing to eat or drink.

Outside in a blur, I saw little barefoot kids waving at us, their long shirts like djellabas floating around their skinny frames. In a field a woman lifted her head and rested her hands on a shovel for an instant, perhaps dreaming of taking that train one day. Where were we? I read "Temara" as we passed the train station. We were approaching the capital and slowing down, a few jolts and hisses, creaking noises, a long whistle and we entered Rabat, the Capital of Morocco. I saw the crowd on the platform with a shudder. As soon as the train doors were opened, a horde of passengers shoving each other hurled themselves up the steps, banging their suitcases against doors and walls. They filled every compartment, every inch of the corridors, even the restrooms. Everybody talked together, or rather screamed to be heard. A real tower of Babel, where Arabic and Berber, French and Spanish were spoken together in a bizarre cocktail of tongues. It became difficult to breathe even with all the windows open.

Three women entered our compartment dressed in the Moorish fashion, covered head to toe with costly djellabah robes in tender pastel colors, embroidered leather slippers and veils over their faces, leaving only a slit for the eyes. They sat, their opulent figures filling the seats, arranging their numerous bundles around them. The perfume they wore was overpowering, jasmine and sandalwood. All the mysteries of Morocco were contained in these women. The covering veil concealing forehead, nose and chin was a teaser, the fabric being semi-transparent. Moslem women certainly knew how to entice or even provoke in a very subtle manner. The eyes said it all. Often beautifully made up with khol, they burned like coals. One could read all the violent emotions of these often sequestered women. I could imagine men lured by their heavy scents, their high-pitched voices and the tingling of their bracelets. They were really masters in the art of seduction, for the competition was fierce in a land where men could choose many wives, and also indulge in several concubines.

The Spaniards had fallen asleep, heavy with food and wine. There was a sour smell floating in the air, perspiration and perfume. My head was spinning – I felt trapped. Getting out for some air without losing my seat would be a miracle, but I could not stand it any longer. Putting my suitcase on my seat, I tripped over the bags on the floor and inched out of the compartment. In the hallway there was pandemonium. A loud discussion, almost a fight, was going on between two fellahin peasants and the French train controller, who was yelling.

"You are not in the right car, your tickets say fourth class, can't you read? Follow me right now."

Obviously they could not read; the controller knew that very well. He was being nasty with those two poor Moroccans. They looked at him with vacant eyes, not understanding. One of them stepped forward, angry.

"But a ticket is a ticket and ours are for this train, so what's all the fuss about?"

They did not move and the argument started all over again. Everybody in the passage was trying to give advice, yelling at the top of their lungs. Retreat into my compartment proved to be an ordeal. Hands were feeling me, eyes and gestures were suggesting lewd things. I was disgusted; was that any way to start a vacation? I was furious to be stuck between all these men like we were sardines in a can. After much effort and discomfort, I finally regained my seat, thinking of what it must be like in third and fourth class. There, people literally walked on each other and lice jumped from one person to the next. Heavy odors lingered from clothes seldom washed, all permeated by the overpowering smell of tar, henna, and cloves, a paste that country women put in their hair for days as a beauty treatment. I felt privileged in my second-class car and resolved to be content about it for the rest of the trip.

I started a conversation with the three Moslem ladies that had gotten on the train when we stopped in Rabat. It was unusual for middle class Moslem women to travel alone. Curious, I asked them if they were going on vacation. They said no. Was it a family reunion? Again they said no and started giggling. I started giggling with them, not knowing why. One of them looked at me aslant and said, half covering her mouth with her hand,

"Hee hee! We do contraband. We go to Tangier to get the goods." She lifted her djellabah robe showing her ample serwal pantaloons. They were stitched with pockets of all sizes.

It was a fact that Tangier was an international city where one could buy almost anything from around the world. It was really a mecca of treasures compared to the rest of Morocco, which had been starved of practically every kind of merchandise during the long war years.

"In these pockets," she pointed, "we put watches and cigarettes. The others are for various goods, nylons and sometimes gold." She lifted a little more of her garment to reveal long sacks attached to her waist.

"Those are for cashmere sweaters and silks, and oh, the tiny ones are for perfumes."

The whole show had lasted a few moments and she was again covered from head to toe, the two other ladies not approving at all by their looks. They really had awakened my curiosity this time.

"How do you come back?" They looked at each other talking in hushed voices. They glanced at the Spanish family, who did not seem to understand what was going on and obviously did not speak Arabic, but who sent suspicious glances in our direction, keeping the two little girls on their knees for protection. The eldest of the three ladies looked at me intensely for a few seconds.

"You seem to be a reliable young girl. We should not tell, but well…" They looked again at each other and the three of them started together. "We travel back to just before the frontier of the Spanish zone, Arbaoua, you know. Somebody comes to get us in a country cart loaded with sacks of vegetables. We dress as peasants for the ride back, with our faces well covered, and after the frontier, being in the French zone again, we take the train back to Rabat or Casablanca depending on the demand." They smiled. "Easy."

I was dumbfounded. In a way I admired their courage; they grew better in my estimation. I wished I could do the same, just for kicks.

Closing my eyes for a moment, I wondered what I would do with my life. Be a fine art painter probably, or perhaps design beautiful clothes. Canvases drenched in color and light danced behind my closed lids, fantastically shaped dresses floated in my head. I would want to travel also. Father had nourished us through the years with tales of his adventures around the world. 'Eighteen times around the world' he always repeated, not quite believing it himself, but it was true. The thought never entered my mind that I might have to work at a real job one day, and very far in the back of my mind was a little niche barely opened. What was inside tried to spell marriage, husband, children. When these thoughts suddenly popped out, I opened my eyes and said aloud, "I'll never marry a guy that wears glasses! I don't want to have girls, just boys." Everybody in our compartment turned around to stare at me questioningly. I apologized, mumbling. What had gotten into me anyway? I could not tell.

We were coming into Kenitra, known as Port Lyautey to the French, a port with an old fort constructed by the Portugese on the Sebou River. It was a large river with an unusual bend, where some of the American forces sent by Operation Torch fought on the second week of November 1942, to take the fort and the only airfield in the region, at the same time that General Patton was fighting for the takeover of Casablanca further south. The place had completely changed since the war. The American Air Force had installed a large base there, changing forever the physical aspect of the town. The station platform was crowded, but nothing like in Casablanca or Rabat. It was mostly filled with Moroccan peasants loaded with baskets of fruits, vegetables and screaming poultry. Trailing behind the men came the women and children. Odd in that colorful crowd were a few Air Force men, immaculate in their spotless and well-pressed beige uniforms, insignias shining on their caps. I looked at them through the window with a mixture of feelings. They had saved our lives in 1942 and for that alone they deserved our eternal blessings. I remembered how in the early days of the American landing in Casablanca, I would follow them at a distance, especially sailors, just for the clean smell of Ivory soap they exuded, the cleanliness of well scrubbed bodies. But whenever I saw an Air Force man, bitter thoughts rose up in me as I recalled the pain, shame, and disillusion of my experience with Jack.

We pulled out at a slow pace; the train seemed to drag its dusty cars in the great heat of midday. Most of the passengers were finally silent, succumbing to the sun's power. The countryside blurred when we started to pick up speed: rivers shining like melted silver, palm trees swaying with the hot sandy wind. Lulled by the rhythmic movements of the train, half the people were asleep, some with their mouths open, some snoring. Flies were buzzing around, landing on lips or eyelids, flapping their wings disgustingly. I kept my eyes open with effort, afraid that if I fell asleep my purse would disappear. The heat became oppressive as we reached Sidi Kacem, a little town also called "Petit Jean" by the French colonists. The stop was a long one; there was a switch of locomotives and a lot of yelling and cursing outside. There were many vendors running along the train hawking their wares. The passengers, me among them, were hanging like bunches of grapes from the windows. I was hungry, and bought fresh baked bread, a banana and a glass of steaming hot green tea, fragrant with fresh mint leaves.

"Al leem! leem! Le zoranze, oranze, ah! Madam ce tre boon le zoranze." 'Oranges, oranges ah! Madam, the oranges are very good', mixing Arabic and distorted French. The air was vibrating, voices shouting between the train windows and the vendors. A little boy presented a live chicken, holding it way above his head.

"Buy it, take it, it's young and meaty."

'Who's going to load himself down with a chicken?' I thought, but someone in third class did after all. Imagine the cacophony in their car if several of those birds had been bought?

How many more hours did I have to endure in this smelly train? I thought of the first class cars with a sigh, probably still half empty, my brief contentment with second class draining away.

We started to move, accompanied by a long whistle. The wind was changing, acrid smoke filling the compartments. I closed the window for a while. We were now crossing the fertile plain of the Gharb, the wheat producing area of Morocco. As soon as the wind changed again, I opened the window wide. The train was running through the middle of orange groves, the trees covered with early blossoms. The perfume of these flowers was so strong, almost intoxicating, that all the bad train odors faded. We passed Souk El Arba, a sleepy village that woke up every week on Wednesdays for its weekly market, hence its name, Wednesday Market. All around me people were stirring. Was it the wonderful orange blossom fragrance? Or were they aware we were approaching Arbaoua, the frontier? The name alone spelled dread; we were entering Spanish Morocco. The customs officers stationed there seemed to exist only to annoy us defenseless passengers. They wore those Napoleonic boiled black patent leather hats, had black mustaches, black looks and dark gray uniforms. These scarecrows represented the Franco regime of the day, and to an extent were copying Nazi attitudes.

"*Senores, senoras, passaportes.* Gentlemen, ladies, passports."

When had they climbed aboard? Nobody knew. Here they were in every compartment, like searching devils. They made us come down onto the platform in a slow trickle, drag our luggage into a small room for undressing. Men and women had separate rooms. They searched us thoroughly. Fortunately my customs officer was a woman, but it was still demeaning and disgusting to have a perfect stranger poke at all the parts of my body, even with white gloves. It made me feel like a spy, an idea that I rather fancied after the search was over. The few minutes that I had stayed in that little customs room, I imagined all kinds of fantastic situations taking place in various countries of the world. It took the gloom away. Soon the ordeal was over, thank God. I thought of the three Rabaty ladies, but they were traveling empty, so to speak; no excitement on the way to Tangier, but coming back would be another story for them.

We were in the north now, mid-afternoon. Suddenly the train sped up as we passed "El Ksar el Souk," an ancient town on the river Loukos. Romans and others had passed through there; there was a medieval fort in the distance; the river made a large buckle of lazy water down below. The

Atlantic Ocean was not far away to our left as we traveled the Jebala hills on our way to Asilah, a sleepy little white port on the ocean that had seen glorious days. Carthaginians, Normans and Portuguese had fought for its conquest. The atmosphere changed completely from the deadly heat of the plains to a cool breeze from the sea. The Rif range of mountains stood almost in front of us now; only a few more miles to reach our destination at last.

In the cars there was movement, suitcases were being lowered, voices shouted, heads were hanging out of windows. In front of us was the shining Mediterranean. We were coasting along the beach slowly. We were almost there. The sun was very slowly going down, painting the sea in orange stripes of light. Cape Malabata was bathed in a fuzzy glow. We came to a full stop. Outside on the platform a controller was yelling.

"Tangier, end of the line."

I scrambled to get out, not even saying goodbye to the Spanish family and the Rabaty ladies. Ouf! Finally out of that train inferno. Nobody was expecting me. I swept the platform with my eyes to see if I knew anybody. The station was almost at the harbor, and the late ferry from Spain, probably the one from Algeciras, was also spilling passengers. I yelled for a taxi; not that I was going far, but my suitcase was heavy.

In the blue light of evening, little shops along the Avenida d'Espagna were still open and badly lit. Still, I could make out colorful Rabat and Berber rugs hanging on the walls, pottery and gleaming copper trays in the windows. The city appeared like a grand circular staircase, its kasbah looming dark and the mosques fading at the top, in the last pink clouds.

"Hotel Continental," I told the taxi driver. In a few minutes we came to a stop. It had been a chic place fifty years ago. Today the hotel was run down, but one could get a decent room with a view for little money. The entrance hall with its beautiful marble floors was still grand, even though the walls needed repainting and the leather armchairs were slightly scratched up. Bellmen and reception personnel had not lost their luster, dressed in rich Moroccan liveries. Lots of foreigners came to this type of hotel: Elderly british couples, Swedes and German women looking for adventures, and occasionally a traveling salesman would show up. Every language was spoken in places like this, but also throughout the city, which was an international enclave at the very tip of North Africa. What a difference Tangier made, contrasting with the sleepy staid towns of Spanish Morocco that we had left behind.

My room was large. I heard the waves even before opening the curtains. Dropping everything, I opened the window, stepped out on the large balcony facing the sea and there I stayed for how long I cannot remember, listening and watching the peaceful night bathed in a blue transparent glow, and raising my eyes to the first brilliant star. I was lulled by that incessant symphony, the sea in motion. It must have been nine o'clock when I went in to take a shower. Here, it was still early for dinner, but I was starving. The inhabitants of Tangier had adopted Spanish ways of living a long time ago; lunch between two and three in the afternoon, dinner at ten in the evening, and theaters starting at eleven every night. For me it was all upside down, being used to very different hours. Here in Tangier, the streets in the center of town were filled with people promenading until all hours. That was in summer of course, because winters were humid, cold, and drenched by rains and wind.

Tonight the Avenida d'Espagna was well lit, but there were few strollers in that part of town. I asked a bellboy where I could find a sandwich. The only place within walking distance was a dingy cafe. I could not afford the fancy restaurants along the avenue. The cafe door was open; music was blaring out of an old phonograph, a wailing flamenco love song. I walked in. Dirty floor, doubtful tabletops, but so what?

I ordered a sandwich of jamon Serrano, a spanish version of prosciutto, and a beer. Sitting in a corner of the room, I felt lonely, nobody to talk to, but this was a small price to pay for total freedom. I sighed. Men were playing cards at another table, drinking cheap wine. I did not like the way they undressed me with their eyes. I looked down at my beer and pretended not to see. Perhaps they thought I was German or Swedish, looking for a man to spend the night with. This was certainly not my goal; I was not against adventure, but it would have to be a totally different type of encounter. The cafe owner, a Spaniard, brought my sandwich, and looked at me with piercing eyes, trying to evaluate the type of woman I was.

"You'd better hurry back to your hotel, senorita," he said, "This is not a place for you."

That was me again, always going forward, loving to explore and often finding myself in awkward positions. Back at the hotel, I was so tired, I did not even think of tomorrow when I slumped into the large sinking bed, not very comfortable. As I closed my eyes, the events of the day swam in flashes behind my lids. Peasants' hard faces appeared and dissolved into sea waves, wailing and vibrating like the train. The three Moslem ladies came dancing on my bed, their skirts lifted up showing all their treasures. A Spanish customs officer all made of black patent leather came running after me. I covered my face with the sheet and soon drifted into sleep.

A warm ray of sun touched my face. Half opening my eyes for an instant, I did not know where I was. When I realized I was in Tangier, I jumped out of bed and ran to the balcony. What a feast, not a cloud in the sky, the sea reflected the sun in millions of broken mirrors, waves sang all the way to the beach. In the street below, a donkey loaded with baskets of freshly baked breads was led by an old Arab man wearing a very white turban. He walked slowly lifting his head, yelling.

"*Hubs, hubs, pan fresco.*" 'Bread, fresh bread.' in Arabic and Spanish. The sight of that bread made me ravenous. I decided to splurge and called room service for coffee and croissants. What to wear today? I was whirling around the room throwing clothes on the bed. Where to go first? Oh well, I had all the time in the world – no chores, nobody to tell me what to do. It seemed too good to be true, so much liberty. I decided I would go to the beach first. It was much too early to meet my friends, I would have to wait until noon. What a surprise it would be! I never thought for an instant that I would not be welcomed. After much choosing, I slipped into a bikini I had designed and sewn myself. I was sure other girls on the beach would not dare to wear something so skimpy. Looking at myself in the mirror, I was pleased. The only thing left to do was to throw a cotton dress over it and slip on a pair of sandals, et voila.

Out on the Avenue, el Levante was blowing, that fierce east wind also called Sirocco and Shergui depending on the region. Today it was blowing sand in eddies, covering car tops, running along the sidewalks, trying to infiltrate every crack in doorways and windows. It burned my eyes, lifted my dress, ruffled my hair, but nevertheless I felt happy and free. Against the wind, I walked and walked, first on the Avenida d'Espagna then on the beach. The sun was burning hot by now. I went down to where the sand was wet and turned east.

There were all kinds of establishments along the way, tents for rent, little beach restaurants; the ones closest to town were unappealing shacks and catered mainly to the less fortunate. Already smoke was billowing from their little grills, a smell of fried fish and piquant sausages in the air. A good mile and a half away was the place I was looking for: El Balneario, a casually

106

elegant place where wealthy Tangier people gathered for lunch and a swim. I was counting on Mr. Abergel, the owner of that establishment, for a free key to one of his fancy bathing huts. He had been one of my adventurous father's school friends and was a great admirer of his feats. What I did not realize was that the moment he saw me, it would take almost no time for the whole town to find out that *la hija de Elias*, Elias's daughter, was here for a vacation. Naturally that included my family.

Father had a fantastic reputation in Tangier, where he grew up. He had been the glamorous hero of his day, confirming the stories he had told us time and again. He had been the leader of his school friends in epic battles against kids from other neighborhoods. They had all mounted horses bareback and had fought with sharpened stones, throwing them at each other. Father had a long thin scar running the length of his nose to prove it.

Later, as a teenager, he had distinguished himself wanting to repay his father's gambling debts. This happened after my grandfather Salomon died in a shipwreck, all the way up in the North Sea. It seems my grandfather had been a somnambulist. Each night he would get up, dress, and ride his horse; nobody knew where. His family did not dare to intervene, as it was dangerous to wake up a sleepwalker. In reality my grandfather was riding every night to gambling houses. How much – if any – of that somnambulism story was real, nobody ever found out.

Father was thirteen years old when his father died. He took a job as a teller in a bank owned by the rich Hassan family. He had quit school and was making very little money working as a teller. He was now his mother and two sisters' sole support. A Scotsman often came to the bank to make large deposits. He liked my father and admired his courage. One day he offered father a job in Scotland to work for Harris Tweed, the wool merchants. What an adventure for a boy of thirteen! Instantly he became a hero in town.

After roaming the world for many years as a traveling salesman for Scottish and British companies he came back to Morocco to visit his mother and sisters. He was now legend. His old friends and his family came to greet him at the docks with a superbly harnessed Arabian horse to ride all the way to his mother's house. As they trotted, a band of little Arab kids followed on foot shouting.

"*Al maalem, l'Inglese, l'Inglese,* Ah! The master, the Englishman, the Englishman."

With all these thoughts in mind, I had walked the distance without noticing. I was almost there, I could see the bathing huts painted white with blue trim. In between stood the open-air restaurant, whose striped awning was flapping in the wind. The bay was beautiful with blue and green waters. White ruffled crests off foamy waves were running, overlapping each other as far as the eye could see. An ocean liner was gliding toward the harbor like a swan. Sailboats were cutting the water at an angle. The beach here was almost empty, except for fishermen mending their nets. A few stragglers were combing the area in hope of finding a lost ring or a full wallet.

I threw my bag in the sands in front of El Balneario. It looked deserted, too early. Only one waiter was there setting tables, trying hard to weigh down the flying tablecloths with plates and silver. I looked kind of silly all alone. She's not one of our guests, was the look the waiter gave me. I turned around, took my dress off, buried my bag in the sand and went for a swim. Entering the transparent turquoise water was bliss. Schools of tiny fish swam around my feet. Would I swim to the raft? It was a little far, bobbing invitingly at the line where the green and the deeper indigo waters met.

In Casablanca I seldom swam far from the beach. The ocean there was treacherous, with ferocious waves crashing on jagged black rocks. Whirlpools could drown one in a matter of minutes. Hammerhead sharks cruised day and night, reason enough to swim only in the many pools along the beaches. Let's go for the raft, I decided, I feel secure here. As I swam, I felt I belonged to the elements, totally blending with them. Had I been a fish or some other sea creature in my multiple past lives? That raft was decidedly too far for my first swim. The tide was receding, pulling me away. I had to swim vigorously to get back to the beach.

Once I was out of danger I started thinking of the friends I was going to meet. These friends were more acquaintances than anything else. They were very different from my usual buddies in Casablanca. These Tanjerinos, as they called themselves, had an aura of big money surrounding them. What was strange was the fact that I would want to seek their company. Subconsciously I was exploring another world, one that I had known as a child, but that was no more. I thought that dipping into their luxuries for a while would be part of a good vacation.

My feet were touching the sand now. Surging out of the water always made me feel stronger and more beautiful, as if I had been anointed by Neptune himself.

Where had I left my bag? That thought brought me back to reality. Oh yes, I had dug it in the sand just in front of that hut on the left. It was a relief to find my belongings; they could have been stolen very easily by one of the beachcombers. I could see people parking their cars behind the restaurant. Reclining in the warm sand, I struck a pinup pose for a while. Nobody was paying attention and that pose was getting tiring; I decided to get up and walk casually through the restaurant. A car was pulling up in the parking area.

"Here they are," I said. Five of my friends were coming out of a top down light blue convertible. They were all laughing, talking loudly, totally carefree in their expensive beach outfits. From the back seat emerged a fellow that I had never seen before. I came up behind one of the boys I knew and reaching up, covered his eyes.

"Guess who?"

He turned around and lifted me up in the air.

"Anit! You're here? I can't believe it, when did you arrive?"

We called him "el Peruano." His father, a very rich man, had gone to Peru decades ago to seek his fortune, abandoning a first wife and a slew of children. He had married again, a Peruvian Indian woman, and the result was here, standing tall, lean, with beautiful teeth and slanted black eyes. In a minute they were all around me, the Pinto sisters, well tanned and very sophisticated. Israel was there also, we were vaguely cousins on my father's side. Alicia Cohen came to kiss me. She was so small, with a tiny waist and hips curved like a china vase.

"Who is this guy?" I asked her, pointing with my chin to the fellow behind them.

"Oh! Him. Mosy, come here, let me introduce you to Anit. She lives in Casablanca, her father is Elias Benaim."

She explained to me that his real name was Moses, but he had been called Mosy when he was a child and the name had stuck.

Was he handsome! Jet-black wavy hair, thick eyebrows shading beautiful green eyes, he was slim, muscular; through his shirt opened to the waist I saw he had hair on his chest. A mischievous smile brightened his face as he said hello. I was impressed; instinctively I thought,"This guy is for me." He looked like Tyrone Power. I locked my green eyes on his, to seduce him; he understood, giving me back an even deeper look. That instant was precious beyond words. Then we started laughing, but I knew I would see him again.

We were all making a lot of racket. Mr. Abergel came over with a frown; I greeted him with a smile. When he found out who I was, he took me by the shoulders and paraded me around the tables, saying to all,

"*La hija de Elias Benaim,* the daughter of Elias Benaim, look how beautiful she is."

Sure enough, he gave me the key to a bathing hut for the duration of my vacation. I felt like the queen of the day; everyone wanted me at their table for lunch, for drinks; what a success. That same afternoon all of Tangier knew I was there, especially after we left Madame Porte's, the most elegant tearoom in town, where my friends had taken me to finish a glorious day. While we were stuffing ourselves with French pastries, I saw people who knew my family. That meant that I could not delay by too much longer my visits to my grandmother Hola, my aunt Simi and my ten cousins, her children. But not just yet – I was having too much fun. My grandfather Leopold, mother's father, could wait a few more days. I did not think he was aware of my coming. He was too remote in his palace of El Marshan.

I got up late the next morning, more at peace now that I knew what to expect for the next few days: going to the beach, meeting my friends, and having a good time – and yes, eventually contacting my relatives. Frankly, I did not have anything serious in mind. I could look forward to a long stretch of lazy days and do as I pleased. I stuffed two hotel towels in a bag. I'd concoct a sandwich for lunch, buying spanish bread and something to put in it, otherwise bread alone was OK. I had not devised anything yet for my regular meals. So far, that was not my most important preoccupation.

What was on my mind was tonight's ball. Who would take me? I hated to ask for favors, so I had to rely on my ingenuity and my charm alone. This seemed very childish, but what were vacations for? At the beach I arrived late, walking leisurely. My friends were all there hanging around, doing nothing. I opened my hut, threw my bag in a corner and called them.

"You hoo! I'm here."

It was like holding court. I sat on the narrow bench against the back wall. Israel came in and slouched on the floor, looking at me as if I were a sea goddess clad in a bikini. The others sat just outside on the sand. Mosy came to the door and stood there looking at me.

"Come in, sit with me," I said to him, but he just stood there looking. I remembered what Alicia had told me about Mosy the day before, while we were munching on cakes at Madame Porte. He had to work every summer during his school vacation. His parents were not rich, even though they had a big house up at the top the hill in the fashionable El Marshan district. It seemed they had lost a lot of money in some unfortunate venture. Was it possible that was the reason he had not asked me to tonight's ball? I wasn't sure. A thought came to my mind: why not Israel? The way he looked at me, I was almost sure I could persuade him to invite me, but I had to be diplomatic.

"Tell me, Israel," I said, "how are the people going to dress for tonight's ball, is it going to be formal?"

"Yes I suppose so," he replied. "These affairs are always formal, but it is summer and I think it is going to be more relaxed. Why do you ask?"

Israel was not handsome, with his reddish hair and the thick eyeglasses he wore, but he was filthy rich. His friends often took advantage of him, even thought they were well-to-do themselves. It was a ritual to go to Madame Porte almost every afternoon for tea. They told me they would order enormous quantities of pastries before Israel came in, and made sure to put the charges on his account. I smiled at him.

"You must be a good dancer, would you dance with me at the ball tonight?"

His mouth opened, but no sound came out. After a long minute he finally said what I wanted to hear.

"Not just a dance! Would you be my date for the ball tonight?"

He seemed not to believe his own words. It was too enormous. For a short while I said nothing, savoring. He was literally held in suspense.

"Yes why not," I said casually. "It will be fun to go with you."

What I really meant was, it will be fun to get rid of you once I am in.

"I'll be at your hotel at ten PM sharp," he said, clearly excited. He started fidgeting, got up, sat down, got up a second time and heralded for all to hear,

"I'm taking Anit to the dance tonight!" His face was flushed, he went around erratically like a headless chicken.

Mosy gave me a deep look. Was he aware of my trickery, or was he hurt that I had not asked him? I got up, went to the door and brushed my lips against Mosy's cheek. He became beet-red.

He tried to grab my fingers in his, but I was already running out to the sea. I yelled.

"I'm going for a swim, are you coming?"

I made a show of myself swimming, fast backstrokes all the way to the raft. As I tried to hoist myself up, I felt two hands grab my waist. It was electrifying. Mosy held me tight against him while he was hoisting me. We lay on the wet planks, I on my back, Mosy on his stomach, our skin touching. We were panting. The waves were clapping against the raft, distant voices came with the wind. It was a moment of pure physical delight, of promises to come. There was no need to talk, our eyes said it all. What a vacation it was going to be.

That night, the ball at the Emsallah Gardens was packed. Music could be heard streets away. As we entered the immense gardens, the sound of the "Bonnet de San Pedro" orchestra transported me to the far away Caribbean Islands. Elegant couples, the women in brilliant summer dresses, wove between tables. Palm trees swayed, waiters were darting here and there like hummingbirds. Everything seemed in motion with the music. Pervading the air was a multitude of heady scents coming from masses of flowering bushes, a paradise for the senses.

I felt exhilarated, beautiful, in my clinging white crepe gown. Reluctantly, I sat down at a table with Israel. He ordered drinks and asked me to dance. God, he kept stepping on my feet every couple of minutes and apologizing for the next five. What a bore! And on top of it all he was holding me tight, to keep his prize from escaping. Above his shoulder, I scanned the garden, trying hard to find Mosy, which was difficult with all the bobbing heads and twirling bodies. There he was, standing at the edge of the dance floor. At last I managed to pry away, pretending a trip to the powder room. Meandering through the crowd, I was passing by him without stopping, on purpose, when I heard,

"Anit."

The rest of the evening was bliss. We tangoed tight against each other, a wave of heat invading us. We sambaed to the fashionable Colombian tune of "Se va el caiman." I had totally forgotten Israel, poor guy. I knew I was being cruel, but I didn't care, and he was too shy to come after me. Mosy walked me back to my hotel; it was three o'clock in the morning and we were exhausted. The night was blue and silent as we went through narrow streets and down steep winding stairs. We stopped in corners to kiss passionately. Fire swept through our bodies, but at the hotel door we said goodnight and he left "until tomorrow." As I went to bed I was trembling in anticipation of what was to come. It was daybreak before I fell asleep.

112

A week was already half gone. I decided to call my aunt Simi. She was shocked that I had not written to her before my arrival in Tangiers, and appalled by the fact that I had a room in a hotel. She was screaming into the phone.

"This is not done, a young lady does not stay alone in hotels! Your father must have gone mad. We will be expecting you for lunch today at two in the afternoon."

She hung up without waiting for an answer.

Good, this gave me plenty of time. I dressed in more conservative clothes for the occasion – a white linen skirt, a turquoise shirt, and sandals would do. Outside it was windy as usual, but cooler than yesterday. I had to cross at least half of the city on foot before I reached my aunt Simi's house. This made me happy because it meant that to get there I had to revisit most of the places I had not seen since before the war. I walked up the hill from the beach to reach Boulevard Pasteur. This part of town looked well tended. Street cleaners were scrubbing the pavement and sweeping debris left over from last evening's promenaders. Stores were opening, overflowing with expensive merchandise: Swiss watches, Italian shoes and leather bags. Jewelers were setting their windows with square cut emeralds, priceless diamonds and gold bracelets. Slowing down, I reached Place de France, the city's hub.

In front of me was the famous "Cafe de Paris". Crossing the square, I noticed it was already full. This was a very special place. Tangier, with its international status, its free money market and its lawless banks attracted all kinds of shady characters. One could meet people from all over the world. There were newspapermen taking notes, gesticulating merchants, dealers in contraband, diamond smugglers, spies! And of course a slew of snobbish aristocrats, British and French for the most part, who came here to live out their fantasies. Also disbarred lawyers, unlicensed doctors and genuine writers in search of the exotic, all of them drinking their *cafe con leche* while listening to other peoples' conversations, making subtle gestures to warn somebody, or to conclude a deal. A fascinating crowd indeed, which typified this city where everything seemed to be permitted.

I felt slightly uncomfortable walking past the tables, knowing countless eyes were following my curves. Walking very straight, chin up, auburn hair flying in the wind, I reached the corner and turned down another hill, Rue de la Liberté, passing our dear Madame Porte, and El Minzah, a sumptuous

Moorish palace that had been converted into a very elegant hotel. I could not resist the temptation and went inside to have a look. For a half hour I steeped myself in luxury looking at myself in all the mirrors, imagining that I was some visiting diplomat. It felt good until a footman gave me an unambiguous look, which made me understand I wasn't welcome.

Continuing downhill on the right, the bay was shimmering green and blue, the wind creating a festoon of white lace on the running waves. I was nearing the "Socco Grande", a daily open market, sprawling across a large plaza and several adjacent streets. In a few minutes I had passed from European sophistication to another world, a place that was so totally estranged from the one I had just left that it seemed impossible they could coexist in the same city.

The Socco Grande was the everyday marketplace of the Tanjawis, as the natives were called. The sellers were mostly Berbers, mountaineers coming from the Rif mountains surrounding Tangier, or from the valleys south of the city. A clamor hung above the crowd, the muezzin's eerie voice was filling the sky atop his mosque. He was chanting the Koran.

"*Allah in Allah! Allah Akbar*", vibrating the name of God above the braying donkeys, the shrill voices of bartering merchants, the cracked honking of old buses. It was covering that noisy, colorful, moving humanity with blessings. Blue smoke rose in spirals from hot grills, where little sausages were cooking, sputtering grease, titillating taste buds with the wonderful aroma of roasting lamb and spices. Colorful peasant women sat on the dusty ground selling little mounds of freshly picked very red tomatoes, green peppers, mountains of yellow squash and onions. Little stalls displayed pyramids of shiny black olives, making the plaza look like a giant tapestry woven into strange shapes and riotous colors. Odors were sumptuous or disgusting, depending upon where one stood. The penetrating fragrance of flowers massed in tin pails was intoxicating and so was the sweet aroma of ripe fruit. Pink peaches, grapes, dark plums, figs, and above all melons and watermelons.

Walking across this enchanting garden of nature, it was easy to round an alley to step on a suffocating pile of rotting vegetables and mule dung, not to mention animal entrails, the whole buzzing with brilliant blue flies gorging on the spoils.

I stopped to buy flowers. The florist had no shop to speak about, just a few planks of old wood nailed together. She sat in the middle of all her bouquets, a young Berber looking like a flower herself. Beautiful, healthy red cheeks and smiling eyes under her wide straw hat adorned with large black wool pompons. I chose a bunch of gladiola of various colors and some wispy white flowers to go with them. The woman gathered and shook the stems to rid them of water. In a minute she had fashioned a wonderful intricate bouquet, looking like a miniature pyramid. She presented it to me, after wiping her wet hands on the blue and red-striped cloth she wore around her hips.

"*Bash hal?*" "How much?" I asked.

She quoted me a price that was clearly too much, but to her surprise, I didn't bother bartering. I gave her the money, pleased that I had thought to buy flowers for my aunt and grandmother. Perhaps it would smooth things over. The Socco Grande was not so different from our open markets in Casablanca, but the native costumes here were unique to the region and so was the color of the sky and the constant wind. I was taken by the magic of the surroundings and continued meandering among the tents and frontless tiny stores with squatting vendors.

Food was not the only merchandise sold here. Suspended on long poles with hooks, pastel colored djellabahs, serouals and kerchiefs twisted in the wind like so many odd flags. Here was a man buying eggs and stuffing them into the hood of his brown wool robe, a precarious place at best. I imagined little yellow chicks popping out of that warm nest. As I walked toward the vegetable stands, I heard a guttural voice calling.

"*A lalla, a ghzalla.* Lady, Beautiful gazelle! Buy my onions, the best in the country, fresh picked this morning with my own hands."

Already he was wrapping the bunch in newspaper.

"I don't want to buy onions," I said.

He seemed very vexed, threw the whole package on a mound of vegetables and cursed me for not buying his precious onions. His neighbor was nicer; crouching in a mountain of fresh mint leaves, he smiled at me. I stopped to smell, closing my eyes.

"*Hak a lalla.*" "Lady, take." He gave me a few sprigs of mint.

"*Barak Allahu fik.*" "Blessings upon you", I replied. I was delighted by such gallantry. Tomorrow I would come back and buy a watermelon for the beach and explore some more, but it was getting late for the lunch. As I walked toward the arch that served as an exit for the giant market and toward the Rue d'Italie, I wondered about these tough mountaineers coming down to the market every day with their loads. Women carrying the heaviest, often enormous bundles of firewood or charcoal, totally bent under the weight, their calves bound in leather leggings, while the men rode donkeys or mules laden with heavy baskets of fruits and vegetables. They were rugged people who smelled of the earth, their skins tanned by countless winds and suns.

I reached the Calle d'Italia. In Tangier all streets names were written in three languages: Arabic, Spanish and French. That street was the continuation of the open market. On my left was the Fez Market, a covered one, that Europeans favored. The rest of the street was lined on one side with wholesale and retail groceries, mostly imported stuff. One could buy enormous wheels of Gouda cheese and tins of salted butter from Holland, english cookies in fancy boxes, sacks of coffee from Brazil and local olive oil sold in barrels. The stores had no doors or windows, only metal shutters rolled up in the morning and noisily brought down at night.

Most of the merchants here were rich Jews, whose families had lived in Tangier for hundreds of years. It was difficult to walk that street during the day, as people never seemed to use the sidewalks. Instead they dragged their feet in the middle of the street. Cars were honking madly, trying to pierce that solid wall of humanity blocking the way. I walked the street in the shade along the walls of the Mendoubia, a park of great beauty. Above, huge dark cedars swayed in the breeze; the sky was intense and very blue.

I turned into the Calle Tetuan, an old and narrow street, tripping on the disjointed cobblestones that smelled of donkey droppings and wood smoke. Old rococo buildings with Spanish wrought iron balconies lined the sidewalk in uneven rows. Crumbling plaster cherubs hanging on flower garlands smiled at passers-by from under the eaves. Here the dust of time seemed to hang for eternity.

I pushed on the heavy door of my aunt's house. I went from intense light to a dark cave-like entrance hall and climbed the marble steps to the second floor. The doors were open on each side of the landing. where a vague odor of fried fish and baked bread permeated the air, along with a smell of bleach and furniture polish. I walked into the large hall and was confronted by a mass of heavy sculpted furniture, waxed to such a shine it reflected the red hues of an old Moroccan rug. Floors had just been washed, and the intricate Moorish tiles glistened wet.

There were so many rooms in the apartment it was easy to get lost.

116

The living room was empty. Wandering down a long corridor, I heard noises. Shouting voices showed me the way; it seemed everybody was in the kitchen.

Aunt Simi was standing in the middle of that vast room, surrounded by a big ancient stove and a stone sink full of dishes. Clad in a blue apron, strands of gray hair flying from her chignon, she still looked regal. Very straight with smooth white skin and the same Roman nose as my father. I knew that she had been a great beauty in her youth. The maids around her were scurrying, mopping floors, washing pots. Rachel and Sete, my two spinster cousins, were setting a long table on the other side of the room, near a large open window with a view of the Mendoubia gardens. I stood in the doorway watching; nobody was paying attention. After a few minutes of this game I burst in.

"Hi everybody." Rachel dropped a plate, Sete looked at me with her big bulging eyes. Startled, aunt Simi rearranged her hair with one hand while she embraced me.

"Anit, Anit." She gave me a big loud kiss. "You look so slim, are you sure you are eating well? Come let's sit down. We'll be eating in half an hour, Mercedes and the boys have not arrived yet." She still had that beautiful contralto voice. Sete and Rachel came to sit with us on one of the maids' beds set in the far corner of the kitchen. Sete had that unpleasant way of looking at me. In her eyes I represented all she wanted, but would never achieve. Rachel was not as jealous, but she was inquisitive about my flirtations and everything else she could extract from me. I chose to be evasive in my answers. Rachel was prone to violent migraines and would closet herself for days in her darkened room. As for Sete, poor thing, she was almost ugly. I had never seen her without curlers. Her face was oily, her nose too big, her body shapeless. Ten years ago some fellow had asked for her hand in marriage; unbelievably, she had refused on the grounds that he was too plain – a bad move that she was to regret for the rest of her life.

Living with their mother was not helping either; aunt Simi was rigid in her morals, it was marriage or nothing. I could not understand her ways. She had lived all her married life sequestered and pregnant year after year. Had she ever been loved? I only knew my uncle from an oval sepia photograph on the living room wall. He was a real mystery, nobody ever spoke about him. After making ten children with his wife he had vanished without a trace. Some said he had left for the jungles of South America, others that he had died of a shameful malady. I was not bold enough to reopen the subject with my cousins.

I was really hungry by now, ready to pounce on a mountain of fried anchovies piled up on a big ceramic platter that a maid had just set on the table. Behind her came other maids, carrying dishes with various salads and a big potato and onion spanish omelet. Three of the boys came in one behind the other. Isake, Abramito and Selomon.

"Ola Mama, Ola Anita, Como estas?" They spoke Spanish like all the Jews of Tangier, originally all descendents of the Jews that were expelled from Spain when Isabella, the very Catholic queen, threw them out of the country in 1492, and they had to drift to other countries. My cousins came to kiss me with a look of anticipation on their faces. I was the foreign cousin, but I was hip to them; it meant that playing love games was possible. Mercedes, the youngest of the girls, came running in, out of breath; she was the prettiest of all. We all sat and started eating. Abramito already had his burning black eyes on me. Selomon, who was sitting next to me, was not wasting his time either, inching a hand on my thigh under the table. I kept pushing it away, but it came back. I was afraid aunt Simi would notice. How annoying this all was. Isake was watching, a smile on his face. He seldom came to eat, said his mother. We all knew he had a Spanish mistress and liked to hang out with the Roma. We were already eating a dessert of green melon and watermelon when Jacobo came in with Moses.

"Sorry I'm late Mama", he said. "Hello Anit, nice to see you here. I went to pick up Moses at the beach. Hortensia and Esther can't make it. They'll see you Friday night."

Esther was the eldest of the ten children; she was married to a rich banker and seemed to be very happy. She would always laugh and giggle no matter how bad the news was. How different was Jacobo, the oldest boy. He looked like a dark bull, with very olive skin and covered with hair. He was far from appetizing. The family knew nothing of his private life. He was gay, a fact that I only found out years later. In those days the subject was taboo. Jacobo was starting a wholesale business. I knew my father had lent him some money to start it. The debt would never be repaid, even when several years later, father would need it most and Jacopo had become a rich real estate lord in Madrid. The youngest of the boys was Moses, only eighteen and the handsomest of all. Tall, well built, he had a winning smile and beautiful blond hair. Sweetly he came to me.

"You are my favorite cousin," he said, kissing my hand.

Both Mercedes and Moses brightened the whole table with their jokes and laughter. Who could have known then that Moses would die the next summer of tuberculosis and that Mercedes, after marrying and having two children, would waste away with cancer before she was thirty.

Toward the end of the meal, while the mood was light and the talk lively, the question I dreaded fell like a stone from aunt Simi's lips.

"Why aren't you married, Anit? At twenty-three I already had four children. How long are you going to wait, what does your father say about it, and your mother Ryta? I do not understand."

It was difficult to discuss the matter with such a rigid person. How could I tell aunt Simi that I intended to live intensely before marrying. I wished cousin Hortensia had come to lunch with us. She was the only one that could have spoken for me. At least she was modern enough to understand. But somebody came to the rescue; Selomon suddenly said.

"Oh! Mother, Anit is so beautiful, she can have anybody she chooses."

Immediately Abramito added, "Anybody!" giving me a long look, while Selomon was squeezing my hand.

With a noise of chairs being pushed, we all got up. It was siesta time.

"Anit you'll go with Rachel for your nap. She has a large bed." Aunt Simi looked at the boys in a way that said, 'I know what you are thinking, I saw it all. Get going and leave Anit alone.'

My thoughts were with Mosy. I longed to take a nap with him instead of Rachel! Perhaps tomorrow. We were going to spend the day together. I counted the hours, imagining so many things.

I visited my grandmother Hola later that afternoon. Grandmother Hola lived across the street from aunt Simi. She knew I was coming; I saw her waiting at the door. A tiny ninety-three year old lady, with piercing blue eyes, high cheek bones and very white hair showing under her navy blue silk coif. She still wore what had been fashionable for Jewish women a hundred years ago. When I came in that afternoon, she embraced me with much love. She was my father's mother and I was her favorite granddaughter. I couldn't get over how small she was, the top of her head barely coming to my shoulders.

"Come, come my dearest, let's have some tea."

Trotting in front of me, in her swishing long skirts and tight bolero vest, she took me into the dining room. The table was set with old china plates filled with delicate pastries she had made. A copper tray with steaming glasses of fresh mint-flavored green tea was waiting for us. I always marveled at the beautiful Moorish tiles covering the walls, the white lace curtains and the tidiness of the place. Was it the sun pouring in from the large balconied windows that made this place so warm, or was it her presence that illuminated the whole abode? What an interesting woman she was, up to date on everything, reading the newspapers daily, and writing long letters. She was way ahead of her time and certainly more modern than her two daughters, my aunts. I told her of my ambitions as a painter.

"Well I believe you should persevere in whatever you set your heart to."

She gave me a kiss and blessed me. The sun was getting low, glazing the walls orange, and we were still talking. It was late when I left. She waved at me from the balcony, a little navy blue shape that I would see for a few more summers and never again. I took a shorter route to go back. Walking fast, I went under a set of arches to a narrow street called the Siaghins, monopolized by the money-changers. Below that street was another small square, a famous one, "El Socco Chico," The Little Market, where the type of merchandise sold was very different. Lined with small cafes, the plaza dealt in human flesh. Beautiful women, prostitutes in search of prey, were competing with young boys looking for moneyed foreigners. One could also buy drugs without prescriptions in the many farmacias around the square.

In Tangier, expatriates found a haven. It was a place where homosexuality was permitted and where drugs like hashish, kif, and majoun were sold freely. The latter was a kind of aphrodisiac jam laced with hashish and spanish fly, strong enough to send one into other worlds. The Socco Chico was also a nest of spies. Here they could mingle undetected with the other riffraff going up and down the street. It was strange to see everyday honest people sipping coffee or a glass of wine at the terrace of "El Cafe Central," or walking by, but the Socco Chico was a square leading from the markets to the casbah and the streets heading to the harbor. I had the guts to dare walking through that neighborhood at dusk, but my heart was beating fast!

At the hotel, there was a message from Mosy. He had called several times, the bell boy said, as he handed me a frantic note; Mosy had looked for me everywhere, on the beach, in town, at Madame Porte; please call him at any time. Well! I had no idea I had made such an impression. I felt a surge of power, a little bit like a spider closing in on her prey. It was awful to

120

think that way. My desires would be fulfilled. At the same time, the very fact that I had succeeded with Mosy started to make me lose interest, but what the hell, I had a beautiful man served on a platter, I might as well enjoy it.

I went to get Mosy at his work the next day at noon, making myself very sexy with a low-cut dress. We decided to go to the beach first. Walking past El Balneario shoes in hand we went almost as far as the Villa Harris, a sumptuous white castle-like mansion in a recess of the beach that belonged to a wealthy Englishman. It was a silent place, except for a few shrieking seagulls zeroing on crashing waves, and the wind playing harp against the mountains behind us. A fierce sun was beating down on the white sand, making it sparkle like crystal. We found an old solitary boat turned upside down on the sand and chose its shadowed side for a hideaway. Peeling off our clothes, we stood in our bathing suits. For a minute we drank of each other before sinking in the hot sand, like in a soft bed. As we tortured each other with caresses, birds circled above in a jealous frenzy, while the sea conducted a rhythmic ballet. For us nothing existed anymore.

One afternoon I went to visit my grandfather Leopold. Instead of walking up the avenue, I took the steps across the Casbah. It was a longer way to go, but much more colorful. Winding through narrow twisted alleys, where houses painted in pale green, tender blue, or yellow created fantastic shadows, I climbed steadily. Now and then I stopped to regain my breath. The climb was steep. Barefoot kids were following me. At every corner, a handful of them joined the group, wide–eyed urchins with sad dirty faces. They clung to my arms, to my dress, begging. I stopped abruptly.

"*Ser, ser fhalk!*" I said. "Go, go away."

It was like talking to the wind. They continued pestering me.

"*Allah Ejib, Allah Ejib!*" "God will provide!" I yelled.

Nothing would deter them, they were like leeches all over me. Opening my bag, I fished out a handful of Reals, pennies, and a piece of bread. They became wild. I threw the whole thing as far as I could down the steps and they disappeared screaming like a band of hungry sparrows. Meandering up the streets, lined with a few small grocery stores I passed blind beggars, a group of jesters in bright costumes and a snake charmer with a cobra sticking out of a basket on top of his head. I finally reached El Marshan. An open plateau full of flowering gardens, perched on a high hill that dominated the city, it was a choice place to own a house. A mixture of people lived up here. Most were old families with big houses, but near the steps and in the back alleys, some poor Tanjawis owned or rented very modest dwellings. The palace minaret could already be seen at the end of the winding narrow street I had taken. It had been one of grandfather Leopold's follies to build a moorish castle and to add a mosque-like minaret, for the sole purpose of having his divinely voiced wife Nejma sing the Koran. It had created a great scandal in Tangier at the time. How could a Jew have the nerve? Grandpa Leopold was arrested for blasphemy, almost costing him his life. He had gotten out of it by offering the authorities an enormous sum of money in gold.

Few passers-by walked the streets at this early afternoon hour. A blinding hot sun made the sky, the houses, and everything else look white. The wind up here was free to play, making the palms sway and the pine trees tremble. I walked in the shade of Jacaranda trees along the walls of the Italian Legation, wondering how I would find the old man. He had always been a puzzle and a mystery to me.

Grandpa Leopold was born in Ismir, Turkey from a very rich and powerful father, whom people called '*El Papou de las liras*,' the father of money, in the Ladino language they spoke. I had only seen a faded photograph of that great grandfather standing on the steps of his house draped in a long caftan, a heavy turban on his head, giving weight to his bearded face. Leopold was the fourth of five brothers. When he was a little boy, the family had moved to Alexandria in Egypt, where he grew up in the middle of splendor, his father being the owner of a very prosperous antiquities business. By the time they were in their twenties, four of the boys already were accomplished antiquarians. The oldest, Ephraim, dreamed of America. He would soon establish himself in San Francisco, under the name of Hadj Benguiat. In time he became one of Phoebe Hearst's favorite art dealers. The second son David became a fine jeweler and left for England. The three youngest were also eager to see the world, but they had little money of their own. They went together to ask their father to help, but despite his great wealth, he gave them nothing. He felt that his sons should make it on their own, the way he himself had done. The three of them, Vital, Leopold and Benjamin, left their father's house disappointed, but determined in their goals. They chose London for their headquarters.

Their brother David was already there; he would at least provide shelter and food in the beginning. Having been brought up in upper class Alexandria, they were not foreign to British culture. Like the other brothers, their abilities and intelligence made them very successful. In a few years, they had become renowned art dealers, and counted Queen Victoria among their clients.

I was walking lost in thought and soon found myself at the palace gate. The groundskeeper saw me and started running to let me in. His wife came out of a little hut-like house at the end of the garden, one hand shielding her eyes from the sun. They were both Tanjawi peasants, good brown wrinkled faces with a ready smile.

"*A benty, tghool! kif kuntsy labas?* 'My daughter come in, how are you?' Your grandfather is going to be so pleased."

I was appalled to see the state the garden was in. Weeds everywhere, figs had fallen all over from the many trees and had been left to rot on the ground. Wild chickens were running in the alleys. My God what a change it was from the well-tended garden I had seen before the war. Why were those keepers not doing their jobs?

"Be careful when you climb the stairs, your grandfather has yet to build a banister," yelled the old keeper.

Inside it was cool, well ventilated, with numerous arched windows around a large patio where a fountain sang a sad melody to the empty rooms around it. I frowned; what had happened? Climbing, I stopped to admire antique Persian tiles imbedded in the steps. But the walls were naked, where once priceless tapestries had hung. At the top of the stairs, I paused; it was drafty, all the windows were open. I did not see the shutters that would ordinarily close them, beautifully hand painted ancient wood panels that had taken grandfather so many years to acquire. Upstairs, his bedroom took up a big portion of the entire floor. Not hearing a sound, I stepped in. An enormous Italian Renaissance baldaquinoed bed loomed in the center. Through its twisted columns and the gold embroidered bedspread, I saw him.

Grandpa Leopold was facing a mirror, trimming his short white beard. What an imposing figure he was, tall, heavy set, very straight for his age. He must have been ninety at the time. Always wearing a well-cut navy blue suit and a white silk shirt. Sensing me, he turned around.

"*Ma petite fille, ma cherie, ven aqui.* My granddaughter, my darling come here."

He was always mixing at least two languages.

"Give me a kiss! What a rare treat it is to have you visit me." I noticed that his tie, a regular one, was made in a bow instead of a knot and that the tips of his expensive leather shoes had been cut off to free the toes. He was a prince, with a tremendous sense of humor. His eccentricities came no doubt from years of wealth and power.

"Darling, how is your mother, my beloved daughter Ryta? How long are you staying in Tangier? Let me show you my latest acquisitions. Why are you naked from the waist down?"

I was stunned.

"I'm not naked, Grandpa, I'm wearing beige slacks."

"You should know better. Young ladies like you should always wear darker skirts or pants, so men will not be confused."

Hmm! This told me that his sight was very bad. As we walked around he held my arm.

"Dear little girl, look at that fantastic painting on the easel, right here in the corner, a student of Raphael painted that Madonna. *Ma che bella!*"

There was nothing there to look at, I was alarmed. He grabbed me by the shoulder.

"See this wonderful statue my dear. I got it last year. It comes from the Roman ruins of Volubilis in the Atlas mountains. Such purity of lines, a masterpiece, that Roman youngster. What do you say, beloved?"

"Well yes, yes it is very beautiful." Tears came to my eyes. Grandfather was going blind. There was no statue there any longer. I looked at the ceiling and saw that all the eighteenth-century Murano blown glass chandeliers had disappeared. Something was very wrong. I realized the whole palace was empty, except for the bed and a chest of drawers. What a tragedy. It did not take me long to figure things out; Grandfather had been robbed of all his treasures. I did not want to think the groundskeeper was at fault, but who else knew the house so well? I had to be alone for a while, all this was too much. I was ready to burst.

"Grandpa Leo, can I go up to the minaret?" I asked.

"Go darling, go. I remember my beautiful Nejma's voice when she sang up there." The tower was narrow, the stairs steep. On that little square terrace, leaning over the sculpted edge, I let go and sobbed uncontrollably. After a few minutes, feeling better, I calmed down and let the sea wind dry my eyes. It was such a lovely afternoon. From up here and across the blue waters, I could see Algeciras, the little Spanish fishing port, all pink and white in the afternoon sunlight. Coming down, I found grandfather smiling. He seemed so happy and totally unaware of what was happening. We talked for more than an hour. Grandpa was telling me of his business appointments, of the purchases he was going to make. As I said goodbye, hugging him he said,

"Querida, darling, this palace will be yours and your sister's when I go. This will be my present for both of you."

Mohamed the groundskeeper and his wife were waiting for me downstairs, all smiles. Hypocrites! They thought they could get away with it, but I was going to call father immediately. Hopefully they had not robbed him of his money, but it was a strong possibility. The whole story troubled me for days. I did not tell any of my friends. Tangerinos were fond of scandals.

Some people would relish the downfall of Leopold Benguiat. Why? Jealousy, of course, of a man that had known such riches from London to Paris to New York, a prominent figure in the arts, one who had roamed Europe and Asia to find unique, priceless tapestries, paintings and objets d'art. He certainly made a lot of people envious when he bought the Palazzo D'Avanzati, a Florentine thirteenth-century marvel, and in the same époque bought Catherine the Great's famous pearl necklace, and the palace of the Duke of Savoy in Nice, France.

Grandfather Leopold and his brothers had often made the front page of the New York Times with the spectacular auctions they had in New York with Park and Bernet, and a very high profile lawsuit against Cartier the jeweler, who had tried to cheat them of several hundred thousand dollars. The crash of 1929 had taken three quarters of the Benguiats' fortune.

After that, Grandfather Leopold had decided to let go of all the hustle and bustle. He wanted peace of mind and decided to live quietly in Tangier. There was also another reason for choosing that city. My grandmother Nejma, who had separated from him twenty years before, owned a house almost in front of the palace. He was still in love with her, even though he had cheated with so many other women. His last dreams were going to shatter when he realized all his precious belongings were no more. In later years he would lose some of his mind because of it. Despite all efforts, none of his treasures were ever recovered.

Fortunately for me, the quantity of dances, balls, and outings at the end of that summer distracted me to the point of forgetting my poor grandfather's troubles. Mosy and I had spent many enchanting days and evenings, sweet unforgettable moments. Strangely enough, toward the end of my stay, I got the notion that I, who never wanted to get married, could spend the rest of my life with him. The day before my departure we drove to the mountain for a picnic. Mosy was sad.

"I'll come and visit you in Casablanca, I promise," he said.

In the afternoon, we went all the way down to Cape Spartel and stopped at the Hercules Grottos. The wind was terrible. A fierce crazy sea was battling the rocks where the Atlantic Ocean met the Mediterranean. It got cold. Mosy took me in his arms.

"I am very much in love with you, Anit."

"I am too."

Suddenly I heard myself ask, "Could you spend the rest of your life with me?"

He dropped his arms.

"Well, I really don't know," he replied, obviously embarassed. "I am so young, I still have to finish my studies. Why don't we let it go at that and see how we feel a few months from now."

I understood immediately that I had made a giant blunder.

"You are right, it is ridiculous, let's stay good friends anyway," I said, trying to put up a good face.

Pride made me say those words. I did not want him to see my distress.

And so we parted that evening, without promises. The return journey was gloomy. Why had I acted so silly? I was mad at myself. For once I had let my emotions rule. I felt angry at the world, sad, hurt. I blamed fate, and even thought the dress I had worn that day had brought bad luck. Sitting in that awful train, I did not even look at the scenery. My beautiful vacation had turned sour and it was all my fault, damn it. My chest was heavy with sighs and I was surprised to feel tears on my face. Self-pity, horrors, that's all I needed. The train stopped. I stared at the window in a daze.

"Where can we be?"

A man stepped into the compartment, looking for a seat. Oh! God, I don't want to be seen like this. I turned my head the opposite way and blew my nose discreetly, saying,

"Hm! Sorry, the train smoke got in my eye."

The man looked at me and I smiled. It was imperative to think of something else, something other than Mosy and his horrible refusal. Little by little, my thoughts drifted to happier things. I remembered that before starting my vacation, I had been asked to play a part in a theater production that was to be given for a charity this winter and I also had to help with the costumes. By the time the train pulled into Casablanca station, I had practically forgotten my woes.

At home, telling the story of my vacation, I only mentioned a few good things. I did not peep a word about Mosy to my parents, but to the rest I embroidered the whole affair a hundredfold to make it seem even more glamorous. No shadows remained of my half love affair with Mosy. At night, I could dream all I wanted about him, to my satisfaction. I had no doubts that another beau would appear soon.

Chapter 11: 1947

Recovery

At the beginning of 1947 Casablanca was regaining its former splendor. People were starting to put the dreadful war years and their aftermath behind them. There was a lot of money to be made, thanks to the Americans. They had kept several military bases in Morocco and employed a great number of eager citizens. Being well paid in dollars meant that one could live almost in luxury. Some Americans had married local girls and they were opening businesses. For the first time ever, we were seeing refrigerators and electric stoves in store windows. My friend Stella had married a charming American fellow, Roy Richie. She was one of the lucky ones. She had found the right man, unlike so many of us young women, who had been disillusioned by handsome but fickle American servicemen.

Stella and her new husband bought a house in Anfa, an elegant neighborhood of Casablanca. They started an import-export business with the United States. When I went to visit her, we reminisced about the war years, when we were two teenagers going through Casablanca's back streets, picking up discarded bottles and selling them for a pittance, just to have a few francs in our pockets. We were proud to have survived all the miseries of that era.

Father also was trying to come back to his former position as a well-to-do businessman. Looking for a lucrative way to make money, he opened a real estate office in the center of the city. Land speculation was very rewarding at the moment. Soon, with his know-how, he was making deals with important landowners and doing well.

For us ladies, there was no end to spending, parties, plays, fashion shows. That year, Christian Dior, the famous French designer, came out with the New Look. Young women in Casablanca were trying to surpass Paris in elegance. We had to get the best of everything. The competition was fierce. Still, something at the very core of my being told me how superficial all this was. I longed for something more meaningful, but I did not know what.

I joined a youth movement with socialist tendencies. I went to exciting meetings, where young militant Moslems were starting to stir up an anti-French movement. The sessions were stormy and vehement against the French oppressor. The young Arabs and the few Jews that attended gave inflamed speeches about freedom, about the rights of men. They also spoke about the discrimination in jobs and schools. Moroccan Jews and Moslems suffered enormous injustices at the hands of the French colonists.

The place where we congregated was a small room in a shack, inside the Parc Lyautey. All of us smoked cheap black tobacco cigarettes, filling the air with clouds of ill-smelling smoke. These sessions stirred in me the notion of adventure, risk and danger that I was so fond of, but how far could I go?

The French police raided the place one afternoon and made arrests. Two of the young men attending were sent to jail. Fortunately I was not present that day. For me it was a warning that this was a dangerous game. I kept all this from father and mother. They would never understand how I could side with rebels for any reason. I was getting involved in such things because of my dissatisfaction with the establishment, of all the taboos girls my age faced in Morocco.

I was twenty-three years old and was still living at home and being treated as a teenager by my parents. When I begged Father to let me go to the Beaux Arts academy in Paris, I felt frustrated not to be taken seriously. I had already exhibited some drawings at the Salon d'Automne in Casablanca with success. It was reasonable to assume that I was ready for professional art classes. Father's answer to my demand was a big No. To him the Beaux Arts was a place of perdition. What his strict mind saw was that living in Paris, alone, and in the Latin quarter to boot, my life would consist of a continuous orgy with bearded artists and other characters of the left bank.

In reply, I told him that if I wanted to live that kind of a life, I could do it right here under his nose and he would not know a thing. It made him furious. How did I dare speak to him in this manner? Once again we were at odds, and I had not gained a thing. I was longing to learn art with real painters, and not with a bunch of old ladies at the Casablanca Art Academy. Anywhere I looked, there was no way out. No freedom. A girl in Morocco was to live at home until she married. Doing otherwise was looking for trouble. I already had had my share of scandal before the end of the war, thanks to my pitiful affair with Jack. I was disheartened, without money of my own.

After weeks of asking, Father at last consented to let me work. That was another taboo; in our country, women in well-to-do families did not work. Father sent me to a maritime insurance company he was dealing with to start as a secretary. It would improve my typing skills, he said. I was so bored with the dryness of the texts, not understanding half of what I was typing, that I fell asleep several times a day. The place was dreadfully somber. Tall narrow windows half covered with dirty blinds gave a yellowish green hue to the whole room. Twenty Remington typewriters going full blast filled the air with a cacophony of repetitious sounds, similar to the sound of machine guns. The people who worked there looked as if they had been molded from the mildewed ceiling, the gray walls and the moth-eaten rugs.

I did not last very long there, only a month. At home, the news was not received well. If I could not stay in a simple job like this one, what was I capable of? But where could I find an interesting job, with interesting people?

The second job I landed was very different, but just as far from my aspirations. It was in a toy factory. My job was to paint the faces of hundreds of dolls lined up on a long and narrow table. In the mornings, I had to stare at these little naked celluloid bodies without eyes, nostrils or lips. It made me shiver. The feeling of cold was accentuated by the fact that it was winter and the room was freezing. The boss, a stingy old Frenchman, yelled each time I lit the stove. Every morning his complaint was the same. I was eating away his profits. In that uncomfortable atmosphere, I was also confronted everyday with his enormous dog, a Great Dane. This evil creature disrupted my work by running around like crazy. He toppled paint cans and jumped for the finished dolls on the table to crunch them up in his ferocious jaws. Preparing the animal's pail of porridge was also part of my daily work. I wondered how much longer I could stand it.

One morning the boss asked me if I could take the dog for his walk. After fitting the beast's collar and grabbing the leash, I turned around to tell my boss I would be back in half an hour. He nodded with a strange smile.

As soon as we were out, the Dane spotted another dog at the end of the street. I was suddenly yanked off my feet at a hundred miles an hour, or so it seemed. The dog was toppling garbage cans and frightening some street kids to death. I was screaming for the animal to stop and the muscles in my arms were hurting. In a few moments I would not be able to hold the leash anymore. I was afraid to let go, to lose the monster, for fear of the boss's reprisals. Losing my strength, I fell and was dragged on the cobblestones at a tremendous speed. Aching, bleeding, realizing I could not do a thing anymore, I let go of the leash.

"Go to hell, you bastard," I yelled after the dog. "I bet I'll be fired because of you."

By now the creature had disappeared, turning the far corner of the street. How true was my prediction. Opening the factory door all scratched and bloody, I faced the boss, telling him I had lost his precious Dane. He looked at me with anger.

"You are fired," he said, looking at my torn clothes and bloody hands with contempt. I was not surprised. I just remembered that little smile on his face before I left with the dog. Asking me to walk his monstrous Dane, he knew very well what would happen. It was a perfect excuse to fire me. It saddened me that I would be without money, but in a way I was relieved.

"Thank you," I said, "I am so happy to get out of this miserable hell."

I only wished it had been less brutal. In the street, I forgot my aches and wretched looks. I felt like a bird escaping its cage. On the way home, I sauntered and whistled all the way, not even thinking of how the news would be received at home. It was better, I thought, not to look for a job, at least for the time being, but without money the day had not yet come where I could be totally free.

Later, in the spring, I met Leonard. He was a handsome young Jewish man spending his vacations in Casablanca. Time had passed since Mosy and that fabulous summer in Tangier that had ended in such a sad fiasco. Here I was, ready for another adventure. Leonard lived in New York, but was born in Morocco. He came from an immensely wealthy family, the Elmalehs. We were attracted to each other almost immediately. He saw in me a free spirit, very different from the other family girls he had met in Casablanca so far. For me the appeal was his good looks, his intelligence, and the fact he came from New York, that fabulous city. Soon we were having a torrid secret affair. This time, I was not in Tangier, free. I was home. It proved difficult to meet in secret. He had rented an apartment in a quiet street. There we met in the early afternoons, when most of Casablanca was taking a nap. It was risky, and I loved it.

Officially, for my parents, we went out together for long walks in the countryside or to the cinema in the afternoons. The evenings he came to get me to go to parties, or a good restaurant. He had a particular whistle to let me know he was waiting for me, Debussy's Golliwog cake walk.

After a while together, Leonard insisted that I meet his mother. She was a formidable woman, tall and plump. When we met, she scrutinized me with a sort of disdain that was very unpleasant. Still, she admitted I was a good-looking and a well-mannered young lady. I was shocked. Was I a horse or some other animal to be bought? But I thought that if Leonard had presented me to his mother he must have some serious reasons in mind.

In June, a business friend of my father's was marrying off a favorite son at his vast country estate. The ceremonies were to take place in the south, near Marrakech. Our family was invited. This was very exciting, because I had never attended an Arab wedding. Non Moslems were not often invited to Moorish houses. It was an honor to be asked by Si Hadj El Mansour, a very powerful and immensely rich man. I thought it would be okay to take Leonard along. He would certainly appreciate the exoticism of the whole affair, because even though he had been born here, he had left the country when he was very young and was completely Americanized.

We left early on a Saturday morning. I had convinced my parents to let me travel with Leonard in his car. My parents went in another car with their friends. The weather was hot in that landlocked part of the country, but still very green, the soil being fed by countless seguias, narrow canals of pure mountain water. To the south rose the formidable High Atlas range, its summits still covered in snow. They loomed like a string of white fortresses into the deep indigo sky.

I was told the wedding festivities were going to last two weeks. Twenty five hundred guests had been invited; that meant more than a hundred people per day. As Moslem custom prescribed, the young man to be married could not meet his bride to be, and would only do so on the last day, when all the guests had departed and the actual marriage would take place.

We arrived around eleven o'clock in the morning. The grounds were magnificent, with a profusion of flower beds, gardens, and fountains. There were meandering lanes of rose bushes, tightly bound together as if they were embracing. Their velvety flowers, opened by the heat, exhaled a heady perfume, enticing us to experience sensual pleasures. Leonard bent over one of the bushes to pick a red rose. "For you," he said and pinned it in my hair. Above us, flowering Jacarandas spread a lilac veil. As we walked further, the erotic scent of jasmine growing on wooden trellises was almost overpowering. I snatched a few flowers and stuffed them in the corsage of my dress. All around us, tall palm trees swayed with a rustling sound in the breeze. Here and there, mosaic-tiled fountains attracted clouds of little birds.

Guests were arriving in droves. They walked the earthen alleys with difficulty, encumbered by their fancy clothes. The French government delegates wore stiff dark clothes that were not made for the heat. Their lapels were ostentatiously embellished with a decoration of the Legion of Honor. Their chatting wives were parading in long silk French couturier gowns and wide-brimmed straw hats. The Foreign Ambassadors and their ladies appeared in all manner of exotic dress.

Moslem dignitaries arrived dressed in the purest white robes, their heads wound in superb turbans. They rode on richly caparisoned stallions, the embroidered saddles flashing silver and gold. Some came with their favorite young son riding on their father's lap. These gentlemen came alone, their wives going directly to the women's quarters, never to be seen in places where other men stood.

The air was vibrating with the sound of flutes, violas and tambourines. The musicians sat on the grass like so many musical bouquets. We finally arrived where enormous Berber tents had been erected on the lawns. I tried to count them, but there were too many. They were beautiful, tightly woven of heavy white wool and decorated with rich black tribal embroideries.

We were invited to partake of the *diffa*, a royal feast. Inside the tents, mounds of sequined and embroidered cushions lined the cloth walls. The light filtered through the tent dome in soft hues, making it comfortable and shading the guests from the fierce sun outside. Our feet were resting on thick, ancient Rabat rugs.

As Leonard and I found our niches among the many cushions, we settled in anticipation of the delicious meal to come. He took my hand and squeezed it gently. We were happy to be here together. Sandalwood burning in little silver cups was a final touch to this paradise of the senses. A light hot wind rose outside. Our tent swayed gently, accentuating a feeling that we were in a strange and magical.

Through the entrance, and coming our way, I saw a line of manservants that seemed to be half a mile long. They came balancing enormous round silver trays on top of their turbaned heads, on which sat large platters covered by conical lids. They walked in silence, little puffs of dust rising from under their feet as they went from tent to tent delivering a feast of sublime dishes; Tajine stews of fowl in various fragrant sauces, then couscous lavishly decorated with fried almonds, vegetables and raisins. Last came the saffron-roasted meats. The smells were powerful: olive oil, butter and spices in a very refined mixture. We ate with our fingers, only with the right hand and only with three fingers. Any fewer fingers meant you didn't care for the food, and any more marked you as a glutton.

Before each course, little boys in colorful costumes washed our hands with rose-scented water from silver flasks. As I ate I watched the French guests facing me. They looked awkward, as they were not used to sitting crossed-legged, nor eating with their fingers from a single platter on a very low central table. Uncomfortable as they were, they still were gorging themselves. I disliked the condescending looks they had toward the Jews and the Moslems facing them. So much antagonism for the people of a country they had brutally colonized and that had made them so rich. With all their so-called superiority, they could never reciprocate such a feast.

While I was reflecting on this, Si Hadj El Mansour, the host, appeared. His huge body inched through the tent's small entrance. He looked around smiling, greeting everybody in turn, as he walked in his light pink djellabah robe. He was a simple person without pretensions and yet he was one of the richest men in the region.

Servants were bringing in the piece de resistance: a whole roasted lamb for each tent. Si Hadj El Mansour swiftly plucked one of the animal's eyes, turned around and presented it to me saying

"Young lady, this is for my good friend Elias' beautiful daughter."

I was taken aback with surprise and revulsion. I paled. Leonard squeezed my hand to give me courage. A man next to me gave me the elbow.

"Eat, it's a great honor," he whispered. And I did, half fainting from the experience. There was applause, exclamations and congratulations. El Mansour smiled, very pleased, and stayed with us a moment more, welcoming and gracious. He then left us, his big gentle body swaying to visit the other tents.

Next came the pastries, served on large engraved copper and silver trays, dazzling us with their richness. Some cakes had strange names like *Kab el Gzal*, Gazelle's Horns, and *m'Hensha*, the Snake, lush with almonds, honey and orange blossom water. A tea ceremony was being performed by a master. Putting strong green tea in giant silver teapots, he then rinsed the tea with boiling water and added pieces of a crystalline sugar loaf. Branches of several types of mint were then stuffed into the teapots, bringing forth an exquisite aroma. The concoction was then poured into small gold painted glasses and passed around.

The meal had been sumptuous, leaving us incapable of getting up. I felt like falling asleep on those soft cushions with Leonard at my side, but we had to let other guests enjoy the same feast. Filing out of the tent, satiated and silent, we stepped into the hot white haze of the early afternoon. It was the hour where nature almost lost its color to the fierceness of the sun. People dispersed one way and the other to partake of the afternoon festivities.

Laughter, song and the strong beat of drums drifted from somewhere behind a group of trees. Leonard and I were drawn to its magnetic appeal. The groom's bachelor's party was going full swing. It was taking place in a beautiful garden, where superb women danced, enclosed by a low fence made of entwined tree branches. Dazzling as the most exotic flowers, they were dressed in magnificent caftans of shimmering silks and gauze, bejeweled like goddesses. They were the Shihats, courtesans hired for the occasion. Dancing to the bewitching sound of flutes and drums, their bodies undulated erotically, inside the low fence. The tops of their robes were open to reveal their breasts, which they thrust forward, so the groom and his friends could pinch their nipples. Foreign guests watching were shocked, ladies covering their faces with false modesty, while their fascinated husbands were trying in vain to get closer to the dancing women. Leonard was also mesmerized and was pulling my hand to get closer to the fence. What could I do? Fortunately he coud not get close enough to touch the shihats!

In wealthy Moroccan families sons were generally very spoiled, as was Si Hadj el Mansour'son. When a son reached his preteens, his father hired a young maid carefully chosen to initiate the young lad in the pleasures of lovemaking. It was discreet and in the safety of their home. Girls did not share this bounty. In the matter of love they were only taught the bare facts, a few days before their marriage and in the seclusion of the harem, if they were Moslems.

Mid afternoon, the heat became overwhelming. A burning Sirocco wind had risen, whipping whirlpools of sand, shaking the tents, obliterating trees and flowers. Guests, musicians, servants were running to take cover. In the big house, we were served hot green tea, a brew for all occasions, and more pastries. The ladies were then asked to bring their presents to the future bride. I had to leave Leonard for a while and was not too happy about it.

The harem was separated from the main house by a meadow and a garden. Fighting the wind, arms full of beribboned presents, the ladies made their way through a field of red poppies that were shaking in the wind. Our pretty dresses were flying around us like so many butterfly wings. Stopping in front of the opened harem doors, we tried to compose ourselves before entering this forbidden realm. At first, the vast room supported by tall columns seemed obscure in comparison with the bright outdoors. The lights inside came from elaborate, lacy silver lamps hanging low from the high vaulted ceiling.

Perched way above us, on a pyramid of thick silk damask cushions, sat the little bride. It was difficult to imagine the young girl was not a statue. She appeared to be a perfectly triangular shape finishing the top of the pyramid. She was wrapped entirely in a striped gold embroidered red and green silk garment, covering her entire body like a cocoon. On her head a heavy gold tiara embedded with emeralds and pearls seemed to crush the little face that appeared below. She was almost a child, barely twelve years old. Her lids were modestly lowered on cheeks covered with brilliant sequins in traditional designs. The latticed pearls hanging on each side of her face and the breastplate of heavy jewels she wore did not help. To me, she looked like a lamb waiting to be sacrificed.

The lady guests and I filed passed her depositing our presents at her feet, saying a few words of congratulations. I could not believe what I was seeing. It was the first time I had been invited to a harem. Chairs had been prepared for us on the right side of the pyramid where the betrothed sat. The bride's mother and female relatives were all sitting opposite us on the left side. I could feel the intense look they gave us. I was wondering what went through their minds, how they saw us. My thoughts and the silence were suddenly broken when two magnificent black women, slaves, came in dancing. Barely dressed in loose tunics of blue cloth, their round breasts half bare, they carried huge metal castanets. With lascivious erotic movements, they moved in tempo with the rhythm of their instruments which they held in front of them, arms extended. The slaves faced each other, moving very close to one another, mimicking the gestures of love. They were sweating, dancing in a trance, the electric blue of their tunics flashing against their polished ebony skin. They were bewitching. The little bride was supposed to look from under half closed eyes and get some clues about what to expect on her wedding night. I felt compassion for the young girl.

I left the harem, thanking God for not being a Moslem woman. I breathed deeply outside, trying to sort out all I had seen and felt that day. Leonard was impetiently waiting for me. We were both tired. We joined my parents for the ride to the hotel we had booked for the night. Unfortunately, I would be staying with my folks; there was no way I could possibly join Leonard and be in his arms on that hot June evening.

Chapter 12: 1947

Strange Vacations

Mother and I left for France in the begining of August. It was the first time after the war that she had taken a real vacation. We were going to Vichy in France to take the waters. It was a fashionable spa where a lot of Moroccans went each year to cure their chronic liver and stomach ailments. Leonard had promised to come and join us. By now we both knew that our love adventure could end in marriage. Only his mother was reluctant: I was not rich enough for her son.

Vichy was a quaint and elegant little town, nestled in a series of green parks and flowerbeds at the edge of the tranquil Allier river. It resembled a wedding cake with all its rococo fountains and buildings. The Marchioness Madame de Sévigné, who had been a regular at the court of Louis XIV and whose writings became well known, had resided here in the seventeenth century. Many foreign languages were spoken here during the summer season, as people came from various countries to wallow in therapeutic mud baths and drink the waters. Hotels were full, and booming restaurants tried to outdo each other with culinary specialties. The town had a casino and every night theaters gave wonderful plays and musicals. In the illuminated evenings, vacationers danced in the parks to the sound of accordions.

Every morning at seven, Maman, already chic in a white suit and a matching hat, came to get me. Together we walked at a good pace toward the thermal spa, where we were taken in by vigorous matrons in nurses' uniforms. After undressing, we were massaged like pieces of bread dough, and showered with water jets that almost knocked us out. Then we were forced to drink many glasses of that foul-tasting water. I marveled that people came here and paid such a lot of money to be tortured this way. Maybe the cure worked, but I was skeptical. After all that good exercise we went each day to a good restaurant and stuffed ourselves with delicacies, undoing, I was sure, all the good that was bestowed on us in the morning.

By now I was impatient to see Leonard, waiting every day for a letter announcing his arrival. I was already feeling like a lioness in a cage. Finally the letter came; he would be arriving in a few days.

At the station, I saw him jump out on the platform. We walked toward each other at a slow pace. He was tall and slim, his shiny dark hair flying in the wind, his blue-green eyes creased in a radiant smile. We stopped short, drinking of each other. He was in my skin and I was in his, both of us anticipating the following days and nights.

Fifteen days of bliss. I did not take the cure anymore; Leonard was enough to cure all my real or imaginary ailments. Every night I sneaked out of my room and walked down a dark corridor, fearful of being seen. I then slid noiselessly into Leonard's suite. We did not sleep all night, exhausting every passion we had for each other. When a pale gray light showed at the window, I regained my room, drunk with pleasure and fatigue. What willpower it took to wake up one hour later, get ready and make up, especially the eyes. It was a miracle to be ready when mother called on me for breakfast. Was she aware of anything? I did not think so, but she was smart and very romantic. Perhaps in us, she was vicariously living an adventure that she never had. I never found out.

During the day, Leonard and I did not have the stamina to do any sports or even to visit any museums. Once or twice, we took a boat and paddled lazily down the river, brushing the tender green weeping willows and letting our hands trail in the silvery water. Most of the days, we only sat on benches, or walked slowly in the beautifully manicured parks, finding friendly trees to shade us and brilliant flowers to dazzle us.

We were surprised when the end of summer came. Days turned stormy, with the gathering of enormous dark clouds, lightning, and wind. The river turned steel gray, and big drops of water fell from the sky. I could feel a certain uneasiness in Leonard's behavior. Several times he started speaking and stopped. What was happening? I knew he was leaving in a few days, but we had made plans for a wedding very soon. The separation would be short, so why did he look so sad?

Three days before his departure, he finally spoke.

"Forgive me for not speaking before, Anit. I didn't want to spoil the magnificent time we had together. I am very much in love with you, but..."

"Leonard, what's going on? Why that look? Tell me."

"Mother has decided I am to study medicine in Switzerland," he said. "I can't get married before I finish my studies, in seven years."

He lowered his head, shamed. The silence that followed was thick and hard as a wall. I could not utter a word, my vocal cords frozen. His mother had found the way to eliminate me, the bitch. How weak could Leonard be?

"Will you wait for me?" he asked, "Please!"

I could not believe what I was hearing. Why was this happening to me again? What was I doing wrong? Or was it that each time, I made the wrong choice? I felt an immense boiling anger rising in my body and was trying desperately not to explode. Summoning all the willpower I was capable of I replied,

"No I will not wait for you, seven years is a lifetime! Marry me now, or it's over."

But in my heart I already knew – he wouldn't go against his mother. I didn't want to spoil the last two days with him, but something was gone. I looked at him with contempt and even a little pity. At the station we said goodbye. He said he would write, and I replied that it was not necessary. For me it was all over. The train pulled away slowly, taking unfulfilled dreams with it. I had a moment of desperate sadness, sobbing, tears drowning my face. The train disappeared round a bend, plumes of smoke evaporated in the thin air. Gone, and a portion of my life gone with it.

The end of summer, the end of a dream. Hotels were half empty, no more kids playing in the parks, no more concerts in the evenings, only a few stragglers finishing their water cure. I was in a somber mood, walking all day along the river with my head lowered and my shoulders hunched. Was there to be no real happiness for me ever? Maman tried her best to cheer me up, taking me to the best restaurants, knowing how much I appreciated good food. My sorrow was deep. It was going to take more than a good meal to bring me out of this.

Before going back to Casablanca, Maman decided to take a trip across the French Alps and revisit Nice in the south. I was sure she did it for me, to take my mind off things. We boarded a comfortable touring bus and traveled first to Lyons, that fabulous city in the heart of France. The few days we stayed there were crammed with sightseeing. The silk museum, the old town with its superb medieval churches. A daily stroll in the Park of La Tête d'Or where deer roamed free among the century-old trees. We ate at famous restaurants to sample their specialties. I had no time to brood or to linger on negative thoughts. I was grateful to Mother who had arranged all this so naturally.

On the spur of the moment, we took a train to Chambery going east and hopped by bus to Mégève high in the French Alps. To rest, Mother said, from the cure in Vichy and the running around in Lyons. I was game, anything to distract me. The first few days she was full of enthusiasm. We went for long walks, ending up one day in a cheese factory way up in the hills. We bought a whole pound of scrumptious cheese, thinking it would last at least a week. I started tearing chunks of it as we turned to go back to town, and by the time we arrived at the hotel an hour later, I had eaten the whole thing.

After a while Mother tired of the long hikes. She preferred reading, sitting in the sun on the hotel terrace. This was not good enough for me. I started hiking further and further every day, exhausting myself, to forget my unlucky fate with Leonard. One morning early, I started climbing the side of a mountain. Following a trail, I went up fast and had to stop several times to catch my breath. The air was getting thin, then abruptly the trail ended. I wasn't about to come down yet; the day was beautiful, cool and sunny. Around me, the landscape was breathtaking. Leaves were turning yellow and orange against a very blue sky. In the distance the Mont Blanc, highest peak of the French Alps, glittered with snow. It was intoxicating. I decided to climb higher through the brush.

At first it wasn't too hard, but after a little while, I had to stop, the grade was getting so steep. For every step I took, holding to brush and high grasses, I would slide back two. Turning around to see how high I had gotten, my head spun with vertigo. Oh my God! Was I really that high up? 'No panic,' I told myself out loud to spur my courage, but I knew I could not turn back; the plunge was almost vertical. There was only one way, and that was up. On my right, I noticed the cables of a ski gondola. I would climb in that direction and was sure that pretty soon I would get to the top of the ridge.

Suddenly it became really cold. I was holding tight to whatever plant I could. The sun disappeared behind huge ragged gray clouds. From one minute to the next, a thick fog obliterated the whole mountain, swallowing everything in its gaping mouth. Frozen with panic, I started yelling for help. Nothing, my voice was drowned in that cottony white fog. Again and again I kept yelling with all the strength left in my body. I was terribly distressed, thinking I might have to spend the night in this Godforsaken place. Surely I would freeze to death.

"Wheeere are youuu," a voice called that seemed far away, distorted by the thickness of the clouds.

"Here I am, here," I replied shouting at the top of my lungs.

I had been heard! My throat was totally raw from yelling, but I would not stop. Again I heard the voices trying to reach me.

"You are not far from the top," the voice said. "Just climb straight up. Courage, courage, you are almost there."

I felt like vomiting, but by God I was going to make it. Gripping, sliding, holding, praying, I was climbing like an animal, half frozen and shaking. The instinct of survival was strong, I was not going to slide back, I was not going to die. After what seemed to be ages, I saw the shadow of a head and arms waving.

"You made it, just a few more steps, here, here let me grab your arms." I had reached the gondola terminus, and the voices were the conductors.

I collapsed like a wet rag at their feet sobbing. They covered me with their heavy coats, patting me on the shoulders.

"Young lady, what you did was very foolish," one of them said. "A lot of unprepared people like you die in these high mountains. Here the weather changes without notice. You learned a hard lesson. Here, drink this in one gulp. It's Schnapps, it will warm you up."

I drank the burning liquor, but I had no voice to thank these men. I just hoped they could see the gratitude in my eyes.

"Well well now, everything will be all right," he said. "We'll take you down with the gondola. In a half hour you will be back at your hotel."

After the gondola ride down the mountain, they drove me back to the hotel, wishing me good luck. I waved back at them with a smile. Their car lurched forward and they were gone. I stood a while on the entrance steps wondering about these two angels without wings, and then I went in.

Maman was not in our room. I was in bad need of a hot shower, but instead I climbed into bed, feeling the softness of the down pillows on my bruised face and the warmth of the eiderdown cover. I did not want to think one minute more of how close to death I had been. I never told Mother about the incident, feeling very ashamed of my foolish actions that day.

Taking the train once more, we stopped in Grenoble, a large town at the foot of the high Alps, the door to many famous ski resorts, and another city full of old twelfth- and thirteenth-century churches and ornate eighteenth century houses. Before we left we bought a bag of huge fresh walnuts, one of the specialties of the region. Following the river Isère was a pleasure of the senses. We were traveling along the Vercors Province, surprised by the wilderness of deep canyons and furious torrents. No wonder it had been one of the main hiding places for the underground fighters during World War II. Soon we found ourselves in a landscape reminiscent of a Cezanne painting when we reached the Maritime Alps. Wild also, but dryer, with landscapes of olive trees and fields of lavender. Peoples' accents were different too and made me think of a good ripe cheese, a pungent tomato sauce and the heady perfume of carnations. We had reached the south of France, and soon we entered the city of Nice.

I had many memories of Nice from the vacations I had spent here with Glad when we were kids. My Grandmother Nejma's big white neo-classical 40-room palace resembled the White House. The huge rooms were filled with tapestries, rare furniture and rich damasks. The garden faced the sea, where as kids we had chased each other around the statues and the central fountain. We had been there many, many times while our parents were traveling elsewhere. We had even gone to a public school one winter, donning black pinafores like the poor children of the city. I had learned to play a dice game with bones as we sat in the dirt during recesses. Glad and I had also caught lice in that school; Grandmother had had to shave our heads until we looked like two dressed-up eggs.

Other memories were less painful. In the garden superb beds of flowers, tall rose bushes and camellias had graced the white graveled alleys. There was Grandma's vegetable garden, where Glad and I helped gather the red tomatoes and the trailing fava beans. There were also chickens in that huge garden. I loved to torture them by running after the poor birds with the water hose. They screamed, trying in vain to fly away. All this happened while on the other side of the monumental gates people were watching us, their hands clutching the ornate wrought iron. What were they thinking, seeing us rich kids playing? Little did they know what the fate of this beautiful palace and its inhabitants would be in the not so distant future.

After depositing our luggage at the Negresco hotel, Mother and I hurried along the Promenade Des Anglais, going west a few blocks, impatient to reach the place of so many of our memories. For mother it was also a landmark; she had been married in that big house and had come back year after year until just before the war.

Stopping at the correct address, we looked around. Where was the palace? The gardens? Instead we were looking at a horrible, cheap, modern building built right where the front garden had been. We faced each other, speechless, big knots in our throats. When Maman had come to get her mother in 1945, she had been too busy with the hospital, the ambulance, the plane that was to take them back to Morocco. She had had no time to go to the house. She had presumed it was and always would be there. Grandmother Nejma probably was not aware that her grand mansion had disappeared. She was still at home in Casablanca, bedridden, under the constant care of a nurse. To us this whole thing seemed impossible.

We walked around the building. On the side, what had once been a lush garden with tall palm trees and beds of roses and camellias was gone. There was nothing left of all the splendor. The renaissance fountain and its cherubs, the Greek and Roman statues, all smashed to pieces. Fragments of marble stuck out of the ground as if in supplication. We cried and sobbed. Walking a little further, we saw that not everything had been demolished; the ground floor was still visible in part. Gaping holes screamed to the sky. What sorrow; both of us were crushed. We walked back to the hotel in silence, holding hands. Things change. Time is ephemeral. I thought of Leonard, of the palace. One day here and the next day gone.

In Marseilles we took the same ship that had brought us to France. Three days at sea was like cutting an umbilical cord. I was myself again, thinking of all the projects for the coming winter.

Chapter 13: 1947-1948

Meeting Charlie

In the middle of November, I was asked to play the lead in a Comedia del Arte play with a new theater company. Like the previous company, this one was a nonprofit organization, mainly playing for charity. I was eager to do it; the role I was to play was the glamorous Columbine. The first meeting of the cast took place one winter afternoon at a friend's house. To impress the group, I came dressed in a new grey flannel suit I had designed and sewed myself, with a matching grey velvet hat. The whole thing was quite elegant, probably too elegant for the occasion. I was presented to the rest of the cast.

To my dismay I found no one to my taste. Charlie Bohbot was to play opposite me as Pierrot, the leading male role. He looked quite wild. A shock of wavy black hair fell to his nose, and he was wearing a wide-open plaid shirt that showed a mat of the same black hair on his chest. Some character! I thought, and I was to be his leading lady? The two others did not look much better. Cake Ettedgui! What a strange name. He was cast as the Doctor, and Albert Botbol was to play Harlequin. He also was bizarre, extremely thin, very nervous, his eyes in constant movement. But when we read through the play and discussed the roles, I realized that they were bright young men. A few days later, I learned that they had found me snobbish and overdressed. Their opinion of me had been as bad as mine of them. Not the most promising start.

At the first rehearsal, I found Charlie much more attractive. His wild hair had been combed back and I saw his eyes, thick black eyelashes shading large deep pools of green. What was even more interesting was the passionate expression on his face.

Within a month, I was trying to capture Charlie's attention. He on the other hand was not aware of it. Cake and Albert in turn fell madly in love with me. It was a very strange four-way game of chess. I could not get rid of these two and I could not make Charlie notice that I was interested. Perhaps I was not forceful enough in rejecting my other suitors, and too discreet with the one person I wanted to attract.

I was designing and sewing the costumes for everybody in the play. They were difficult to make and I wanted them to be perfect. This meant many fittings. Cake and Albert were always looking forward to these sessions because I had to touch them, pinning fabrics here and there, to their delight. Albert's eyes would roll ten times faster and Cake's look was that of a cow in heat. When it came to Charlie, he was always in a hurry to meet some girl, to my dismay.

We started to rehearse in costume. The play was delightful. With the lights on and in full dress, we looked very professional. Only Pierrot could not remember his lines. Very at ease on stage, he would invent dialogue as he went along. It was almost impossible for the rest of us to follow, and the director was furious. This situation gave me an idea. One evening when Charlie walked on stage in his superb Pierrot costume, I came close to him and whispered in his ear.

"Charlie, if you can say all of your opening speech without missing a word, I will kiss you when you finish."

He looked at me as if he was seeing me for the first time, surprised and delighted.

"I am going to try my best, I'll do it, just wait and see," he replied.

Now I was anxious; would he do it? It was very forward for a girl to show openly that she cared for a boy. It was almost scandalous, but I did not care, I had my eyes on him and wanted him.

We were all astonished at how well Pierrot delivered his opening speech. At the end, he bowed with a smile and in two seconds flat I was on stage giving him the long kiss I had promised. The whole cast was flabbergasted, Albert and Cake realizing that their case was hopeless.

Often after rehearsal we all walked home together. One time Charlie asked me to hold his trench coat. While he was lacing his shoe, bending to the ground, I walked ahead talking to Cake. When I turned around to see if Charlie was coming, nobody was there. He had disappeared into thin air and I was left with his coat on my arm. Where did he go, I asked?

"Oh! He had a rendezvous with a French officer's wife and he was probably late, that's why he didn't say goodbye. You should know that he usually has at least three girlfriends at any given time."

Cake looked at me, his eyes shifting here and there as if to say, 'I am the serious one, perhaps you should reconsider.'

I did nothing of the sort, and waited patiently for the chance to be alone with Charlie. The day of the opening it was raining hard. The play was a great success. I was given a bouquet and there was thunderous applause for all of us. People came backstage, there was champagne and laughter. Then, tired and happy, our guests and my parents with them filed out of the theater and into the rainy night. The cast stayed to remove makeup and change clothes.

"Charlie, I said, "will you share a taxi with me to go back home? It's pouring outside."

"That's a good idea," he replied, "get ready while I call a cab."

Two minutes outside and we were already drenched. Inside the taxi it was warm and comfortable. We eased ourselves on the red plush seats and Charlie grabbed me and kissed me hard. I looked at him surprised.

"You are very sexy, Anit," he said. "Would you like to be my girlfriend?"

"Yes I would." Finally!

"But I warn you," he continued, "I only take girlfriends for a week. Are you game?"

Well, the nerve! he was treating me like a teenager, or god knows what. I was furious, but did not show my feelings. I was really piqued, and said,

"I'll take the challenge, and I bet it will be for much more than a week. Let's see who wins."

After that evening in the taxi, I asked myself whether I had been foolish to attach myself to such a conceited young braggart. He seemed so sure of himself, so macho, but the very core of my being told me I would be the winner. For one, I was four years older than him, and I believed that even though he had gone with more women than I with men, my experience was greater.

It was at the beginning difficult to make heads or tails of the way he behaved. Not normal, his friends would tell me, erratic. To discover the real person underneath I had to become not only his lover, but also his friend.

Little by little Charlie unveiled some details about himself, but guardedly. He was very strange; that was part of the strong attraction I had for him. I learned that a few months earlier, he had had two severe sunstrokes, one after the other. The second one happened because he had completely disregarded the doctor's orders not to return to the beach; the result was a severe loss of memory. No wonder he couldn't remember his lines. He was treated with electroshocks, which later proved to be totally inappropriate for that condition, and created more complications.

This temporary illness did not detract from his charm, his good looks, and his intelligence. He also was a very well read young man and had a great love for music. About twice a month during all of 1948 Charlie and his friends would organize musical afternoons. We gathered in one room, sitting on couches or lying down on the floor with all the windows and shutters closed. These sessions had an almost religious character. We listened in the utmost silence to the great ones: Bach, Bethooven, Mozart, Mendelssohn, and many other composers that touched the divine in us.

The other side of Charlie was more down to earth; his youth and muscular body demanded physical effort. Running track was one of his routines. Several times a week, we went to the sports coumpound situated in the Parc Lyautey among the palm trees, bougainvillier and Cana lilies. I waited for him, sitting on a wooden bench, admiring his elegant body in the speed of flight, the jet black mane of his hair flying in the wind. Another sport he was very fond of was making love to women, and being the chosen one I was full of expectations for our budding love affair.

The beach at Sidi Abderaman was where Charlie and I made love for the first time. Dusk had invaded the sea shore, and the place was totally deserted. Dark shadows at the edge of bushes made us uneasy, and the sand was gray and wet. Enormous crashing waves filled the foggy air with the sound of thunder, drowning our panting sighs. Above us a pale moon was rising into a dark blue sky where stars winked on one at a time. Far from the ideal place, but our bodies were hot with desire. We ignored the cold wet sand and the roaring waves, our bodies melting in a fiery bliss. It was also dangerous to stay on a beach at night, prey to thieves that could kill you to steal one Franc, but it was almost impossible to find a place were we could be alone in town. Only when my parents left for a weekend was the house mine. After dismissing the help, Charlie and I would spend the whole time making love. We only left the bed to drink a cup of coffee and eat a piece of stale bread. It was a marathon, as if we had to win some kind of Olympics. We finished these sessions totally washed out, but very proud of our performances.

Unknown to me was the gossip that the maids spread in the neighborhood. They knew very well why I dismissed them every time my parents went on a trip. I saw them more than once talking on the sidewalk to a fat young man whose sister I had gone to school with. He and his family lived just across the street from us. I knew little of him, just nodding when we passed each other. It seemed odd that Yacout our maid or her sister our cook would stop to engage in a conversation with him. One Monday morning I was going out to get the newspaper. As I opened the door, I stepped into what looked like a small puddle of water. Surprised, I looked around, who could have done that? I cleaned it up and forgot all about it. The next day, I found the same puddle of water at the very same place. It was intriguing. I asked the cook if she knew anything about it. Her shifty eyes averting mine, she shook her head in denial. I was troubled. A puddle of water in itself was nothing, but why was it there again, and at the exact same place? I asked Yacout to clean the spill. She shrugged, uneasy, and answered that she could not do it, too busy. So I cleaned it again myself. On Wednesday as I was going out the door, there it was again, the puddle of water at the very same place. Aïcha, the woman who came to clean the stairs twice a week, was there cleaning the marble landing.

"Aïcha, look, I found a little spill of water right there, three days in a row. What does it mean, do you know?"

Aïcha became agitated.

"Miss Anit, do not step in that water! Be very careful, somebody is doing sorcery to you, death is in that water."

I stopped short, petrified.

"I stepped in it once and cleaned it twice, oh my God, I touched that water! Am I going to die? "

"Well," she said, "I'll see to it that you don't. Come with me to the terrace, I am going to try to undo the spell. I think I know who is doing this to you. Give me your confidence and all will be well. I shall deal with it."

Somebody was trying to kill me, but why? I followed Aïcha upstairs to a small room where she kept her buckets, mops and brooms together with a few of her belongings. Soon she had a brazier going and was throwing various herbs, stones, and seeds into the fire while mumbling weird

149

incantations. A smelly violet smoke rose in spirals. I coughed; this was strong stuff. She grabbed the brazier with her rough bare hands, not even feeling the burning heat and swirled it around my head and my body, doubling the pitch of her incantations. I was in a daze, totally at her mercy, hoping she was doing the right thing. At last she put the brazier on the ground and asked me to spit on one of the white stones bubbling in the hot coals.

"I knew it," she said. "Look at the enormous black eye that formed in the center of the stone. Somebody is jealous of you and your boyfriend. I bet he or she bribed your maids to do that kind of sorcery. Now urinate on the whole thing and I think you will be safe. Be careful, they may try again."

For years after I never stepped outside without looking at the ground for a puddle of water.

Sometimes I forgot we lived in Africa. We were very Europeanized, wearing western clothes and speaking French most of the time, but this was a land where ancient customs were very much alive and sorcery was a daily occurrence among Moslems and Jews and even some Christians. I had seen people waste away for no apparent reason; people that were in perfectly good health would slowly lose their appetite until they became as thin as rails, then they lost their minds and died.

I had gone once to the sorcerer's market with my cousin Chewing. We both knew it was a place of evil, but we were attracted by the danger. Nobody in their right mind would think of going there for a visit, but for us it was a forbidden adventure. We took the bus all the way up the colorful Mediouna road where wholesalers had their shops, showing their wares by hanging samples around the entrance doors. As we approach the dreaded place, I grew uneasy, and so did cousin Chewing. The market was a vast expanse of dirt and stones, black tents scattered here and there forming irregular alleys. Hungry yellow stray dogs wandered around looking for scraps of meat, a rat perhaps. Each witch and each sorcerer had their own tent filled with repulsive merchandise. Here, hanging from the rafters were desiccated birds of prey, talons all out ready to scratch. There, swinging in the wind were tails, heads and bodies of various unknown animals.

Displayed on counters, tall transparent glass jars containing disgusting white snakes and various types of frogs, lizards and worms told of somber deeds. The alleys in front of their shops were spread with more dead animals, but also an array of powders and ill smelling herbs, some of them in small containers full of burning coal. One of the witches called out to me, offering all kinds of potions to make my man virile, she said. She was a frightening sight, a tall skeletal woman all draped in black. One of her eyes was missing, like somebody had pierced it with a sharp pointed object, creating a circle of wrinkles around it like a desiccated sun. Her other eye was shining evil with blackness in her yellow parchment face. I recoiled, but stood my ground. Her image is still in my mind today sixty plus years later. It was amazing to see how many people were buying that stuff. Was there really so much hate in the world?

In early June, Grandmother Nejma, who was still bedridden at home, got much worse. Her terrible suffering was intolerable to watch. Now she had a nurse with her day and night; she knew she was dying and called Glad and I to her bedside.

"Queridas hijitas," she spoke Spanish more readily than French, "I have put aside a present for you, Gladita, because you just honored us with beautiful twins, a son and a daughter."

She reached to her side table, took out a small jewel box and opened it to reveal a stunning star sapphire ring, set in gold and diamonds. With great effort she put it on Glad's finger. Looking at me she said,

"You will have as beautiful a ring when you get married and have a son, Anit."

I was speechless: nothing for me, Grandmother smiled.

"Come here, don't make that face! Here is a little something to remember me by until you get married."

She extracted a long box that she had hidden under her pillow. In it was the most magnificent gold chain I had ever seen, at least forty inches long with emeralds and enameled medallions. What a present! I kept winding it nervously around my fingers, not believing my good luck.

Grandma sat up straight on her bed.

"Anyway, I do not believe in marriage," she said. "Listen to me Anit, the best life is that of a courtesan. If you choose to be one, you will always be well taken care of and spoiled. Marriage often finishes in disaster, I warn you. For Glad it is already too late."

I had just discovered a new grandmother. How modern she was, how young and daring were her thoughts, what a shame she was dying. I regretted not to have known her better. To me she had always been just Grandmother Nejma, a little eccentric perhaps, but still just a grandmother.

In the days that followed, she invited all her friends for a last afternoon of music, singing, and poetry reading. They came with lutes and tambourines and sat around her bed in a circle. They played Andalusian classical Moroccan music. Among them was a famous singer, La Hannabia, who had been Marshal Lyautey's mistress as well as a spy. Lyautey was considered the founder of the French protectorate in Morocco. Hannabia sang sad love songs and a young man read Arabic poetry. Late in the afternoon Grandmother asked me to open her wardrobe, where she kept her most precious antiques and what she had left of her fabulous jewels; cherished items that had been hidden in her Tangier house before the war.

"Friends, I want to thank you for all the wonderful years we had together. Each of you choose a present from my wardrobe as a souvenir."

They all got up together and rushed like demented people, fighting each other, insulting one another, almost breaking the wardrobe doors and plundering everything to the last item. It was a horror to watch. So those were the good friends! Grandmother never said a word. She sat propped up by pillows. On her face was an enigmatic smile of derision.

A week later she was dead. Mother asked us to kiss Grandmother Nejma goodbye. I had never seen a dead person before and was terrified to see her cold and rigid, all wrapped up in pure white sheets. It seemed impossible that she had been alive less than an hour ago and now she was gone forever. It left me pensive for quite a while.

Little by little Charlie was recovering his memory, thanks to my incessant efforts to make him totally well. To be able to see me more often, he had found a job in a wholesale shop very close to where I lived. It was tedious work, selling spools of thread all day long, but during his breaks he would run to have a moment with me at home. Mother liked him very much. She baked wonderful desserts just for him. I could not say the same for father, who disliked him for no reason at all. Sometimes father came back early from his office. We could hear his heavy step as he walked to the door, while Charlie was still in our kitchen stuffing himself with cakes. Mother and I, hearing the key turn at the front entrance, would swiftly smuggle Charlie out the kitchen door, but not before filling his hands with sweets for the rest of the afternoon.

It was about that time that Charlie introduced me to his parents. I was in for a surprise. They lived behind a square called Place de Verdun by the French colonists, but in reality it was an old Jewish neighborhood. It was like going back in time. Nothing here seemed to have changed for centuries except for a few buildings dating from 1920 or so. Behind the square unrolled a maze of old unpaved streets where two of our synagogues stood. The smell of hot Moroccan Kesra filled the air, a wonderful wheat bread that was kneaded daily in Jewish houses. Domestics could be seen going to and from the public oven, carrying large wooden trays filled with bread or cookies barely covered with a white sheet. There were tiny stores like the ones in the Medina where the Moslems lived. They sold olive oil from large metal drums, French cheeses competing with flies and a few other dusty groceries and fruits. Children played in the street, yelling like banshees as they threw their footballs made of newspaper high in the air. Charlie's parents' house was a whitewashed two-story high moorish construction that dated from the nineteenth century. The street was narrow and bordered by garden walls lush with flowering trees spilling their petals in a fragrant carpet. In contrast, here was also a charcoal seller all black with coal dust, sitting outside his dark store among huge burlap sacks.

It was a Sunday morning. We stood at the foot of the house looking up. Charlie was showing me his room's window on the second floor. He opened the old wooden entrance door painted green and we climbed twisting narrow steps. Up here was another door. We stepped into a large square room lit by a domed skylight whose tinted glass gave a greenish yellow light. There was a faint aromatic smell of meat soup coming from a tiny kitchen.

His father was a man of about fifty, short and round with steel grey crew-cut hair. He was fixing a kerosene cooking contraption on a large table covered in flowered oilcloth. He looked busy with all his tools spread around him on the table.

"Father, I want you to meet my friend Anit."

Looking up from under suspicious eyebrows he said,

"Enchanté" the usual French greeting formula, but with a terrible Moroccan accent, and went right back to work as if I were nonexistent. Charlie was walking to the other end of the room yelling,

"Maman, Maman, I want to introduce you to my friend Anit."

The lady sitting low in an old armchair did not answer. She seemed to be eons away, her nose plunged in an open book. Charlie shook her gently and she looked up smiling.

"Ah! My son it's you, where have you been? I haven't seen you today."

In the meantime I had timidly advanced to the middle of the room.

"Mother," Charlie was shouting in her ear, "meet my friend Anit."

"Your friend, Ah! Very pleased to meet you. Are you from Casablanca?"

"Yes I live on Rue Guynemer with my parents."

She nodded and went back to her book. Charlie looked annoyed. His parents appeared to be totally disinterested. For him it was uncomfortable, he was so sophisticated. Obviously his mother was deaf and his father not friendly at all. What a strange couple; oddly, it made me want to know more about them. We said goodbye; nobody heard us and we left, I going down the steps first, thinking how lovely Charlie's mother looked with her sad blue eyes and wavy red hair, and realized that her burly husband must be a tough cookie to live with. In the street, Charlie apologized, saying he should have told his parents of my coming, that perhaps we had embarrassed them.

We were approaching midsummer 1948. Charlie had been invited to be the delegate from Morocco to represent a student conference in Marseilles, and he asked me to go with him. How wonderful it would be, to be alone together every day of that vacation. Unfortunately I had no excuse to go to Marseilles. I knew better than to ask father, and sadly had to refuse the invitation. This meant a separation of sorts for us. I knew that Charlie would very probably be unfaithful, too tempted by French girls, but I could not prevent it and said goodbye to him, hoping for the best.

A month passed and he had not returned. The conference was supposed to last only a week. In the beginning of August I received a postcard from Paris; Charlie had decided to extend his vacation and was having a very good time with some friends who had traveled with him. He would be back in early September. My thoughts were troubled; would he come back to me? After all, we were not even engaged. The week Charlie had set for our affair was long past. I had so far been able to keep him to myself, and he seemed to care for me a lot, but that trip!

A week later I received a letter from one of his friends. What was in it was shocking; a photograph of Charlie in bed with two women and a note saying "that's what Charlie is doing in Paris." I felt a knot clutching my entrails. That good-for-nothing! Well, that meant it was all over.

It was painful, but I decided I'd better make the best of it. After all we had been together for more than sixth months and had shared some sublime moments. I decided to have some fun too. For the rest of the summer I went out with various male friends. The very rich ones immersed me in

Champagne and fancy dinners, trying to gain my favors, but I was hard to catch. I preferred the guys that took me dancing. Tangos and Paso-dobles were fashionable and we danced close together in those smoky cabarets so famous in Casablanca, whirling in billows of cigarette smoke under the flashes of a mirror globe. I was trying to forget, dancing night after night, but still Charlie was in my mind more than ever.

The doorbell rang one mid afternoon during the third week of September. I was expecting no one. In the doorway stood Charlie as I had never seen him before. He looked like a skeleton, his face drawn, his hair a huge black mop waving all over his face, his eyes burning.

"Forgive me Anit," he said, "I know I look like hell, but let me explain."

I thought I was facing a man from the fanatic tribe of the Aïssawa, whose rituals involved trances where they hacked their heads with hatchets until they were covered in blood. I was speechless!

"Come in," I finally said. "What happened to you, are you sick?"

"I'm going to tell you everything, Anit. As you know, I went to Paris after the student conference and I shacked up in a cheap hotel in Montparnasse on the Left Bank. I was almost penniless; the money my father was supposed to send me had not arrived. My friends and I met a few girls that lived in the same hotel, and they were nice to us. They brought us food that they had cooked and cakes that they had baked. What could we do to repay them? Well, we slept with them. Please understand and forgive, please, Anit. I'll make it up to you, I will."

In my head there was a revolution. What Charlie was telling me I knew from the photograph his friend had sent me, but I had hoped it was only a joke. So it was really all true. Was I going to forgive such a monstrosity?

"Charlie, what can I say?" I told him, flabbergasted. "You betrayed me. I know we are not married, not even engaged, but after being together so long, I thought your intentions were more serious."

"They are serious, Anit, I really want you with me, that is the reason I told you everything."

I was hurt and could not give him an answer.

"Give me a few days, Charlie, a week to sort things out. I'll meet you at the Milk Bar in one week to give you an answer."

Conflicting thoughts fought from the core of my belly to the center of my brain, like so many blades crisscrossing, creating intense lightning and shaking my whole body. Was he really sincere? Did he mean what he said about wanting me with him? It was so hard to make a decision. Physically I was very attracted to him, and he was one of the very few men I had met with an interesting and nonconformist mind. Also I really wanted to be his wife. For better or for worse I told myself, walking toward the Milk Bar exactly one week after our conversation.

So we stayed together. That winter we produced many plays, busy with décor, costumes and rehearsals. Somehow Charlie and I were restless, tired of always the same routine. We wanted real adventure, more than the youth hostel's camping weekends and the same friends day in and day out. We also needed to be alone together, to feel our closeness and to discover more of each other.

Chapter 14: 1949

An Incredible Journey Begins

A bold idea came to us almost simultaneously. A long trip together would be fantastic, but where, how, when? Those were the big questions. We had no money for such a venture, and my parents would never give their consent. It was almost hopeless, but we were stubborn and we decided to make it happen. Our first destination would be France, and once there we would decide where else to go, depending on if it was the beginning or the end of summer. I had to find a way to convince my parents to send me to France.

But in the meanwhile, we prepared. To save a little more money, Charlie took a job as a substitute teacher at the Alliance Israelite, the same school he had attended. The wages were not great, but certainly better than what he was making as a clerk at the wholesale thread company. Every possible franc was saved for the trip. My job was to make a waterproof tent big enough for both of us, and buy our sleeping bags and travel equipment. I was also knitting several pairs of heavy socks and a couple of woolen shirts. How exciting it was.

We needed some advice and let my cousin Chewing in on the secret. He designed the blueprint for the tent very professionally, and I started working almost full time on the project. It wasn't too difficult to hide all this activity from Father because he was gone most of the day, but Mother started asking questions. I told her my friends and I were planning several weekends for the summer, and had decided to have better tents and better clothes for the outings, and that each of us had been assigned various chores.

In late spring of 1949, almost everything was ready for the trip. One of Charlie's colleagues at the school fell madly in love with him, but this time I was not jealous at all. That poor girl was ugly as sin, with a big hairy mole on her cheek, and on top of that she was a fanatic Seventh Day Adventist. Charlie did not know what to do and to calm her down, he asked her to knit one woolen sock for the trip, while I was knitting the other. In her zeal to please him she made an enormous deformed sock big enough to fit an elephant leg. When I saw this horror, I could not stop laughing and made several nasty comments on the girl's amorous accomplishments. Charlie was more charitable. He gave her a small present to thank her for the hard work she had done.

Very suddenly I fell quite ill, high fever, terrible pains in my stomach. I had caught an intestinal flu. This was a nasty affair with a long treatment. The doctor prescribed a new drug that came from a plant in West Africa. In Morocco almost everyone suffered either a liver or intestinal ailment, but at this time, when I was ready for the great adventure, it was quite a blow. The trip would have to be postponed at least a month until I was better.

The effect of the drug was terrible. I had nightmarish hallucinations, waking up drenched in sweat, not recognizing my surroundings. The Fabergé lavender cologne Mother was splashing me with in the evenings turned sour on my feverish skin. The fragrance, so lovely in ordinary circumstances, made me feel like retching. Ideas of suicide controlled me day and night; I felt like a stranger to myself, as if I were in a deep hole unable to climb out. What was happening was terrifying; I was sure the medicine was killing me. The illness and the drug had weakened me to such a state that I decided to stop taking that poison. Slowly I got better, but not totally well. On my next visit to the doctor's, a flash thought came to me. Why not use my illness to justify my trip to France? Wasn't there a town called Plombière in eastern France, I asked him? Wasn't this place famed for its water cures, particularly for the intestines?

"Yes," he said, puzzled.

"Can you tell my parents to send me there, doctor?" I asked. "I am sure the waters would cure me completely."

"You know, this is a bright idea. I think you should go as soon as possible," he replied.

"Thank you, doctor," I said. "Can you write the note to my parents right now?"

I waited while he wrote the note to my parents that meant freedom, and smiled, profoundly satisfied when I had it in my hands. I had found my escape route.

As soon as I was out of there, I ran toward the Milk Bar, where I was sure to find Charlie. Brandishing the note like a banner, I yelled like a banshee intoxicated by the thought of freedom.

"Charlie, Charlie, we are going, I am free!"

After so many months of hard work, of defeats, of wishing, a simple little piece of paper written by a doctor made everything possible. It was finally settled, we were going.

Mother decided she would accompany me part of the way to Plombière. We traveled together up to Lyon, the medieval city on the river Rhône. There on the train platform we said goodbye. She was going to Vichy for the waters, and I was taking the next train east to Plombière, near the German border. We were to meet in Paris in three weeks at the end of our respective cures. I had not told her about my plans with Charlie, who was to join me at the same time in Paris. I was counting on Mother's indulgence to let me stay in France for an extended vacation, letting her return to Morocco alone. It was somewhat cruel on my part to let her deal with my severe father.

Plombière was an old town with narrow cobbled streets and medieval buildings. It looked sleepy, nestled in verdant rounded mountains millions of years old. Its inhabitants looked quite conservative, including the lady in whose boarding house I was to stay. The guests were past their forties and too serious looking for my taste. No fun here, was my immediate thought. I had nobody to talk to, except the local doctor and the people at the spa.

After a few days of this regime, I had pangs of anxiety and tried my best to divert myself by reading books and going for long walks in the country. Nothing could take me out of that curious depression. I had moments of total blackout and was frightened to death. What was happening? I could not call Mother, as that would jeopardize the whole trip, and I would not let Charlie know about my state either, afraid he would cancel our plans. I had to endure and get well on my own.

One evening I woke up in sweats, not recognizing where I was. The window was wide open, its lacy white curtains moving in strange patterns with the hot breeze. In a daze I got up, attracted by the balcony and the emptiness beyond. Feeling the cold stone under my feet, I walked past the window to the very edge of the iron railing, ready to jump. 'I have to go now, there into nothingness,' I remember thinking. Suddenly I gripped the railing's cold metal. 'No, no, Anit don't do it, don't.' Somebody was calling me back, who? I did not know, but I retreated slowly toward the bed, shaking violently. Opening a drawer in the night table next to my bed, I retrieved a handkerchief and, climbing into bed, I tied one of my wrists to the brass headboard, deciding not to sleep. The next morning, I woke up still tied to the bed. I felt very weak. I must have fallen asleep from exhaustion. At breakfast one of the guests, a woman, noticed how pale I was. She came to sit besides me.

"What happened?" she asked. "May I be of help? I'm a registered nurse."

She had a sweet, concerned face. It turned out she was from Cairo, and had tended to soldiers during the war. She too had come here for the intestinal cure. I was so distraught with what was happening to me, I decided to tell her everything, from the beginning. She was horrified when I told her what drug I had been given.

"My little girl, you could very easily have died," she said. "This West African drug has been banned - I am horrified that your doctor gave that to you. Many patients on whom it was tried did not survive, and there were many suicides reported too. It takes a long time to get it out of one's system, but I can help you, I have some experience with treating the effects. I shall be at your side every moment of day and night."

An angel had been sent to save me, yet the fight was terrible. Over the next three weeks the hallucinations and thoughts of suicide came back again and again, but less every time. At the end of those three weeks, with the help of my Egyptian angel, I had licked it.

On the train back to Paris my only thoughts were for Charlie; I was anxious to see him and to get on with our daring plan. It was a hot July in Paris that summer of 1949. The city was deserted of its inhabitants; only tourists, cameras in hand, were to be seen in the streets. Mother was waiting for me in a small but chic hotel near the Opera. We fell into each other's arms. She was as elegant as ever in a pale linen suit, her long dark hair in a chignon, a luminous smile on her lips. I realized that I might not have seen her again if I had jumped out of that window. I had to forget all of that fast, never allowing myself to dwell on it ever again.

We went for lunch in a good restaurant near the hotel. I had not eaten like that for some time now and Irelished every morsel. While eating dessert, I told Mother that Charlie was coming that same afternoon to

My parents, Elias and Ryta, on their honeymoon in Venice, 1921

I'm at bottom left, a flower girl at a society wedding in Paris around 1929

Glad and me, ages 5 and 3, in Paris, 1928

Left: Visiting Father in Settat, 1941.
Back row: Me, Rene, Glad, Stella,
Henri. Middle row: Father, Mother,
Chewing, Pastor Green, Lison. Bottom:
Robert

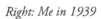
Right: Me in 1939

Below: Taking a bow - on stage, 1943.
I'm second from right.

At home with our american army photographer friends, 1943. From left: The pianist, Father, me, Glad, John Vergis, Leon Chooluck (standing), Mother.

Glad's wedding, 1946. Back row: Me, Gabriel, Cousin Mercedes;
Front row: Cousin Lycie, Glad.

Left: my summer in Tangier, 1946, with El Peruano and Mosy (right)

Below: Meeting Charlie - on stage in our first production, 1947: from left: Albert Botbol, me, Charlie

Bottom Left: A costume party, 1947. From left: Me, Charlie, Lulu Mouyal and Chewing

Bottom right: Charlie and me in 1948

Right: In Sweden, modeling traditional Moroccan burnooses and hats, and the subject of a newspaper article, 1949. Translation: The Moroccans in traditional attire. The hats are made of palm leaves. Anita has her eyes downcast, as women tend to do in that country. The small pipe with the little bowl is filled with very strong tobacco.

De båda marockanerna i sitt hemlands klädsel. De bredskyggiga hattarna är gjorda av palmblad. Anita har ögonen nedslagna liksom kvinnorna brukar ha som gå med slöjor i Marocko. Den smala pipan med litet piphuvud röks med en särskilt stark tobak.

Our wedding, December 20, 1950

Above: Saying goodbye to Charlie's family on our way to America, 1953. From left:
Simon Amsellem; Charlie's father Abraham Bohbot; Nenette Amsellem, Charlie; Rosette
Dayan; Charles Dayan; Charlie's mother Gracia; me; Cousin Armand.
In front: Nenette's eldest child, Monique.

Left: At Beulah Roth's
house in Hollywood,
1953

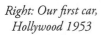

Right: Our first car,
Hollywood 1953

meet us at the hotel. She seemed agreeably surprised. This was as good a chance as any to ask for an extended vacation.

"Maman," I started, a little hesitantly, "I'd like to stay in France a little longer. I want to go down south to the region of Cavaillon to help in the melon harvest. Its good exercise for the body and mind, and it will help me to get completely well working in the fields."

Mother looked at me sideways. She understood. Her eyes had an expression of longing; the freedom she had never been able to achieve was transmitted to her daughter.

"Your father will not approve, of this I am certain," she said. "Will Charlie accompany you?"

"Well...yes he will," I replied, "but Chewing said before I left that he would join us in a week or two."

"Really, I had no idea," she said. She thought for a moment. "In that instance I believe I can let you go, but only for three more weeks. You understand how difficult it will be for me to deal with your father when I get back alone."

My heart had been beating hard all throughout the conversation. I was unable to say a word. That was it, I finally had achieved what I desired most, total freedom. Tears came to my eyes from the emotions. I threw myself upon her, heedless of the restaurant's guests, and kissed her again and again, repeating thank you, thank you.

Charlie was waiting for us in the hotel lobby. It took a lot of control not to throw myself in his arms. Was he ever handsome in that very short-sleeved shirt showing his muscles! His hair was combed back with water and shined blue black. I kissed him on the cheek as was customary for friends, but I really wanted to bite his lips. His green eyes were flashing with suppressed desire, when he returned my kiss his body was trembling. We went up to the hotel room for tea, Charlie dragging all our equipment, two enormous backpacks that were not yet full, but already very heavy. I was anxious to tell him that everything was OK, that we were free to go, but had to wait politely until Mother opened the conversation on the subject.

"Charlie, I have given permission for Anit to stay in France for three more weeks. Please take good care of her."

Her voice was hesitant as she said these words. I could see that she had second thoughts about leaving me alone with a man. Did she know we were lovers? I wanted to think she did not, but her look said a lot.

We took her to the station the next morning. I kept telling her that everything would be all right, not to worry so much, but still she had tears in her eyes. I was twenty-five years old and I could certainly take care of myself, but I was unmarried, and therefore she and Father treated me like a girl, who had to ask permission for everything.

When the train pulled out, a handkerchief waved at us desperately until it faded in the distance, like a white bird disappearing in a cloud of smoke. Charlie and I were all alone on the platform.

After a minute or two of total silence, we realized that we were free, totally free and together. From our two throats came a tremendous yell that filled the air around us like an aura of joy. We started dancing around, jumping like mountain goats on a summer slope, and after exhausting ourselves we stopped, took a deep breath and joined our bodies in a long passionate kiss.

Dragging our bags, we got off the metro at St. Germain des Près and looked for a cheap hotel on the boulevard. The room we found in a questionable hotel was only steps away from the Café de Flore. This was Paris' existentialist center, where the action was. Our room was extremely small with an enormous ornate bed taking up three quarters of the space. In front of it, a massive chest of drawers left no space to move. No bathroom, but there was a washbasin coupled with a shaky bidet, the only appliance never missing in a French hotel! For us it was paradise. In a café we bought two ham and butter sandwiches and hurried back up our little room. We were dead tired from that long day full of emotions.

Unable to sleep because the bed was sagging with every move, we made love all night, sweating and laughing regardless of the hotel neighbors. In the morning we hurried to the Café de Flore for a cup of strong dark coffee and a croissant. Our main reason really was to have a glimpse at Albert Camus, the controversial existentialist writer who spent most of his days there, composing and writing his new philosophical treatises and his wonderful novels. Perhaps we would be lucky enough to also see Simone de Beauvoir, his lover, herself a great author. Camus was already there in his favorite corner dreaming away under thick eyeglasses. We were fascinated by this man whose books we had read avidly, books that had shaken a good portion of the western world with new ideas. Not daring to disturb him, we drank our coffee absentmindedly, staring at him like two hillbillies in town for the first time. It was difficult to tear ourselves away without making contact with such a formidable man, but we did not have the guts. We came back every day, each time sitting a little closer to him. At last he noticed us and waved hello to us. We were in heaven.

It took us a few days to look at maps and decide where we would go first. In reality it was too early yet to go down south for the melon crop. Closing my eyes I pointed at the map of France that was spread all over the bed and to my surprise my finger fell on Normandy. So be it then, it would be the northwest. Charlie did not care one way or the other. One thing was sure, we had very little money, including what mother had given me for the three weeks of my stay. The word was frugality.

For the first time in our lives we were alone on the roads of France, on foot. We planned to hitchhike, but it proved more difficult than we had anticipated. Tired to the bone after four days of hard walking, we flagged down an old truck coming toward us, and to our amazement, it stopped for us. It was rickety, full of farmer's tools. The rusty owner in blue peasant garb resembled his dusty truck. In a cracked voice he asked us where we were going. "Wherever you want to drop us is OK," we said. The old wrinkled man became suspicious, his eyes squinted while he was trying to discover who we were. Did we have bad intentions? Were we thieves? After a moment of reflection that seemed an eternity to us, he yelled,

"OK climb in, but I warn you, I am cutting the motor. We'll go down the hill and whenever the truck stops, that's where you get off. I don't want to spend my gasoline on vagrants like you, understood?"

Down the hill it was. The grade was steep; we could have been on a roller coaster. The old man seemed to enjoy it as much as we did, but for other reasons; he was saving his precious gasoline. Little by little the truck tired of running like mad, slowed down, coughed a few times and stopped.

"Well kids, off you go, and you're lucky, that old jalopy of mine went much further than I expected. You're really lucky."

Opening a huge toothless mouth he grinned. Grateful, we thanked him and waved goodbye. Back on the asphalt we walked on deserted roads, the sun beating down on us, sweat running down our backs staining our armpits and our backs. We only had a vague idea of where we were going. The only thing that mattered was that we were totally free, that we had not a care in this world, stopping whenever we pleased, eating when we were hungry. Yellow fields shimmering in the sun competed in hues with the very green patches of apple orchards, some of the fruit on the trees already blushing pink. I had never experienced such well being, finding my true self in that gorgeous nature. I was realizing how free one can be without owning a thing and swore to make it last as long as I could. That night we slept in a ditch along a country road. Rolled together into Charlie's big white wool burnoose, we stared at the immense dark sky studded with thousands of bright stars. Holding tight because of the sudden chill, we were happy. The world belonged to us.

Waking with the cock's crow, it was still a surprise not to be in our beds at home. We were stiff with cold and in great need of something hot in our stomach. Should we go right or left? At this point we were quite disoriented, our eyes still half open. A good two miles away, we spotted an inn at a crossroads. A few trucks were stopped around the back. Rough male voices could be heard cursing. The smoky joint was filled, truck drivers having breakfast at a long wooden bar. We looked at the menu chalked on a blackboard.

"What will it be?" the guy behind the counter said. "We have good salami, cheap, and it comes with a large piece of country bread."

Charles and I looked at each other.

"OK, we'll have that and two cups of coffee."

"Coffee? That's for sissies! Why not a good shot of white wine, you'll see, its much better, it will warm you up."

We sat outside on the sidewalk devouring our bread and salami and getting tipsy at seven o'clock in the morning drinking white wine. Looking at the map, we found out we were already in Lower Normandy and we decided to go to the region of Argantan where there was a fourteenth-century castle to visit and fifteenth- and sixteenth-century churches. It was also the great painter Fernand Leger's birthplace. Surely there would be some of his work in a museum. Walking across fields slightly shortened the distance. Lazy cows heavy with milk ambled slowly, stopping here and there to graze on lush grasses and multicolored flowers. Where were we? We had lost our bearings. Approaching a young man working at mending fences, we found out we were near Camembert, where the famous cheese was made. This was certainly worth a stop. A few more miles and we would enjoy a fabulous lunch with a piece of that good cheese and the rest of our bread.

So far our trip was a success. That afternoon, after having eaten a whole very ripe wheel of camembert and a few apples, we napped at the edge of the river Orne, well protected from the sun by huge leafy trees. Life was wonderful; undressing, we splashed in the cold water trying to wash clean all the grime we had accumulated. Getting back into dirty pants and shirts did not feel that good, but so far, there had been no opportunity to wash our clothes; too bad, it would have to wait. It was already evening and we had not yet reached Argantan. Tired and hungry, we were ready to settle for another ditch to spend the night when I spotted a feeble light in a field. Vague dark shapes suggested a farm. Would we have the nerve to go and ask for food and shelter? Looking at each other was enough of a decision. Walking through the wet field, our shoes sloshing with water, we reached the farm's door, accompanied by fierce dog barks. Now it was pitch black and we had to control our fear of being bitten by an unseen foe. We were cold. Abruptly the door opened on a tall farmer holding a lamp. Looking at us with steel blue eyes that matched his overalls, he said roughly,

"What do you want at this hour of night?"

"We are hungry, wet and very tired, sir," I said with a weak smile.

"Where are you headed, young ones?"

"We tried to reach the Argantan youth hostel, but we couldn't make it, too late, too tired."

"Alright, come in, you can sleep in the horses' stable. There's straw to keep you warm, and I'll bring you some bread and a pitcher of milk. Beware not to sleep to close too the horses, you could be kicked badly." He gave us a kerosene lantern to light our way, with stern warnings to put it out before going to sleep, and to be careful with it around the staw and hay.

Yes, we got warm in the straw and yes, we calmed our hunger, but the time we spent in that stable was nightmarish. It seemed that every time we closed our eyes, the horses, big heavy Percherons, started kicking their feet on cue, scaring the hell out of us poor humans. In the dark stable we had no way of knowing how close to us the beasts were and so it became a sleepless night. Somehow the ditches on the road appeared to be friendlier. In the very early morning, I heard the barn door being opened.

"Young ones, it's time to get up, it's already five o'clock in the morning. Here, I brought you something special to drink before your morning coffee, it will give you strength for the rest of the day."

Presenting us with two small glasses he continued, "Calvados, the best of Normandy's spirits. I make it myself, you have to swallow it in one gulp."

And so we did. It burned down our throats, our stomachs, our guts, until our whole bodies were aflame and charred. The farmer burst out laughing, saying that us city folks were weaklings, that we did not know what was good for us, and told us to follow him to the kitchen where his wife was preparing a breakfast of pork roast, cheese, bread and butter, and strong black coffee. Nothing could stop the burning sensation in our guts, no matter how much we ate. We left, thanking them profusely, and started down the road still totally drunk and totally unaware of our surroundings. After walking several miles, we meandered for the rest of the day in and around Argentan. We visited here and there, the castle and a few churches, but were too tired to go to the museum, and we ended up sleeping on the road again.

Summer was getting on. Now we had to go south if we wanted to reach Cavaillon, to pick the melon crop. Spreading our map once more, we traced a route that would take us there in a slanting pattern, first to the Aube province and the medieval city of Troyes. By now we had lost a few pounds and were tanned like old leather. Before leaving Casablanca I had cut my hair and I was wearing shorts and army boots; it was difficult to distinguish me from a boy. I liked this feeling of being so totally different from the well-dressed young woman I had been, as it seemed to give me even more freedom. Another pleasing thought was that none of my family or my friends knew where I was.

Several days of hard walking and little rest took us to our destination. It was morning when we arrived at the outskirts of Troyes. We had slept the night before close by, in a meadow. It was not a very large city, less than a hundred thousand inhabitants, but it was an important hosiery and spinning mill center. What attracted us here was the beauty of the place. Dating from the early middle ages, it was renowned for its several magnificent churches. The oldest, Sainte Madeleine, dating from the twelfth century, and about six others including the superb gothic Cathedral St. Pierre and St. Paul, each church rising century after century. Both Charlie and I were lovers of architecture and of all the art and the treasures to be found in those churches. The small streets had changed little – they were crooked and narrow, and some of the houses seemed to be toppling in toward each other acorss the cobblestones.

We made our way to the youth hostel, which was a large house with several rooms and a huge kitchen. It seemed like the whole place had been invaded by British hitchhikers. Seeing us, they let us know that we were not welcome, but the landlady disapproved of them and their conduct.

She welcomed us, but told us we would have to fend for ourselves, *"avec ces Anglais."* After two days under the same roof, I found out how dirty they were. They did not wash their dishes. The whole kitchen stank of rancid food. Their dirty smelly clothes were strewn everywhere, yet we had to endure, we could not afford a hotel room. Fortunately we were out most of the days enjoying the great beauties of the city. I bought a softcover book of the stories of Percival, the story of the Grail and the story of Lancelot, by Chrétien de Troyes, who had lived here between 1135 and 1183.

The day of our departure was a sultry one, the air heavy and humid. While we were crossing the main square, noon struck and all the church bells rang in unison, drowning us in loud heavenly sounds. I could not envisage a long walk at this time and both of us were hungry. We had very little money for food and were planning to look around for the cheapest meal to share. Charlie and I sat down in the shade for a while to choose the best possible route to the south. Sitting in the street with our backs against a wall and our sacks against us, we had the benefit of a shady tree above our heads. It felt good. Both of us were sweating profusely, sponging our brows with our doubtful handkerchiefs. What would we have given for a glass of cold water, but there were no fountains on the plaza. Charlie closed his eyes.

Passersby were eyeing us with disdain: Bohemians! Across the street, I spotted a nice house. The people must be on vacation, I thought, all the shutters were closed. My eyes followed the alley leading to a gate that was also closed. Looking up I marveled at what I saw, an apple tree full of pippin apples toppling over the gate. Nudging Charlie to wake him up, I silently pointed towards the apple tree. We looked at each other; our lunch was right there in front of us. Choosing a medium-sized stone, looking around to see if anyone was watching, Charlie shot his small weapon with dexterity and here rolled toward us a big round apple. Unbelievable how easy it was. With what pleasure we sank our teeth in that juicy apple. Five minutes later we got another one and a third one. We could not have been happier.

While I was munching the last bits of the juicy fruit I held in my hand, I saw with horror the door to the house open and a skinny man all dressed in black come out with a big stick in his hand. He walked directly to us slamming the gate to his house behind him. His eyes were glowering.

"You good for nothing thieves! "I watched your little game behind my dining room shutters. I'll teach you to steal." He raised his knotty stick to strike Charlie.

But sir," I said, "it's only a few apples and they were not in your garden, the branches are sticking out above the gate in the street."

"It's still my apple tree and you are going to pay for this, you foreigners. Our children would never dare steal apples. I am the Chief Administrator of this city. I am calling the Mayor to deal with you scum."

By this time a few people had gathered around us gawking, including a gendarme in his ill-fitting blue uniform who kept lifting the peak of his cap to sponge beads of sweat running from his head. The official sent him running to get the Mayor, who it seemed was at an official luncheon. My God, what fate had pushed us to be in front the Prefect's house and to steal his apples? We had to keep our cool no matter what. The circle of curious onlookers was growing. Half an agonizing hour passed before we saw the Mayor appear, panting, rolling his round body up the hill, followed by the Gendarme. I bit my lips not to burst out laughing. All this looked like a scene from a cheap operetta. The Mayor reached our group out of breath, all dressed up in tails, a huge silk red, white, and blue ribbon edged with a gold fringe around his bulging stomach.

"So those are the bastards who stole your apples?" he asked, looking at the mean Chief Administrator. And turning to us he continued.

"You will have a fine of one hundred francs to pay for your theft, and eighty francs more not to be arrested as vagrants. We want the money in cash now, or you go to prison."

Did we have that much? I did not think so. Fumbling in our pockets we took out every penny we had, plus we had to look in our bags for more. It was a very embarrassing moment, while the crowd that had now assembled was taking bets on our account. We finally gathered the money and handed it to the Mayor. At last we were free to go, but not before the Mayor's sententious voice yelled,

"I am throwing you out of this city, you are undesirables. Where are you from, Morocco? no wonder. You have fifteen minutes to get out. Out!" he shouted.

To which I replied as soon as I was at a safe distance,

"You provincial bigots, you can cook in your nastiness and stew in it forever. We will never set foot in your town again. You don't deserve this jewel of a city!"

On the road our woes continued for a while, when we found out that our hated British hitchikers had taken the best spots on the road to flag down passing trucks. What a day. At that moment I thought of my parents, how shocked they would be to learn that their beloved daughter had almost been arrested for theft and almost put in prison for vagrancy. For me it was an unpleasant story, but what an experience, something to add to my life.

With almost no money remaining, the only solution was to go back to Paris, where we had left most of our money entrusted to a good friend. That meant delaying or trip south again instead of what had been planned. We flagged down a truck going in that direction, but the driver was only going a little distance. As the sun was disappearing in red splendor, we were left at the edge of a wood, the driver then turning right towards his home. At least we would be protected by all the trees around us, I thought.

I had not counted on the millions of mosquitoes that assailed us as soon as we sat down to eat a piece of dry bread and the last rolling apple that I had stashed away in my bag. The only light we had was from our flashlights, it had to be used sparingly, but we had cigarettes to add a little glow and to keep us company. I noticed that the smoke we produced seemed to push away the insects that were eating us alive. Charlie had the idea to mix our saliva with some tobacco and smear it all over our bodies. It worked; not a mosquito would touch us, too bitter. As I was fumbling in my back pack, I felt a little bag where I kept a spare comb and a nail clip, I opened it, lighting it with my flashlight. What a surprise! There was money in it, three hundred francs that I had totally forgotten about. Plans had to be changed once more but for the better. The truck that picked us up the next morning was going to Orleans, south of Paris. Well so be it, we would go to Orleans. Could it be fate, that we had been pushed here and there toward Orleans, where an adventure we had never dreamed of was about to unfold?

Arriving in town, we were told that the youth hostel had been abandoned and that the city was in the process of building a new one. Where could we sleep, then?

"Well," the man we spoke with told us, "You can still go to the old one, but you'll have to be very careful, half the floor boards are rotten and there are no more tiles on the floor, but there is a big fireplace. So if you do go, you won't be cold at night. There is plenty of wood in the garden, and as for water there is a well in the yard among the apple trees."

Apples, I winced, remembering our sad story in Troyes. Seeing my face the man said, "You can eat those apples, they are good. Well, good luck to you both."

About four good miles to walk. Our backpacks seemed much heavier at the end of the day. It had been hot at midday, but now a cool wind suddenly rose, raising dust and debris from the road, getting into our eyes and nostrils. It was difficult to walk against it. The sky took a sickly yellow color before turning an intense dark steel color, erasing the last of the sun's rays lingering on the green fields. Charles was holding his head with his two hands with a splitting headache, one of the numerous bad ones he was plagued with since the time of his sunstroke two years earlier. Big zigzagging lightening bolts tore the heavy clouds. Heads bent, we were running now, pelted by rain that felt like bullets on our heads and bodies, the formidable thunder engulfing us.

"Come on, only one mile left, we're almost there," I shouted. Anyway we had to continue, there was not a tree in sight to hide under.

At last we saw the house on the right side of the road. It looked abandoned all right; windows were broken, the fence was askew and when we pushed the door to enter it almost fell to pieces. To us it was paradise, a shelter, a whole house to ourselves for as long as we wanted and nobody to chase us or to question us.

Letting our gear fall to the dirt floor and forgetting how tired we were, we started exploring the house. Half the stairs were missing when we climbed upstairs to find out how bad the floor planks were. It was bad; one of every two boards were missing, and walking across was like dancing a dangerous ballet, but we found a large corner that looked solid enough to put our sleeping bags. Up here it would be warmer, only one window was broken, which could easily be stuffed with newspaper. By now the storm had abated, leaving the outside washed and clean. We went out to find the well in the garden. Clouds were now receding in the background leaving a perfect dark blue sky aglow with a sliver of bright moon. Drops of water were falling from the trees, their leaves glittering in the dark. What peace! We just stood there in awe, in absolute silence, breathing in the night, the land. After a while, overtaken with fatigue, all our plans to build a fire and eat some of the apples were drowned by the imperious desire to sleep.

Waking up the next day was a nice surprise. A warm yellow sun had invaded the room, its dancing spots playing on the walls. I woke up Charles and together we concocted a well deserved breakfast of apples, stale bread, and instant coffee; a feast. Today we would explore Orleans and perhaps find a job in the fields.

The city had existed since the fifth century, well before Charlemagne. Already in the middle ages it was a place of great learning, with several universities of renown. Orleans became a royal city where kings were crowned and in 1429, after a long siege, Joan of Arc took back the city from the British. All that history was fascinating to us; we knew our days here would be filled with wonders. Approaching the city center we heard people talking about the Loire river on which the city was built; they were mentioning about how dry the river was this year. We heard other pedestrians saying the Loire had not been so dry in a hundred years. Everybody seemed to converge toward the river where they said treasures were to be found, so we followed. The sight was astonishing. The large span of water had turned into an immense field of mud. In it, at least two hundred people were in the muck, some up to their waists, digging for treasure. We looked at each other.

"Well let's go," we said almost together, taking our shoes off and tying the laces around our necks. We descended into the cold wet mud and started digging. People were shouting.

"Hey! Look what I found, a real beauty. That silver tray is all embossed, I would say it is Renaissance." Another fellow was waving his arms at us, showing a better place to dig. At first we did not find a thing and were discouraged. It had been three hours already and the sun was beating down on our naked heads. Looking around we realized that most of the diggers were closer to the bridge. As we tried to navigate across the muck, a young fellow approached us.

"Hi! My name is Serge Boulez, I can help you, I know the best places," he said. "You see the bridge? It has medieval houses on it. In past days the bridge was an important passage, people did commerce on it. Whole armies went over it. There were battles fought right on top of it. Weapons and various objects were lost in the river. Besides, it was the custom since the very early days to throw a coin in the water for good luck." When he found out we were from Morocco, he was captivated.

"Why don't we meet after the dig, let's say five this afternoon," he said. "I'll be right there on the steps."

He turned around and walked away. How wonderful, we had made a friend. With renewed ardor we resumed our digging bare-handed. By four o'clock, we had found several objects. Roman spear-heads, old silver coins, and the prize was a gold ring wrought like two entwined hands. Charles gave it to me as a gauge of his love. We kissed, a romantic moment in a sea of mud. The funniest moment came when plunging my hand in for the last time, I retrieved a Mickey Mouse watch – definitely not an antique, so I put it back way down in the mud. In a hundred years, somebody would find it and perhaps it would then be a treasure.

Over a cup of coffee with Serge we found out that he was on vacation and had just completed his military enlistment. For the moment he was working as an instructor in a youth camp. This was a government-sponsored vacation for the sons and daughters of French postmen, and they were housed in a beautiful chateau a few minutes out of Orleans. Serge had recently been married and his wife was also part of the team. She took care of putting plays on as well as musical events.

"We have done a lot of theater," I told him. "We can do almost anything – set design, costumes, directing, acting, and we both are looking for a job. Do you think there's any chance to work with you?"

"This is unbelievable!" he said. "Micheline, my wife, is at this moment looking for people to make the sets for her next play and also to make theater masks. There's no pay, but you will be fed two good meals a day. I just have to tell the camp director, but I am sure he will approve. Where are you staying?"

"At the old youth hostel." Charles said, "It's a wonderful place, drafty but OK, and it's free." We all laughed.

"I'll send somebody for you tomorrow morning, be ready at seven AM."

Half of our worries were over; at least we would not starve. How long did he say we could work? I remembered now, two weeks. The chateau was imposing, with turrets and a moat. We were introduced to the director and immediately put to work making masks. It was a huge room with long tables covered with tons of old newspaper, big pots of dripping glue and small ones containing gouache paints. We were to make the heads of angels and demons for today. Later we met Micheline, Serge's wife. She came bursting in the room, a big smile on her face. A tiny wiry woman, she had magnificent blond hair that came down to her waist.

"Am I so happy to meet you," she said. "You are a godsend, I was really despairing to find the right people." She was dancing around us, a real ball of energy.

The meals at the chateau were quite elaborate. We took real advantage of that free manna and stuffed ourselves with all the delicacies that were presented. Some of the lady instructors eyed me with coolness to say the least, because I wore the same pair of shorts and the same shirt every day, while they would change before coming to the dining room. I did not care, my clothes were washed and clean if not pressed, and frankly this was the last thing on my mind. I was thinking that the time to go to Cavaillion for the melon crop was nearing; we would have to move out of that dream house of a hostel, where we had spent so many wonderful evenings roasting apples in the fireplace, sitting in the garden at night under a roof of stars and being in each other's arms for as long as we wanted with nobody to interfere.

Serge and his wife came to see us one evening with the most extravagant proposition. We sat around the low wooden table with a bottle of wine while a big fire was roaring in the fireplace behind us. Serge and Micheline had six more weeks of vacation, and they asked us if we would join them. Charles said we already had plans for the rest of the summer, but we would listen to his proposition and decide.

"As you know, I just finished my tour of duty in the army. I was stationed in Baden Baden, near Fribourg in Germany. I have a permit from the army to travel across Germany for myself, my wife Micheline, and three close kin, a brother...a sister... you see what I am coming to. We would love you to come with us, we consider you like family now."

While he was talking, my mind was racing a hundred miles an hour. It was the total reverse of our safe little plan. Western Germany at the time was occupied and divided into three sectors, the American, the British, and the French. The country was far from being recovered, and the cities were still in shambles. Charles said yes right away. He was fearless and I went along with him, even though I was terrified of going to Germany. I could not forget the war and all we went through, but the lure of adventure was too tempting; I was going!

The last nights in Orleans, Serge and Micheline stayed with us at the youth hostel. Feverishly we wrote names of places we would go to, far beyond Germany: Denmark, Norway, Sweden, Lapland perhaps. Drawing routes on maps that Serge had brought, we dreamed of faraway lands that we had never thought we would see. We had to think of the practical side of the trip too. The food we would carry, the tools we might need, the weight each of us was capable of handling, and the all-important visas and papers that would be required for the foreign countries we were about to cross.

That meant going back to Paris; all the foreign embassies were there and we had to get the rest of our money and some extra warm clothes that we had left at our friend's apartment. The date was settled, we would all meet in Baden Baden, where Serge had to get his permit signed. We said good-bye to each other, embracing warmly, knowing we were going to see one another very soon. Closing the door to our Orleans dream house, we did not even look back. What was in front of us now was so incredible it gave us wings.

Chapter 15: 1949

Germany

We were ready. Each of us carried rucksacks on our backs, heavy with a tent, a hatchet, rolled blankets, a portable gas stove, and clothes for various climates. Tins of sardines and other edibles purchased for the trip weighed the bags down even more. Charlie's pack weighed fifty kilos and mine weighed twenty-five, a lot to carry on our shoulders. On top of the rucksacks we perched Moroccan straw country hats embroidered in bold colored silks and brilliant sequins. People were turning around to stare at us as we walked the platform of the Gare de l'Est, the train station that would take us east to Germany.

It was just before midnight when we boarded. With a long whistle and clouds of steam the train departed, taking speed and wailing in the night, the black machine tearing the dark, taking us to the start of a unknown, risky journey. The adrenaline was high and we loved it.

Standing in the passageway crowded with travelers, we stood up most of the night, elbowing a few in the stomach and others in their sides to be able to breathe. Toward the end Charlie and I collapsed on top of each other, not caring anymore who was trampling us.

"Strasbourg!" yelled the controller; the train stopped and more passengers came on, disrupting our half-sleep. Soon after we reached the frontier of Germany. I jumped up shaking Charlie to wake him; our eyes were burning, refusing to open. Customs officers climbed aboard to look at our passports; an uncontrollable fear took hold of me when I saw the German uniforms. I could not even answer their questions. Charlie came to my rescue; the officers looked at me with a cold suspicious gaze that froze the blood in my veins. In the wee hours of morning the train halted again, and we heard the controller's voice once more.

"Passengers for the northern train step down, ten minutes stop."

Gathering our stuff we stepped down onto a deserted platform to wait for the connection to Baden-Baden. It was cold and so foggy that only a long whistle told us our train was nearing. Then in a flurry of noise and steam the long gray beast entered the station. In the compartment all eyes turned on us; did we look so foreign? Charlie and I felt uneasy; we kept silent, listening to but not understanding the German spoken around us. It was a relief of sorts when we stepped down in Baden-Baden and were once more by ourselves.

The weather was cold; fortunately we both were wearing the heavy red wool shirts I had sewn so many months ago at home in Casablanca. Big dark clouds were racing through the sky, a sharp cutting wind freezing our hands. We reached the center of that pretty town running, trying to find cover before the deluge. Already large drops of rain were falling, but we could not make it fast enough, it seemed the whole sky had opened. Drenched to the bone, shaking with the cold and wet sticking to our skin, we finally made it to the entrance of an old Rococco building. We had to change our clothes or we would catch our death, but how? and where?

"Behind that heavy door," said Charlie, "we'll take turns."

I went first, dragging my heavy bag with me, inching my way as far as I could behind the large ornate entrance door. It had curlicues of wrought iron. Could I really undress completely? The glass on the door was translucent..

"Hurry up, nobody is coming, the street is empty," Charlie said.

It was a real battle; wanting to go fast, I put my pants on the wrong way and the right sleeve of my sweater on the left arm; Damn it, it took me ten whole minutes before I stepped out of my corner. Now I was to be the lookout while Charlie went behind the door.

"Charlie, somebody is coming toward the building! What do I do?"

"Block me, lean on the door, smile, use your charm."

A man stepped in looking at me with surprise; I said hello in English, nodding, and smiled my most radiant smile while all my insides were frozen with fear imagining the horror if we were caught undressing in a public place, and in Germany to boot.

Charlie changed much quicker than I had. We felt so much better in our comfortable dry clothes; now we had to find our friend Serge who was stationed here with the French occupying army. It took us a while to locate the garrison headquarters. After asking the sentry for our friend and giving his rank and serial number we hadn't long to wait. We saw him coming and then suddenly running when he realized it was us. We hugged and kissed and yelled at the top of our lungs all at once. The sentry stood there in amazement wondering what the hell was going on.

Micheline and Claude, a cousin of hers, joined us soon after. We all went to a konditorei, a sort of tea room, and sat in the back. Serge ordered coffee and pastries for everybody. I was surprised at how well he spoke German; he certainly would be handy during our trip.

We had serious business to discuss. Our departure was set for the next morning, Serge said. That meant Charlie and I would not even have an evening to relax, and God knew we needed it.

"Alright, Serge," I said, "shoot."

"Well this is the deal. As I told you before when we were in Orleans, I have a vacation train pass through Germany. The paper says Mr. Serge Boulez and his immediate family, so I am going to add your names to the pass as a sister and a brother-in-law. Claude is Micheline's first cousin anyway. If we play it right, we can all travel at least to Frankfort-on-Main for nothing."

Charlie looked suspicious and asked all kinds of what-ifs. I on the other hand was all for it. It was daring all right, but I was sure we would manage. The conversation got heated, we were all talking together. Guests were turning around staring at us in disapproval. Serge motioned us to quiet down or else our plan might very well fail.

"Tonight we sleep at the Baden-Baden train station. Our train will arrive at four-thirty in the morning. At four o'clock the ticket booth opens and the man or the woman manning it will be half asleep. I'll give her my pass to sign and I am dead sure there won't be any questions. Then we'll have to pass the control at the platform gate. That bit is going to be a little tricky. You will stay a few paces behind my wife. If I see the controller frowning as I give him the pass, I'll give you a sign. You'll then dash through the station garden, jump the white fence and run for the train."

Everybody was silent. This was dangerous stuff. What if we missed the train? What if we were caught? But Serge was convincing and anyway what else could we do, we hadn't come all this way to chicken out, I told Charlie. So it was decided, we would meet at the train station at seven that evening. Serge, his wife, and Claude had to go get their stuff and Charlie and I would stroll around for about two hours. We could not really go very far dragging our heavy packs. It wasn't raining anymore, but the streets were still shiny with the water of that sudden downpour.

Where to go? The smell of grilling sausages lured us down a cobblestone street. Stores were being lit one by one, illuminating the facades of ancient houses. Older people were passing us with bags of groceries, walking toward their homes. The sky was slowly darkening to a teal blue. It was too late for a tour of the city. From far away we could make out what seemed to be a Renaissance castle. We passed an old twelfth-century church, all shadows at this late hour. I knew this town was renowned for its waters and that it had been famous since Roman times; unfortunately we wouldn't see any of this, having time only to grab a bite before walking to the station. We ate some lush fat pork sausages in a bun from a cart vendor and tried to tell him, speaking with our hands, how the wonderful smell had brought us here.

The station was one very large room with windows on one side, two entrance doors and harsh lights above. Inside, the place was packed with passengers. Many young French soldiers were milling around among German civilians, all of them carrying old suitcases, some tied with rope, or various-sized bundles. As usual Charlie and I attracted attention with our colorful sequined Moroccan hats hanging from our rucksacks. Where could Serge, his wife and cousin be in all that crowd? Stretching our necks left and right, trying to look above moving hats, military caps and kerchiefs, we finally located Serge and his little family sitting under a huge oak table covered with timetables, newspapers and travel magazines. They seemed very at ease eating sandwiches and fruit, not caring at all about the passengers' furious glances.

"This is going to be our hotel for the night, not uncomfortable at all," said Serge. "All the people you see here are taking early evening trains; soon we will be alone in the station. Charlie, Anit, make yourselves comfortable."

We opened our packs and retrieved our large double sleeping bag, another of my sewing projects, made for two lovers. Heads were turning as we were preparing for the night. Somebody bent down and threw this sentence at our faces:

"You Bohemians, we don't need people like you."

A French soldier came by and said,

"*Vous en avez du culot!*" "You have some nerve."

To all this we smiled back, feeling comfortable, warm and fed.

"How about a little jam for dessert," I said, opening a two-pound can of apricot jam from Morocco, one of the goodies mother had sent me while we were in Paris.

"I am going to the bathroom to change into my pajamas," Charlie said, walking off nonchalantly carrying his night stuff on his shoulders. The look on the people's faces when he came out of the bathroom dressed up in baby blue pajamas and slippers was comical, but the shouts of disapproval grew louder when I joined him in the sleeping bag. This was really too much for the Baden-Baden crowd.

The noise in the station was too loud to fall asleep; it took about an hour for the passengers to disperse to their various trains, then all was silence around us. The lights were dimmed. Charlie was already snoring, Serge was tossing around, uncomfortable on the marble floor. Claude and Micheline did not move, sound asleep. Fatigue was pulling me down toward unconsciousness, but I was still awake, thinking of tomorrow. It was difficult to imagine what would happen, because I had never been in a situation where I took a train without buying a ticket. This was fraud and it fundamentally displeased me, but now that I was in it I would not back down. After all, it was part of the great adventure, and even though I had a measure of fright I was also curious about how well we would pull this caper off. How long I stayed awake I could not say, but slowly my thoughts became all mixed up and I drifted into sleep.

Somebody shook my body several times before I painfully opened an eye. Serge was waking us up. I was so sore from the hard floor I could not move; Charlie was still snoring. There was a line in front of the ticket booth. My God, these people were early. Serge went to stand behind them, waving at us to get ready. I was watching his progress toward the ticket booth with anxiety. A loud speaker announced the train would arrive in fifteen minutes. I could not wake Charlie up; frantic, I threw cold water on his face and he jumped up, furious.

"Charlie the train is coming, hurry up, everybody else is ready, just put your jacket on, come on."

Serge was at the booth and all the rest of us behind him, Charlie still wearing his pajamas and bare feet in his boots, Where were his socks?

185

The lady behind the booth was half asleep all right, she was reading Serge's pass at a snail's pace, not understanding what was written on it. The train had arrived, passengers were already in their compartment and we were still here.

"The train is leaving," I said. "What are we going to do?"

The woman behind the counter had finished stamping the pass, but she said we couldn't make this train, we'd have to run to the next station.

"You can make it," she said. "If you run fast enough, the train will be in the next station for at least twenty minutes to take water and the station is ten minutes away from here." She was speaking German and Charlie and I did not understand a word. We did not realize for a moment that with all the commotion the woman had forgotten to give us our tickets!

"Run," said Serge, "as fast as you can, we can still catch the train at the next station."

We left as the train was picking up speed, running like mad down the road, five demented figures half dressed, our heavy packs bobbing on our backs, disheveled and out of breath. It seemed we were flying alongside the train but could not compete with the smoking engine that was going faster and faster. I was carrying the precious open can of apricot jam in both hands.

"Drop the damn thing," yelled Charlie, "or you'll never make it. Come on faster, faster."

My lungs were ready to burst, almost there, almost there. "I am not throwing away that jam!"

The noise of our five pairs of boots resounded in my head like kettledrums. "We're there, we're there, I can see the station, the door, the fence. We made it."

The train was ready to leave, we could hear the "All aboard!" from the station master. Serge shouted.

"Anit, Charlie, straight to the fence, we'll meet in the train somewhere."

Trampling a few flowers beds in the little station garden, we threw our packs before us and jumped over the white fence. A loud whistle almost stopped us; looking back in panic we saw a running man in uniform yelling what seemed like "Stop, stop." The train was leaving, we had to make it. Charlie took my pack and jumped on the train steps. I was just behind him panting. He tried to grab my fingers, but the train was moving faster now. Leaning as far as he could, holding with one hand to the side rail he finally grabbed my wrist and yanked me up the steps with all the strength he could muster. We rolled together inside the car, more dead than alive. When I regained control of myself I realized the tin of apricot jam was still cradled in my left arm. I was tenacious; we looked at each other and started laughing. It was all too much.

We had landed in one of the front cars very near the locomotive and had been seen climbing on by one of the drivers, who had yelled at us, raising his shoulders in disbelief. Now that we had been spotted, the train controller would be looking for us. The trip proved to be a game of cat and mouse. Inching our way in the corridors of that long train we at last found Serge, Micheline and Claude coming our way. Serge pointed with a finger toward an empty compartment and we filed in silently. We were all of us exhausted and ravenously hungry; dipping our fingers into the tin of jam, we ate like animals. Claude was standing at the door as a lookout.

"The controller is coming our way," she said. "He's carrying a huge open book with what seems a thousand pages. We have to scatter fast. Whoever sees the controller first will yell, *Le Mille Feuille*, you know, like the Napoleon pastries that are made of so many sheets of dough."

Fortunately there were people in the passageway and mingling among them we disappeared from the controller's view. Charlie and I locked ourselves in the nearest toilet wondering how long we could stay in there. Sure enough not ten minutes had passed when there was a knock on the door. We did not answer. Two minutes passed, and the knock became more insistent. We had to get out of there, there was no other way. The man waiting outside was literally dumbstruck when he saw both of us emerging from a men's room, me carrying an open can of jam.

This little game of hide and seek lasted the rest of the trip. Every so often we found ourselves together with our friends, had a few laughs and had to scatter again each time the controller came around with his big book. The train stopped a few times to let passengers down and take on new ones; Heidelberg, Mannheim, Darmstadt. Places I had heard or read about; their universities, their castles, and their factories. I had never dreamed I would see them, let alone after that terrible war. Today many of the bombed buildings looked like open wounds, still bloody and festering after four years of peace.

At last we reached Frankfurt-on-Main. We stepped out on the platform anxious about the immediate future, but relieved to be in the open air again and with no controller on our backs. Readjusting the heavy packs on our shoulders, the five of us filed into the noisy station. Crowds of people were milling around, Americans military, displaced persons going to their next destination, German police. We must have looked awfully haggard and ragged, for we were asked to follow a policeman into a booth and to produce our passports to the authorities. We were scrutinized from head to toe one by one as our passports were read by two men dressed in the detested grey German uniform. What were they going to do? They could not detain us, after all this was American and British controlled territory and I had a British passport, but Charlie was now in front of them; the policemen were looking at his passport and they looked terrified.

"Maroccaner! Maroccaner!" they said, their eyes coming out of their sockets, "Murderers! You are the ones that came with the French troops. You are the ones that cut our women's hands, necks and breasts to steal rings and necklaces. Get out of our sight, we do not want to see the likes of you anymore."

As Serge translated the fact to us, we only had one thought: to get out of there fast. Regrouping outside the station, out of sight from the dreaded police, we all started to speak at the same time.

"Is it true that the Moroccans did this?" Claude looked shocked.

"Would the French Army permit such horrors?" Serge asked in disbelief.

"I never knew any of this," I said.

"God knows what went on during that awful war," was Micheline's comment.

We all looked at Charlie for an answer. I knew how violent an Arab or a Berber could be when he fought, but Charlie knew more than I did.

"I had not heard about this, but it's true that Arabs and Berbers can be very refined in their cruelty."

He went on, telling us stories of prisoners' misfortunes, like the ones buried alive with only their heads sticking out of the ground, the head smeared in honey, the captors opening bags of bees and releasing them. Another cruel way of killing a prisoner was to have several prostitutes make love to the prisoner using wild methods to excite him without interruption until he died. Those were chilling stories, but we had more pressing needs for the present, like finding food and looking at our maps to find our way.

Frankfurt had been more than fifty percent destroyed during the war, it would prove difficult to find our way in among the ruins of the city. I asked myself what twist of fate was bringing me to cross Germany, to walk into the dragon's lair. I now realized how naive I was, not to have thought of the tragic path we would have to walk.

We had to ask for directions; otherwise we would lose too much time here. After going in circles for a while, we found a group of students who spoke a little English. In answer to our multiple questions, we found out that two fifteenth-century churches were still standing along with a tower gate from the same époque, and that Goethe's house had not been damaged. They also gave us directions to places along the river Main where we could eat good grilled sausages and drink one of Frankfurt's specialties, apple wine. As usual we were starving and went directly there first. We would have no time for a complete visit, but I wanted to see the house where the great German poet had been born and at least one of the two magnificent medieval cathedrals.

After an exhausting day sightseeing, it took us a long time to get out of the city center through miles and miles of industrial neighborhoods. By late afternoon, We finally found ourselves in open country.

The County of Hesse was a complex and twisted terrain. We were walking on a high plateau of rounded hills and beautiful forests. That night when we disappeared into our tents pitched at the foot of tall trees, we went to sleep like logs, not feeling the cold or the wind that was shaking our meager dwelling. In the morning, after a hasty coffee brewed on a small camping stove, bundling ourselves as best we could, we started the long walk north.

It was raining, a soft and steady rain. On each side of the road greenish fields were sloping down in rounded shapes. In the distance the forest was still draped in soft ribbons of fog. We were the only color in that dreamy gray landscape. We sang in rhythm with our martial steps to give us courage and also to warm our stiff bodies. It was cold this morning and we were already hungry, but that would have to wait. We had decided to walk between fifteen and twenty-five kilometers a day. Our goal was to reach Sweden before the big snows. Five days of this regime proved to have a terrible effect. My shoulders had bleeding sores from the rubbing motion and the weight of my pack. The others were not faring much better. The solution was to dump the heavy stuff from our bags. Day after day Charlie and I threw out cans of wonderful sardines from Morocco and delicate patés from France. It was impossible to eat it all at once and we could not bear the weight anymore. We almost cried when we saw the cans dwindle away behind us, a glint of gold in the sun before being swallowed by the fields. Now we were walking light, but we had no more food.

Nearing the town of Kassel we stopped, dead tired and dead hungry. On our right above the road stood an all white little country store. Outside three cows were eating grass. Micheline and I decided to go in to buy bread and milk. We were aware of how unkempt we looked and tried our best to put a little order in our disheveled hair and dress before going in. The boys were anxiously waiting outside. The store looked more like a kitchen, varnished woods, lace doilies, chairs, a cat and in the middle a red faced plump lady with blond hair, a big white apron covering her generous chest. She smiled as we showed her the coins we had to spend. I pointed to the golden loaves on the shelves and the big metal milk pails on the floor.

"Bread, milk," I said in English. The woman looked outside where our three men were waiting. She made gestures for them to come in. She did not speak English and Micheline and I did not speak German, but somehow she knew that we were traveling; she saw how young we were and she sensed we had no money. We bought the milk and bread and went outside to sit on the grass to enjoy our food. Not ten minutes passed before we saw our lady coming out of her store with a huge tray full of hot sausages and bread, a big round of cheese, hot coffee and pastries.

"For you," she said, making large gestures to us all, a big smile illuminating her face.

Many thanks dear lady, an angel come down to feed us poor globetrotters! We bowed and bowed again to let her know our appreciation and Serge made a thank you speech in German which delighted the good woman. I never knew there were such good people in Germany. This little incident started me thinking in different terms about the people of this land. I was elated, but then a twisted thought came to spoil it. What if the woman had known that two of us were Jews?

We all felt like sleeping after the feast and stretched for a moment of delight on the humid grass, the cows mooing around us.

"Up, up," said Serge, hoisting himself. "Come on Charlie, Claude, ladies, we need to discuss important things."

Charlie got up first.

"Yeah, I am tired of walking, my feet are full of blisters."

"Let's take the train in Kassel," I said. "We will never make it to Sweden otherwise – too far and too cold. I am sure we can pull it off once again without paying."

Claude and Micheline looked at each other and got up.

"Well let's make plans then," they said almost simultaneously. This time we were a little more prepared and chose to hop on the midnight train. It was dark, cold and raining, and the platform was deserted. We waited hidden in shadow against a wall. Then the stationmaster in a big oil-cloth raincoat came walking along the halted train swinging a storm lamp and shouting. We waited, seeing his form diminish as he reached the very end of the platform. The train gave a big jerk and started very slowly, a cloud of steam joining the strident whistle.

"Now!" I said, running like mad and jumping high on the rung of a car, not even knowing if the others were following me. Trying to pierce the darkness, I saw several shapes on various cars. All right, they were on, now we had to get in before the doors were totally closed.

It was nice and warm inside, but we had to stay awake lest we were caught by a controller. In an empty compartment I found a train map; there were no stops before Hanover. This meant that if by now the controller had not verified our tickets, nobody was going to bother us until then and we would be able to crash on those seats and sleep.

At three o'clock in the morning we were woken suddenly by a big jolt. I had no idea were I was, totally confused, then I heard "Hanover." I shook everybody, we had to move out of this car. We could hear voices shouting outside when Serge opened the window. He was bending as far as he could to hear the conversations. Turning around and closing the window, he said, rubbing his hands, half frozen,

"It's cold out there. It seems we will be here for a while, they are changing engines and adding some cars. I also heard that the last stop will be Hamburg."

At daybreak the train pulled out. All we saw of Hanover were miles and miles of sidings, big black locomotives maneuvering back and forth, while conductors halfway out of their machines gesticulated like so many clowns. Once more we started our game of hide and seek, each time escaping by a hair from the clutches of the dreaded controller.

That morning we traveled through a bleak landscape, a northern plain that had no end, despairingly flat, a yellowish grey sky diluting its color with the rain soaked ochre grass, not a tree, not a house for miles upon miles.

Our spirits were low, wondering if it would be impossible to go further north with such weather, but by afternoon a pale sun came out of the clouds, the rain stopped and we passed a village and then another one; a few trees bending in the wind gave life to these swampy fields. It was enough to bring our courage back. The train stopped briefly in Luneburg, probably to take water for the engine. Nothing much to see from our compartment; also we had to lay low again to avoid discovery.

We sighted Hamburg in the early afternoon. The city was huge, set far inside a fjord. As we moved slower and slower we could see huge ships at anchor, a very high bridge and a mass of buildings totally destroyed. There was nothing left of the Hamburg that had existed before the war. It looked as if a giant had torn it to shreds, a very troubling sight. At last we reached the station and had to come down. We were all dreadfully tired and so hungry, having had nothing to eat since Kassel. But before finding food, it was imperative to find out when the next train to Flensburg would leave. Flensburg was the German frontier with Denmark.

The station was very busy with all kinds of people. Hamburg was then under British occupation. The place was full of Britons in their ugly khaki uniforms mixing with the German crowd. Charlie went to a ticket booth to inquire about our train and was told the next one would leave in one hour. Relieved, we sat at the station cafe and ordered one order of sauerkraut, potatoes and sausages, bread and beer for the four of us, when we could have eaten two portions each. No matter how little, it was delicious and warm; we ate very bit of it, not leaving one crumb on the plate.

At the platform, belching steam and rattling its massive frame, the shiny black engine entered the station, dragging behind it a long series of polished cars. "Train to Flensburg!" the stationmaster yelled. Very naturally we threw our rucksacks on the steps and climbed aboard. What a surprise when we saw that every compartment was luxury itself, every seat covered in plush red velvet with lace doilies for headrests, and to boot, all the cars were empty after the train started. I looked at Charlie wondering, our friends looked at us, we could not believe our good luck; a whole luxury train for us and no controller to be seen, what a relief!

Micheline and Serge sprawled on the cushioned seats, Charlie took me in his arms and kissed me, Claude, a little embarrassed, fumbled in his sack. Then we all started to dance like crazy, jumping up and down on the fancy seats, singing bawdy student songs at the top of our lungs.

"What are you doing on this train?"

The voice was loud and severe. We turned around as one with our mouths open in disbelief. Here in front of us, oh horror, was a high ranking British officer, stiff as a rod, covered with medals, coifed in a rigid cap and beating a short stick on one of his gloved hands.

"Nobody is allowed on this train. It is reserved for the British high command. How did you get on without permission? You will have to come off at the first stop, or you will be arrested."

From where did this jack in the box spring out, with his waxed blond mustache and his eyes of steel? At first the five of us were speechless, then I ventured,

"Sir, the train master never said it was a high command train, I distinctly heard him say this was the train for Flensburg and that's where we are going."

"May I see your passport, Miss," he said with an expression of disgust.

Producing my British passport had its effect almost instantly, though while leafing through it and looking at me simultaneously his eyes were disbelieving. I had upset his strict attitude.

"Oh! Oh! so you are British, born in Folkestone, eh? Well, hm! As I said, no civilians are allowed on this train, sorry Miss, but you and your friends will do as I said, you will all have to get off."

Making a rigid about face he walked away unsteadily along the corridor.

What a silly man, we could not just jump out of the train while it was running. He also knew very well that there would be no stops until Flensburg.

We were lucky once more, nobody had asked for our tickets, but we were on our guard for the rest of the trip. No more songs, no dancing or jumping on the seats. Getting out of our plush compartment, we sat just behind the train door on the floor, expecting to see our clown officer appear any time to throw us out.

The sun was already slanting when we rode over the Kiel canal, soft hues of pink lighting the pitiful ruins all around. What an irony of nature to brighten in glorious colors the dead fishing port in such a way. We sat silent for the rest of the trip, each of us with our private thoughts. It would be night before we arrived at the frontier. I had absolutely no idea what Denmark looked like except for what I had read of Hans Christian Andersen's fairy tales.

Chapter 16: 1949

Denmark

Flensburg. The train slowed to a snail's pace, coughed a few times and stopped. We were the only ones to get off the train. Very few people on the platform. The British officer had disappeared like a ghost, thank God. Stepping into the station was an agreeable surprise. The floors were so clean, we saw our reflection in the highly waxed wood planks; the place was heated and inviting. After showing our passports, we asked the officer in charge if it was all right to stay the night in the station, because it was too late to find our way to a youth hostel. He responded with a large warm smile, like we were all his children. And he spoke English. The man told us where we could find sandwiches in the station and even went so far as to give us the money to buy them. He knew just by looking at us that we had little money and no Danish Kronë, naturally. Could people really be that nice? It was difficult to believe.

Copenhagen was our goal. It was decided we would walk forty kilometers each day to reach the capital in five days. Hitchhiking was another way to get there, but we had no idea as to the Danes' reaction to that mode of transportation. Certainly it was worth a try.

I was surprised at all I saw on each side of the road. The neat, charming houses and tiny gardens around them looked like they were made to play with. Everything was small, colorful and reminded me of a box full of toys. The air was crisp, as it had rained the night before. Sparks flew from under our pounding boots in rhythm with our loud singing. The province of Jutland that we were crossing was a rich and fertile land, its plowed fields the color of chocolate, dotted with groups of black and white cows here and there. The hours passed and all we could see around were more cows and more brown earth. A few trees dotted the landscape, the last of their copper leaves whirling in a mad windy dance. At sundown we were exhausted, having walked hard, stopping only briefly to eat brined herrings and brown bread for lunch.

"We have to separate and hitchhike," I said, "otherwise we'll collapse before reaching Copenhagen. I'll stay with Charlie and the three of you make a separate group."

"How about meeting at the town hall in the capital, let's say in three days?" Serge suggested. "Whoever gets there first waits for the other, in case we miss each other. The first one there will also leave a message at the main post office."

Serge was always so efficient, so sure of himself. It was the reasonable solution, we all agreed. As soon as we separated, Charlie and I were lucky. It was almost night and there were no youth hostels on this road for another fifty kilometers. The day had been a long one. We stood at the edge of the road. I waved a little French flag I had fished out of my sack to attract any passing vehicle. The only lights now were coming from a green glow lining the horizon and farm windows shining yellow on the darkened fields.

Not ten minutes had passed when a silver car screeched by, reversed, and stopped abruptly in front of us. A big red faced round man came out inviting us into his car, first speaking Danish and then when he saw our blank looks, English. Yes he would be happy to take us where we wanted, a youth hostel? All right. His eyes sparkled in the dark. Was he an angel coming to our rescue or was he something else? It was difficult to say, but as we rode we realized that he was drunk, and continued his drinking on the road, taking long slugs from a bottle before passing it to us.

"Aquavit," he said, "Good good."

What a jolly fellow. He wanted to know everything about us, where we came from, why we were doing this trip and seemed very interested in the story of our adventure. By now it was more than an hour of driving, I was really getting suspicious; where was the man taking us? Then suddenly without warning he stopped in front of a large wooden building, got out and said to wait for him, he would be back in a few minutes. Charlie was half asleep. I kept watch, not knowing what the fellow was up to. Here he was coming back with a big smile on his face waving something in his hand.

Two tickets for bunks tonight and four more for dinner tonight and breakfast tomorrow, all paid. This is your youth hostel."

We stared at him in disbelief. He waved us off.

"It's OK, good luck."

Not giving us time to thank him, he almost pushed us out of the car and abruptly took of.

I looked at the tickets in awe.

"Can you believe this, Charlie? This really must be Hans Christian Andersen's fairy land."

Walking next morning, after a good long sleep, was not as demanding as the previous day. The sky seemed bluer, the little houses along the road looked more colorful. Also we were alone together, without the rest of the bunch. We stopped often, sat down, kissed and held each other. It had been a long time since we had spent a night together and we longed for it, not knowing how long it would be before it could happen. Around noon that day we reached Odense. The day was warmer than usual; Charlie's red woolen shirt was soaking wet in the armpits, the chest and the back. I was not faring much better. That morning, wanting to cover some distance, we had left early and now we were longing for a cool drink, but also for a strong cup of coffee.

What a charming town, old houses and cobblestone streets. People were smiling at us. Walking slowly, looking around, we were trying to find a cafe, but no building seemed to have one. At last we asked a passer-by, mimicking somebody drinking coffee. He understood us quite well and took us across the street to the entrance of a house. Here he pointed to the inside. We found ourselves in a bar that looked more like a home dining room; perhaps it was also a restaurant. A few men roughly dressed in working clothes were sitting at a large round table drinking from small glasses. They talked loudly, but when they saw us come in, they stopped, staring at us. It was embarrassing. We stood there for an instant not knowing which way to go. I went to the bar and asked for two coffees. Somebody tapped me on the shoulder; one of the men that had been sitting at the table motioned to Charlie and I to join them. As soon as we sat among them, they ordered Aquavit for us.

I said, "No, no, coffee."

They answered, "Yes, yes Aquavit!"

The bartender arrived with two cups of coffee, the Aquavit and several bottles of strong dark beer. With hand gestures the fellows told us to drink a bit of coffee, a sip of Aquavit and a big gulp of beer. When they saw us hesitate, they motioned that it was all paid for and insisted we drink with them. They laughed and sang together holding arms, inviting us to do the same. They asked questions about where we came from and looked at us with unabashed curiosity when we told them we were from North Africa. They touched our hands and faces, not believing white people could be Africans. This really puzzled them. What were we doing in Denmark? Many more rounds were ordered. An hour passed and we were still drinking; by now we were all buddies.

Charlie looked at his watch.

"One o'clock, Anit we have to go, we can't miss the ferry, and we still have quite a few miles before we reach Nyborg for the crossing. Come on get up, I'll help you. We have to go."

His speech was so slurred, I did not understand a word he said. He repeated the sentence again loudly. OK, I understood, but when I tried to get up, I was glued to my chair. The whole room started spinning around. It took ages to stand up, the guys helped put our sacks on our backs; were they ever heavy!

"Goodbye," they said, "have a good trip, come back and stay with us."

They all stood up swaying, took out handkerchiefs and waved from the door as we started. What beautiful people.

Charlie and I were drunk, and it was an ordeal to put one foot in front of the other. The houses on each side of us seemed to melt in strange shapes. Reaching a stone bridge on the fjord we stopped, turning around, leaning our rucksacks on the parapet. Charlie said, "Ah! how wonderful," and in a second both his legs went flying up. Oh! My God, he was going overboard. I pulled him down just in time. This incident sobered us instantly, especially when we looked at how far down the shining sea was. We stood there like two idiots looking at each other. No more drinks for us. From my sack I took out two pieces of bread from our distant breakfast. This would steady us a least for now. On our way out of this quaint lovely town, we passed several old churches nestled in rustic gardens, and as I looked at my travel book to make sure we were on the right path, I discovered that this was indeed a fairy tale town, for it was Hans Christian Andersen's birthplace.

At noon the third day we were in Copenhagen, proud to have made it in such a short time. Looking for the Town Hall we tramped around until we found ourselves in front of the imposing nineteenth-century building and its tall belfry. Now to find our friends. Charlie went inside to look for them and I stayed out walking right and left, up and down, but in vain. Charlie came out again with a grim look on his face. Not a trace of them. Tired and hungry as usual, we trekked to the main post office to leave a message for our friends. Double-checking I asked the woman behind the counter if perchance there was a message for us.

"Yes there is," said the lady, handing me a crumpled piece of yellow paper.

"Well what do you know," I told Charlie, "they're already here. Serge says that they found a truck that took them straight to Copenhagen. How lucky can one get? Here's the address for the Hostel where they are staying and he also reserved beds for us."

They were there waiting to cheer us with a good bottle of wine and were surprised when we declined the offer, telling them about our adventure in Odense.

There were so many things to do and visit in this city of Copenhagen, we did not know were to start. Micheline suggested the Tivoli Gardens for the first day, a wonderful amusement park. At last we could walk through a city without being weighed down by our packs. We had all decided to remain a few days in town and make the most of it.

From far away we could hear the music. We entered the gates at Tivoli to the sound of "The Persian Market". Charlie was quite a sight, wearing his white wool burnoose on top of his Tyrol leather shorts, British army boots and heavy wool socks. The fact that he wore a well trimmed black beard added to the picture. As usual we attracted stares from the crowd milling around. The afternoon finished in high fashion with a parade of soldiers dressed in rich uniforms of red, black, and gold marching to the sound of trumpets and drums.

The days that followed were full of surprises. We discovered the old neighborhood of Christianshaven on the island of Amager. Its old fortifications were still there, the canals lined with ancient houses, their colors reflected in the water from delft blue facades and green roofs to yellow painted fronts with red tiled overhangs. Little stores full of beautiful china and rich silver objects lined the streets. I had no idea that the china and silver in the windows were manufactured in Denmark. The evenings found us often in pubs sampling some of the country's potent beers, Tuborg or Carlsberg – the real thing, not the wan imitations they would later export - while eating meatballs in a sweet sauce and trying to converse with guests.

Our last day in that joyful city had come. Early in the morning, strolling on the Langeliny Promenade Charlie and I decided to swim to the Little Mermaid. The statue was set on a rock in the middle of the harbor. We undressed right there in full daylight, Charlie in his briefs and I in my panties and bra. Plunging into the black and cold water was not inviting, but it was a challenge. Could we swim that far without being frozen? We did. Hanging onto the rock, out of breath, we touched her slippery fish tail and even reached for her arms and shoulders. Talking to her, we told her how far away we had come from and how well we knew her story.

The morning after, our gear strapped to our backs ready for the next stretch, we took a local bus north, forty five kilometers to Helsingør and the 1577 castle of Kronborg. At the sight of the green-roofed tower and the imposing castle we were impressed, but in reality what interested us was being at the site where previously had stood the fortress about which Shakespeare had been inspired to write his famous play, Hamlet. Later that afternoon we would leave Denmark for Sweden, sailing across the strait of Kattegat. Going down to the harbor we bought a dozen live mackerels for our evening meal. I had those wiggling creatures in a net hanging on my back as we boarded the ferry. The sun was going down, painting the ship, the rippling sea and us in gold. Leaning on the rail, breathing the salty cool breeze, my thoughts went back to Denmark and all the jolly people of that land, thanking them for all the help they had freely given us and wondering what was going to happen next in that far north country of Sweden.

Night had fallen; from a distance harbor lights could be seen here and there through the dense mist. Helsingborg, our first Swedish town, was nearing. It was a rocky coast where many ships had capsized in the past. Drifts of fog were obscuring the landing, and sirens going full blast created a distorted eerie sound. At last we bumped the wharf, the captain shouted orders and the sailors threw a big rope around a pole. The ferry was now steady enough to disembark. We were finally in Sweden.

Chapter 17: 1949

Our Swedish Adventure

We walked down the gangplank and found ourselves on a dark deserted square. Which way to go? Left? Right? We had no idea. A cold wind was blowing. All of us were starving; we had not eaten a thing since morning. The fish we had bought in Helsingborg was the only thing we had for tonight's supper. So far the fish was still fresh and hanging on my back, but by now they were dead and limp.

A man walking with a shiny bike came out of a corner of the square.

"Sir, sir," I called, running to meet him. "Mister, mister, please."

The man stopped short, a little frightened I believed at such a sudden apparition.

"We need some directions," I said in English, using my hands to emphasize that we needed a place to eat and to sleep, pointing at our group huddled together in the middle of the square. He looked at us with blank eyes for a few minutes. I was wandering if he had understood a word of what I had said.

"Yes, yes," he said with a heavy accent. "I shall help you."

He pointed north, saying there was a nice beach there to camp, about a mile away. We could not miss the place he said, there was a big clump of fir trees going down to the sea at that spot and some fancy houses on the hill above. He walked a little with us, than said good night and disappeared on a side road, swallowed by the night.

We walked and walked and walked, no sight of beach or trees. By now the mile was stretching into five. Dead tired, we were dragging our boots on the asphalt wondering how far we could go. The sea was near, we could hear the waves crashing on the shore; occasionally the white flash of a crest shone for an instant. The fish on my back were starting to smell; hopefully they had not rotted yet. Charlie spotted the trees first, shouting.

"It's here, it's here," he said, running down toward the water. It was pitch black. I could not see a thing on the beach side, but on the other side of the road I could make out some houses up on a hill, a faint light coming from a door.

Seated in a circle on the wet sand, everyone was assigned a job. Micheline would go for wood, Claude would gather stones to put the wood on, Charlie would make the fire, Serge was going to put the tents up and I was sent to wash the damn fish in the sea and gut them. I came back stinking of dead mackerel and soaked with sticky cold sea water, cursing at everything and everybody; I felt miserable. Later as a punishment for my ill behavior, the group sent me up to one of the fancy homes to get some drinking water. I must have stunned the woman who opened the door, with my wild flying red hair and my rumpled wet clothes, for her look was one of panic and I had to reassure her that the only thing I wanted was water.

After gorging on half-boiled mackerel, bones and all, we all went to bed, thankful for being inside a tent protected from the wind that was now howling outside, and the high-tide waves that were eating up three quarters of the beach.

A gray and drizzly morning awaited us as we opened the tent flaps. Our bones were sore from having slept on sand that barely covered the stones we hadn't known were underneath when we had pitched the tents the previous night. It took almost an hour to build a fire and boil some water for a cup of tea. Holding our tin cups with two hands we were grateful for the burning sensation and the hot steam on our faces. Once more we all stood on the road ready to go.

The next town north was Halmstad. Five minutes had not passed when we saw a heavy truck coming our way. I stepped into the middle of the road waving, and to my surprise the driver stopped. Screaming pigs were sticking their heads through the lattice work in the back.

"Can you take us all?" I said showing the group. The man hesitated. I smiled, and Micheline waved at him, her beautiful blond hair flying in the wind. He nodded for us to climb on. Lucky we were this morning as we hopped in the back of the truck, silencing the pigs for an instant.

By noon we had arrived in Halmstad, home to about forty thousand souls. It was a fishing port on the Kattegat, the same body of water we had crossed the day before coming from Denmark. We were left in the center of town. While traveling in the truck this morning Serge had suggested that we hold a powwow to decide what to do next, but for now food was the most important thing in the world. Last night's fish had long been digested and this morning's tea was no food. All of us stopped to count our money and to our dismay there was very little left. Charlie suggested that in the afternoon we should go and try our luck singing in the city park we were passing now. We all knew several songs and Claude had a harmonica; maybe we could make a little money that way.

Sure of ourselves now, we descended like wolves to the harbor where we spent some of our precious remaining money on food, devouring an enormous quantity of salt herring, dark bread, butter, and lingonberries, the whole washed down with a doubtful cup of coffee.

All that food had made us sleepy. As we reached the park we sat on benches and decided to take a nap before singing so we would feel more refreshed. The sun had made an appearance, it felt good and warm, and my clothes were going to dry while I slept wonderfully.

A falling leaf on my face woke me up. Oh my God, it was almost night. Jumping up, I went to wake the others. It was freezing cold, Serge was sneezing, Claude had a sore throat. We got ourselves together to form a choir. Hurried people were crossing the park going home after work. We started singing a Russian folk song. I was out of pitch, the sounds Claude got out of his harmonica were pitiful with his sore throat, and Serge kept stopping to blow his nose. The only one who could really sing was Charlie; he had a beautiful tenor voice. People stopped to listen, but in the end when I passed the hat around not a single penny was given. I felt ashamed to have had to sing in a park for money and thought about my parents. Thank God they would never know. Later we all sat around a bowl of soup to discuss our future.

"We have decided to go to Norway first." Serge was looking at Charlie who in turn was looking back at him questioningly, why?

"Well, my dream was always to go to Norway and before we run out of money that's where I would like to go," said Micheline. "You are welcome to go with us, but we know that you had your mind set for Sweden and you are already on the spot. Serge, tell Anit and Charlie our plan."

If you choose to stay in Sweden, we will meet you later on our way back from Norway. We'll correspond as always leaving messages at post offices and you will do the same."

What a blow, it was so unexpected. Being five travelers gave us strength, even though it was sometimes difficult to hitch a ride, but breaking up the team?

We did not show any resentment though, and the next morning we parted on an optimistic note. They took a ferry to the frontier and we started walking north again to reach Gothenburg. In the early afternoon it started snowing. We stood on the edge of the road trying to get a ride. The cold, accompanied by a strong north wind, was getting fierce; the snow was now falling diagonally, whipping our faces. Cars passed on the black road, ignoring us. Where were our wonderful Danes that had stopped every time we needed them? By the end of the afternoon we were exhausted. First from the long walk and then by the endless waiting on road corners for rides that never came. We were ready to collapse.

A distance from the road among tall spruces dusted with snow, a farmhouse painted dark red and with all windows lit seemed the logical place to find refuge. It reminded me of that evening in Normandy where we had begged a farmer to let us stay the night. Sloshing in wet snow and mud a good mile, we finally made it to the entrance. Charlie knocked a few times before the door was opened. A giant of a man answered gruffly; this one did not speak a word of English. Using sign language, we made him understand that we were students in need of sleep. He took us to the horses' stable, same as the French farmer. That night we slept one on top of the other covered with straw and a horse blanket that stank; we had never been so cold in all of our lives.

Where was our beautiful Morocco, the sunshine and deep blue skies? Why were we punishing ourselves? What did we want to prove? That we were tough? We already knew that, but both of us were proud. There was no question of turning back and losing face with our parents and friends.

The morning after, very discouraged, but still determined to reach at least Stockholm, we went to thank the farmer. No Calvados this time, but a pitcher of hot milk and a loaf of rye bread to keep us alive. Walking to the edge of the road, we talked and decided it was no use to go on the way we had. A few days of this regime would see us sick or worse, frozen on these icy roads where no drivers were charitable enough to stop. No trains left from where we were, so we had to summon all our courage and walk back to Halmstad, the closest town.

At the station we inquired about trains for Stockholm and the price of tickets. There was a slow train leaving within the hour, and there would be a transfer to a faster one about half way. As for the tickets, our only option was third class. We were warned that a lot of Roma traveled in that class and that we could not fall asleep for fear of being robbed. It seemed these people had nimble fingers and were experts in the matter.

Climbing aboard, I saw the compartment was large, well lit and heated. Several rows of varnished wooden benches were facing each other. We had difficulty finding a seat, as it seemed that a whole village of Roma had invaded the place. The noise was appalling, they all talked together very loudly and in a language that resembled nothing we knew. It smelled of food and sweat, while in a corner a competition was going on, or so we thought. Two men were playing guitar, another the violin and two more were strumming on a sort of balalaika. A frenzy of sounds went up and down the scales at a vertiginous pace.

As we tried to make our way through the aisle we were pulled to one side and the other by women dancers in bright colored skirts and kerchiefs trying to show us their wild steps.

Hey, This was fun! in a few minutes we were perspiring, something I had not felt for quite a while. At long last we found two seats. Nobody spoke a word of English, but these wonderful lively people wanted to know where we came from. They thought Charlie was one of them because of his jet black hair. They pointed at him asking,

"Tziganare?"

"No, no," said Charlie. "Maroccaner."

Seeing their blank faces, I took a sheet of paper and drew a rough sketch of a map showing Sweden, the countries below and at the bottom of the page Africa, where I put a cross and pointed to Charlie and me.

"Africa," they all said and repeated, putting their hands to their faces, saying, "Nay shwarzt". I understood what they were trying to say, that we were not black, how come? As a matter of fact Charlie and I were much whiter than all the people around us.

We knew we were accepted when they opened their baskets of food and insisted that we share. After several rounds of Aquavit, meatballs and bread, I was falling asleep and so was Charlie. We took turns in closing our eyes the rest of the night, but finally both of us slumbered. In the early morning one of the men woke us up with a tin cup of coffee.

We woke up, startled. My God, the money! Charlie carried it under his shirt, and was not too delicate in looking frantically for it. The train stopped in a cacophony of brakes. Where were we? I had no idea. Charlie was relaxing, looking through the window. A controller came to the door of our compartment and yelled something in Swedish.

"I'd better go and ask," I said to Charlie. Sure enough, I was told that if we were going to Stockholm, this was the place we changed trains. We shoved everything into our bags and scrambled down the steps onto the platform, to find all our Roma friends already there, blowing on their hands for warmth.

We walked briskly up and down the platform not to freeze, talking in French as we usually did among ourselves.

A strangely dressed man with a black beret and a huge black cape approached us.

"I hear you speak French," he said in a Swedish singsong. "You must be campers, are you going skiing?"

"No we are going to Stockholm," I replied.

"Oh! I see."

"We decided to take the train, because it was too cold on the roads to hitchhike, and we spent our last money to buy train tickets."

He now addressed himself to Charlie.

"Did I hear that you had no more money? You must be out of your mind. Stockholm is an enormous city. You'll be begging in the streets, and you'll starve to death." He took a good look at us and resumed, "I can offer you lodging in my house for a few weeks until you find jobs and make a little money. How about it? I live only twenty miles away in a town called Skövde."

Charlie looked at me, undecided. Our train for Stockholm was pulling in. Who knew where that strange man was going to take us. He looked funny; how did we know to trust him, we could end up dead, I whispered in Charlie's ear. We really did not know what to do and started toward the train, ready to climb on.

"No, no don't go," the strange man in the black cape caught me by the shoulder. "You will see, I have a nice house on the outskirts of town. My wife, Ingrid, will take good care of you."

By the time he finished speaking the train was pulling out in a cloud of steam. That was it, mentally we had decided to follow him. I looked at the last train car as it rounded the bend with mixed feelings. What bizarre fate had brought us here at the same time as this man. Was he real? Was he God sent? An angel perhaps. His black cape flying behind him made me think more the Devil, and I shivered.

We walked a few blocks to the bus station. He paid for the tickets.

"My name is Erik Ekhart," he told us. "I went to Paris last year to study. My wife and I walked all the way from our town to France."

"But this is crazy," I said. "You mean you walked, without trains or buses? How long did that take you?"

"About three months, but we were not in a hurry, you see."

I wondered what he went to study in Paris for, but did not dare to ask. His French was atrocious. It was nighttime when we arrived in Skövde. The streets were deserted, it was very cold and snowing. The eerie glow of street lamps showed a nondescript town, where walls of packed snow lined the sidewalks and factory buildings succeeded one another making the scenery even gloomier. What were we getting into?

After a good twenty minutes walk bending under the windblown snow, our packs weighing a ton on our tired backs, Erik stopped in front of a house and said in Swedish,

"Vashegood." Which I took to mean Welcome.

It was a small wooden structure two stories high all painted white, the roof heavy with snow and hanging stalactites. There was a small landing downstairs and a steep flight of steps in front of us. Erik yelled.

"Ingrid, I am bringing two guests."

She appeared at the top of the stairs, a plain woman in her thirties, pale blond hair hanging to the shoulders of her brown wool dress. She repeated, "Vashegood." Upstairs we entered a small kitchen with a large double glassed window, a wooden table, two chairs and a big cast iron stove on the opposite wall. How warm it all was. A pink lampshade gave the whole room a relaxed happy feeling. At that moment I realized Erik was an angel and not a demon as I had feared. He was an honest man trying to help a brother in need.

His wife Ingrid never complained about having two total strangers invading her home and privacy. There were not many people of this caliber in this world. Charlie and I were very grateful for so much generosity.

Somehow they did not fit the mold. We had up to now proof of the contrary on the roads of Sweden, where car after car had passed us coldly without stopping.

Ingrid opened a door on the right kitchen wall and we found ourselves in a large room that served as a living and dining room. In the middle was an unusually long rough wooden table with benches on either side. In a corner a huge cylinder that looked like porcelain crackled and belched flames through a half open door at the bottom, a mighty stove that heated the whole floor. Pushing a curtain over, we discovered their bedroom, with a huge bed in the center piled up with thick eiderdowns, a chest of drawers with a broken mirror and nothing more. Ingrid turned to Erik and started talking fast, he translating for us.

"You will sleep in the kitchen, in your sleeping bags, under the table. Before you retire you may have a pitcher of hot milk and a piece of rye bread. Feel free to heat the milk yourselves, the bread is in the cupboard right there. Oh! I forgot to tell you, we do not have a bathroom, the outhouse is in the back of the garden. In winter it's too cold to go out so we use a chamber pot, but now that you are here us we will do a little differently. We go first and I shall pass you the pot through the kitchen door, and when you are finished it will be pretty full. One of you go downstairs, open the back door to the garden and throw the contents outside. Don't worry, it will freeze immediately. Good night now, sweet dreams."

The days that followed were full of surprises. Erik told us early the next morning that they only ate one meal a day. It consisted of raw vegetables, dark rye bread, milk and sometimes cheese. And he said the food was taken at five in the afternoon.

For us it was a disaster, one meal a day and no meat or fish! We were already starving early in the morning, but there was nothing we could do, we were completely out of money.

We also found out they belonged to a strange congregation called Philadelphia Churka. Could this possibly be one of the bizarre American churches? And we were asked to attend the coming Sunday, to thank the Lord for his compassion toward us.

Erik told us that he was a part-time carpenter, while his wife, Ingrid, worked in a coat factory. They would be gone most of the days. In the mean time Charlie and I were going to find jobs. One thing we could not do is read the Swedish newspapers.

Those first days in Skövde were gloomy, to say the least. There was food in the house, but we did not dare steal anything for fear of being thrown out. We walked aimlessly the streets of that small town day after day. Stopping in front of the butcher shops for hours, dreaming of the day we would be able to buy a steak.

The evenings were dull after a meal of raw potatoes, raw beets and cabbage all mixed together without any trace of a dressing. They brought home some friends of theirs to meet the strangers. Because we could not converse in Swedish, all we said was translated by Erik. God knows what he was telling them, because these people looked at us as if we were savages.

That first Sunday, dressed in the only pairs of pants we possessed, our cleaned red woolen shirts and borrowed sweaters on our scrubbed bodies, we were dragged to church. It was extremely cold that morning. My whole body shook. Neither Charlie nor I were dressed for that type of climate.

There were no statues, not even a cross in that church. The place was already full when we arrived. People were sitting on long wooden benches greeting each other. The place was lit from large windows on each side. An alley separated the benches and in front of them there was a stage with three chairs. Our appearance at the door hushed the congregation. I was dead sure they all knew who we were by now. We were looked at curiously, some smiled at us, some said *vashogood ok sita,* 'welcome be seated'.

Then it all began. A man in shirt sleeves jumped briskly on the stage. He looked possessed and started yelling to the audience as if accusing.

Curious, I whispered to Erik, "What's going on?"

"Shut! The Devil is in this room," he said. I relayed the sentence to Charlie who looked as puzzled as I did. What happened next was pandemonium. Everybody except us started to wail, their arms flailing as if disjointed. Tears were running down their cheeks, they seemed stricken with the utmost fear and started hiding under the benches. That was too much for me; I almost burst out laughing and had to stuff a handkerchief on my mouth not to explode. Charlie was also biting his lips not to laugh. This crazy behavior lasted at least twenty minutes and suddenly there was silence.

A young man rose slowly from his bench and walked to the stage. He was carrying a guitar. The first demonic preacher stepped down, head bowed, as if resigned. The young man sat on one of the chairs and played while he sang. Little by little the congregation dried their tears and sat on their benches once more.

Now what?" I asked Erik.

"Shut," he said again, "Christ has just arrived, he is here in this room, listen and look around."

The transformation in the church was unbelievable. People who a minute ago were the picture of distress and total madness were now smiling, singing praises to the Lord and kissing each other, including us. Both of us felt totally out of place among these loony Swedes, but we had to go with the flow and kissed them in return.

For me the only positive thing about this weird church came after the service, when the pastor distributed big round loaves of warm rye bread and huge chunks of a whitish cheese. Charlie could have jumped on it on the spot and I too, but we had to wait until five o'clock that Sunday to enjoy the meal; no cheating was possible because Erik and Ingrid were there watching.

It had been almost three weeks since we had arrived. So far we had not found a job; in the meantime we had written to Serge in Oslo to let him know where we were and what we were doing. No answer from him yet. Our morale was low; we felt that by now we were imposing on Erik and Ingrid, even though they never mentioned a thing to us.

One evening, late, we heard loud banging downstairs at the entrance door. We had gone to bed early to keep warm. Outside the wind was howling, glazing the snow into sheets of ice, even the stove burning full blast was not enough. I got up reluctantly and went down the narrow stairs, grabbing a wool scarf on the coat rack, to see what all the commotion was. The banging was still going on. I could hear voices, but they were distorted by the wind. As I opened the door, three people fell on me, covering me in snow. Oh my God - Serge, Micheline, and Claude! By this time Charlie had appeared at the top of the stairs in his long johns, his wild black hair all over his face. At the sight, we all burst out laughing and made such a racket that Erik came out to see what was going on.

"Your friends have come, I see. Well, you will have to share the kitchen, the five of you. Good night."

In the morning Erik came to talk to us, before he went to work.

"Friends, as much as I would like to keep you all, it's not going to be possible. You understand that we are both working people and we do not have the means to entertain the five of you. Ingrid has inquired about a job for Anit in a men's clothing factory. I am sure there will be a job for

Micheline also, they are now hiring. Anyway you can all stay the week, this will give you time to find a place."

That day the five of us went out. We just needed to unwind with our friends. By now I looked like an elephant with three layers of borrowed heavy sweaters and two pairs of woolen stockings, my head and face buried in a double ski mask. I was afraid to look at myself in shop windows. Charlie did not look much better, but both of us had slacks that were too thin plus boots with serious holes in them and no money for repairs. It was imperative that we find jobs and a place to stay.

Serge had a little money left. He invited us to a pastry and tea shop. The place was dainty; little round tables with pink lace coverings, older couples and spinsters sitting munching delicately on little sandwiches and cakes. The look on their faces when we entered like a whirlwind banging the door shut, talking too loud and in French to boot, was hilarious. The lady in charge of the tea room asked us politely to lower our voices; this was an elegant place, she said. As we sat and devoured the delicate pastries, Serge told us about their trip to Norway. It seemed that Norwegians were wonderful people in all aspects; they would have stayed longer, but their money was dwindling and they also wanted to see Sweden.

Going back, we took them through the center of the city. By now stores were closing. I noticed a synagogue in a side street. I had had no idea there were Jews in this town. As we walked we were throwing snowballs at each other, screaming and laughing, when a young man stopped us.

"Vous parlez Francais, c'est merveilleux!" he said. "My name is Jacques Gustavson. I am French, though my mother and my father are Swedish. What a pleasure to meet you all. Let's walk together."

Jacques was a lanky, tall, and good looking young man. He was probably in his early twenties, with a ready smile, soft brown eyes and a rebellious lock constantly falling on his forehead. We all had so many questions to ask. Why was he in Sweden if he lived in Paris? How could he be French if both his parents were Swedish? Was there a possibility of finding a place that would lodge us all in the center of town? Was he working or was he on vacation and if so why in Skövde of all places?

Soon we found out almost everything we wanted to know. Jacques was the type of guy who could not stop talking, interrupting his own explanations with funny jokes. Before arriving at our destination we were already good friends. We found out that Volvo's headquarters was here in

Skövde. Jacques had been working there for his summer vacations as an apprentice in mechanics. Tomorrow he would inquire about jobs for Charlie and Serge; it was a sure deal he said, Volvo was hiring every day, and he also knew of a big mansion-like place that was advertising rooms for rent. Pure luck had brought us together that afternoon. At last we could give Erik some good news. That evening the meal of raw potatoes, cabbage and beets seemed less obnoxious; I could already smell an enormous sizzling steak on my plate.

December was upon us; only one hour of a pale washed out sun appeared between noon and one o'clock. How sad it was to be plunged in darkness, day after day. The temperature got to thirty five below zero. We had to summon all our will and courage to withstand such punishing weather. One good note, though; we were going to visit the rooms for rent that Jaques had spoken about. Armed with all our sweaters, bonnets and heavy socks on us, but our feet freezing in our shoes full of holes, we braved the snowstorm that was raging that day. It was difficult to make out any structure in the streets of Skövde, but in the end we found the place.

The house was imposing, resembling a castle of old gray stone flanked by a tower. It had many long narrow windows and a green roof laden with snow and hanging stalactites. Would we be able to afford such a place? There was a garden around the house piled up with snow up to the top edge of the wrought iron fence. Huddled together for warmth we rang the bell. A tall, skinny old lady opened the door. She looked half frozen herself swaddled in a lacy wool shawl. "

Vashogood," she said.

This welcome word seemed to fit every occasion. One behind the other we entered a long carpeted dark corridor. The walls were adorned with portraits; some were paintings and others yellowed photographs, perhaps defunct family members. Several double doors could be seen on each side of the hallway. They were all closed. A particular smell that I could not define impregnated the premises, not mildew, not grease, but more like the stale odor of an old house where windows were seldom opened.

She led us to a Victorian looking sitting room. The lady of the house introduced herself as Miss Yohanson and again she repeated the magic word *Vashogood ok sita*, which this time meant please sit down. Tea and dainty little cookies were waiting for us on a table covered in a red plush velvet cloth and embroidered linen doilies. It was like going back to the nineteenth century. The five of us certainly did not fit the picture in our bizarre borrowed accoutrements. Miss Yohanson than sat herself on a tabouret, very dignified. Then, lowering her head, she said:

"I inherited this house from a wealthy uncle, but recently I had some reverses of fortune and I now have to rent rooms to survive." She seemed to be ashamed of that fact. "For the moment I only have one room available, it's quite large and it has two single beds. Are you interested in seeing it?"

We looked at each other, wanting to say a hundred things, but kept quiet. Serge motioned with a nod, yes we would be interested. Miss Yohanson had not mentioned a price yet. This worried me and somehow Serge caught my distressed look.

"I'll pay for the first month," he whispered in my ear, "you will reimburse me when you and Charlie get a job."

I sighed with relief and gave him a thank you kiss.

The room was huge, twenty-one feet by twenty-one. The very narrow beds were at the two opposite sides of the room and were framed with wrought iron headstands. Two of the tall windows we had seen from the outside flanked the garden wall. The room was freezing cold. In one of the corners stood a blue porcelain cylindrical stove reaching to the very high ceiling. Between one of the beds and the door stood a small wash basin and completing the furniture a large oval table covered in oilcloth and four rustic chairs filled the center of the room. The bathroom was at the end of the corridor for all the tenants to share.

So this was going to be our new home. The price she finally quoted was reasonable and the five of us could certainly manage in that big room. Miss Yohanson mentioned that she filled the stove only once a day. She also showed us a cupboard full of dishes, pots, pans and glasses. She did not ask too many questions. We told her we were students and we were writing papers on the various countries we were visiting and that was that.

As soon as she departed we all held hands and danced around the table singing at the top of our lungs. The problem now was how to divide this room among us. There were heated discussions on who would use the beds and when. In the end it was decided that two of us would enjoy the beds for a week while the rest would sleep under the table, that meant three people. Thus we would make a weekly rotation.

This was really a so-so arrangement; it was not very funny for Charlie and me or, for that matter, Serge and Micheline to be separated one whole week and then have to sleep uncomfortably and with someone else under the table. Claude was the problem; being the fifth person in the group, he felt awkward. For the moment there was no other way to do things, we tried to comfort him, saying that everything would be OK.

Then to our dismay we found out that there was no stove in the room to cook our meals. What were we supposed to do? Miss Yohanson gave us access to her kitchen only to cook dinner! Were we to starve all day the way it was in Erik's home? No, no, this would not do. We decided to use our camping stoves incognito for all the extra meals.

A week later we were all working. Things were getting brighter, but not without hardships. Micheline and I had found work in that men's clothing factory that Ingrid had spoken about, Libo. The trouble was the distance we had to cover every morning and every evening, five long kilometers on skis. No buses – the roads were impassable with the amount of accumulated snow. This meant getting up at five in the morning in freezing cold, gulping a cup of tea and a piece of stale bread, and washing the indispensable areas only. Miss Yohanson never seemed to put enough wood in the stove, if she put any at all. When we returned in the evening the porcelain stove was always cold. We had to stuff in all the newspapers and all the available packaging cartons we could find to get a decent fire.

The Libo manager who interviewed us was a young man without any color whatsoever. His hair was so blond it was almost white, and so was his skin; even his eyes had no color. It was strange for me to converse with a person that seemed to have all the life drawn out of his body, but the fellow was sharp, to the point, and he spoke English. I told him that as students we were looking for a temporary job, that I could sew very well and so could Micheline, which was not true, in her case. Our aim was to learn all the special machines. I think the man was more interested in our looks and the fact that we were foreign than in our abilities. We were hired on the spot.

Most of the factory workers were women. The noise in the factory was appalling. Above us were long tubes of blinding neon lights. The manager, 'Mr. Libo' as we called him, not knowing his real name, showed us around the vast compound. Most of the clothes manufactured here were men's coats and jackets. Downstairs was a vast refectory-like cafeteria where employees took their meals. Outside, the dense pine forest, heavy with snow, reached to the very walls of the factory, almost hiding it. The only sign of life, a plume of blue smoke coming out of a brick chimney.

All this was exciting in a way. I had never worked in a factory, except for
that little place in Casablanca where I had painted dolls all day long. This
was going to be very different. Here the employees were all professionals;
how were they going to react to our being hired? As we walked around
with Mr. Libo, they looked at us with curiosity. Were they going to be
friendly? In later weeks Micheline and I discovered the factory girls wanted
to be more than friendly with us. The bathroom was the place we usually
congregated to smoke a cigarette; soon we found out that most of the
women in the factory were lesbians. All kinds of things were happening
in the bathroom stalls and pretty soon they were after us. I was horrified,
and so was Micheline. We let them know that both of us liked men and
to please leave us alone. This created a big gap; none of them would speak
to us anymore. We felt totally isolated and had only one thought, to make
enough money this winter to get out of this place.

Charlie and Serge had also found work at the Volvo plant through
Jacques Gustavson. Jacques worked on the assembly line, and Charlie was
given odd jobs which at first seemed like fun, but proved to be boring. It
took Charlie only two weeks to find a more effective way to sort the nuts
and bolts he was assigned to fix. In the beginning he was showed how to
painstakingly take each nut and bolt from a big box where they were all
mixed in sizes, and put them individually in various boxes according to
size. Charlie's new method was revolutionary. He found a swivel chair and
sat on it with his back to the table where the various boxes stood. Putting
the box of mixed nuts and bolts on his lap, he took a handful and swiveled
the chair and threw each nut and bolt in its respective box. This created
a scandal among the workers, but also some admiration. They called him
"Crazy, Crazy Charlie". Pretty soon their manager showed up to find out
what it was all about. Instead of reprimanding Charlie, he praised him for
his inventiveness and the speed with which he was doing his work. The
manager was impressed and was interested to meet Charlie personally; this
probably meant advancement.

It took little time to make new friends. Saturday nights became potluck
nights around our big table. Everybody wanted to meet the new Moroccan
and French tenants at Miss Yohanson's. This was 1949, and Sweden was
still riddled with war refugees from many countries. Our place became a
real Tower of Babel. German Jews, Hungarians, and Russians mixed with
local Swedes and Lapps from the North. The trouble was we could not

understand each other. I was sure every one of them had an interesting tale, and certainly in return they would be eager to hear our story, but it was impossible. So we spoke with our hands and eyes, but mostly we sang together, songs that we had learned in youth hostels. One fellow played the guitar, another the balalaika and Claude played his harmonica. There was in these get-togethers a true camaraderie that I seldom found in future years.

At work things were going well until one morning I severely wounded myself. Working these powerful factory sewing machines was a challenge. Trying an automatic hemming machine, I managed to put a finger under the needle, which repeatedly made holes just under my right index fingernail. I screamed like a hog being butchered, unable to stop the damn thing with my left hand, the switch being too far on the right side. What a commotion! The pain was atrocious even when a worker switched the machine off and retrieved my poor finger from under the needle. The manager came running and gave orders for somebody to drive me to the hospital. I felt faint from the ordeal, but also a sense of shame. Was I incapable of manning a simple hemming machine?

At the hospital, while the nurse was cleaning and putting a bandage on my wound, she mentioned that accidents of the sort were common. It seemed they had several cases every month of wounded factory employees. It was not a consolation, but in one way it made me feel better: hopefully I would not be fired. I returned home to sleep it off with some pain killers, waiting anxiously for Charlie to come back. I needed his warmth and his powerful arms to give me reassurance.

During the week of my convalescence, I was exempted from washing the tower of dirty dishes piled up on top of the wash basin, a chore that none of us liked and that was always left until the last minute, when there was not a clean dish left.

Back at work, I kept trying other machines as if nothing had happened, but I was cautious and made sure I was not day-dreaming of pleasanter things while working these tough factory monsters. As a matter of fact I grew to dislike the work; it was tedious: the long walks in the pitch black freezing mornings, artificial neon lights burning my eyes all day long; and the food at the cafeteria. It seemed that most Swedes, at least the working people, ate herring every Monday, yellow pea soup every Tuesday. On Thursdays they ate pancakes with lingonberries and on Fridays meatballs. It never changed. Where were our superb Moroccan dishes and French cuisine? But I had to endure and put on a good face. After all, nobody had pushed me to come here but myself. We needed the money badly and I was longing for the moment we could free ourselves from work in order to visit more of the country. So far I was not yet ready to go back to Morocco, nor was Charlie. Strangely, we had less freedom here than we had at home, having to work long hours, never seeing the sun shine except on Sundays from twelve to one in the afternoon. The real reason for staying so far from home was that here we were a couple, free to love each other without restraint.

Chapter 18: 1949-1950

Christmas and Beyond

We were nearing the middle of December. The streets of Skövde started to look like decorated Christmas trees, tinsel everywhere. The reflecting colors on the snowy roads and the walls of ice lining the sidewalks transformed the town into a fairyland.

I found out about a holiday I had never heard of before, called Santa Lucia, held on the thirteenth of the month, the same day as my birthday. When I told my Swedish friends, they got all excited, telling me I had to be part of the procession that was taking place that night. All the unmarried girls in Skövde would attend. The wish to Santa Lucia was to get married before the end of the following year. We would each don a long white robe and a gold crown specially made to carry thirteen lit candles. I agreed, for the fun of it. Charlie, Serge and Claude went along with me, but I could feel Micheline was a little jealous of all the attention I was getting.

One of my new friends was Irma, Jacques Gustavson's fiancee, who was the daughter of a very wealthy farmer. Blonde, tall and strong, she had gone to some of the best schools in the country. There was a faint trace of snobbishness in her manner at first, but then when she saw that Charlie and I did not pay any attention to her rich kid airs, she reverted to being a simple, wonderful country girl.

It was Irma that procured all the fineries I was to wear on the night of Santa Lucia. I had invited all my old and new friends for the event: Erik and Ingrid, the German Jews, the Russians, the Swedes, the Lapps, Jacques and Irma. They would accompany me at the procession and come home after for a birthday party. Micheline and I would provide the traditional saffron buns and other specialties eaten on the feast of Santa Lucia, and the other guests would bring wine and spirits if they could. Sweden was not a dry country, but all alcohol was sold through government stores; one had to be a resident and more than twenty-three years old. This did not make things easy and therefore a glass of wine or a sip of Aquavit was drunk with utmost pleasure when available. There also existed a thriving black market in sprits for those who could afford it, which was not the case for us.

The evening was magic. The town's windows were decorated and lit with the thirteen prescribed candles, which reflected their dancing gold auras on the fresh fallen snow. The streets were full of people in a merry mood waiting for the procession. Underneath my beautiful long white gown I had to dress as if I was going to cross the Himalayas, otherwise I would have been unable to walk at a slow pace in such cold weather - fifteen degrees below zero centigrade! Under the golden crown of candles my head was kept warm with a tight woolen bonnet I had covered with a long white silk scarf. The most difficult part was to walk very slowly so the candles would not blow out and in pace with the other girls.

We were at least twenty four young women, eager and unmarried. Walking two by two in a long glittering ribbon, we dazzled the crowd on the snowy sidewalks. Flaming goddesses in all that white, we were the triumph of youth. If only my parents and Glad could have seen me – a passing thought. I felt a pang of guilt for abandoning them and being so far from them; they always made a big to-do for my birthday. People in the streets hushed as we approached the center of the city where we stopped and formed a circle of lights to sing an ode to Santa Lucia.

Where was Charlie? I looked around, but I could not see him. Instead, I saw a short blond man with curly hair escaping from his cap looking at me intensely. He seemed mesmerized, his eyes and mouth wide open. Why was he looking at me that way? Did I look like somebody he knew? Then I saw Charlie coming toward me. The ceremony was over, the procession was dismantling. I took off my heavy crown and blew the candles out. We were all going to our respective homes in little groups. By now I felt like an icicle, I was trembling. Charlie was rubbing my shoulders as we walked.

Somebody was following us; I could hear the crunching of shoes on ice. Turning around, I saw the short man following us and making gestures for us to stop.

"Charlie, I don't know what this guy wants, let's find out."

"Hello, I heard you speak French," he said in halting English. "Do you understand me?"

"Yes, we do. What do you want?" Charlie seemed annoyed with this interruption.

"Is this your wife or only a friend?" the little man was trembling as he spoke.

"What is that to you?" Charlie said. "We don't know you, again what do you want? We have company waiting for us at home, we have to hurry."

"Please, please, She is so beautiful," the young man said raising his two open hands toward my face.

Charlie and I were speechless; the nerve this fellow had; but secretly I was flattered.

"Please may I come with you to your house? I will be quiet, I just want to look at her."

In an instant we realized that the fellow must be simple minded. Who else would dare to be so bold?

"You've made quite an impression on the poor man," Charlie said to me a bit testily, I could see that Charlie was piqued and I loved the game.

"Let him come home with us," I said. "I don't think he's dangerous at all. Come on, be a good sport."

Lief, that was his name, came home with us. As we walked Charlie and I spoke French, hoping he did not understand. We made fun of him, but gently. After that evening and for the rest of our stay in Sweden, Leif became a friend of sorts that Charlie tolerated only because he was harmless in his unfulfilled love for me.

Ringing our bell every Sunday morning at seven, Leif brought hot rolls for breakfast, his arms always full of flowers that he deposited at my feet while I was still waking up. Falling on his knees, he read love poems he had written for me in Swedish. I didn't understand them, but that was fine. Sometimes Charlie got miffed and threw him out of the room unceremoniously. Many Sundays he came carrying sheets of newspapers he had painted in oils, dark powerful abstracts in the manner of Rouault. His suppressed desires seemed to explode, splashing the newspaper's torn pages in violent colors. Spreading them on the floor, he waited for praise, his very blue innocent eyes almost begging, then with a royal sweep of his arms showing his masterpieces.

"They are all for you Anit, with all my heart."

At which point I would get a dark look from Charlie. I did not see any harm in all this; if anything I only had pity for the poor guy.

The holidays were nearing and so far nobody had invited any of us for Christmas. Jacques told us that in Sweden, Christmas was a very private affair. No outsiders or foreigners were ever invited to join families for the occasion.

"I am having Christmas at my future in-laws," Jacques said. "Let me see what I can do, I'll ask Irma to ask her parents to invite you."

In the meantime I had sent a long letter to Father telling him where I was and what I was doing, pleading with him to be patient, and not to condemn me without hearing my point of view. I wrote several pages telling him that I knew he always had wished I were a boy, so why was my being independent and daring so bad?

"Dear Dad," I wrote, "you should be proud of me, of my endurance and my curiosity to discover the world. You were the one who gave me the taste for adventure with the tales of your travels around the world. You disobeyed your father too as a youngster! I am your true daughter. Instead of worrying so much, why not proudly tell your friends the courage it took me to leave a plush and secure home for the uncertainties and pitfalls of the world outside. Please forgive the pain I must have caused."

So far I had had no reply, but I was not too worried about it; I had other things on mind. I also had written our friend in Paris to send my trunk to our new address, but nothing had arrived yet. I was tired of wearing other people's ill-fitting clothes and wished for my personal things.

A week before Christmas, Charlie and I received a formal invitation to spend the Yule holiday at Irma's parents on their big farm. With it in the mailbox we found a torn piece of paper with another invitation scribbled by Leif. We were invited to spend New Year's Eve at his parents' home. Leif's parents were rich merchants who lived in an upper class neighborhood. I was curious to meet his family. Were they as odd as he was?

Our French friends had not been invited with us for Christmas or New Year, but then I found out they had already made plans for the holidays with other acquaintances. All was for the best then.

The town was awfully quiet on that twenty-fourth of December. A pale sun barely lasting one hour disappeared fast. I was at the window expecting to see Jacques any minute now. We were ready to go, anticipating a great

Yule feast in the country. Jacques finally showed up in a pick up truck covered with snow.

Crossing the deserted city was eerie; all the inhabitants were already tucked warmly in their houses, drinking and making merry. The windows of each house were aglow with tall fir trees glittering with colored bulbs and shiny ornaments. It transformed the whole town into a silent white surreal place bathed in a heavenly rainbow of light. Above us the sky was a strange color of black mixed with an orange glow, a sure sign of more snow. We drove the twenty miles almost in silence, as if being quiet would bring us there faster.

Irma came out to greet us. The big house, covered in festive lights, sparkled like a jewel in the miles of white snow around. Inside it was warm and plush with colorful country furniture made of roughly-worked local woods. Embroidered pillows in cross-stitched patterns, mostly red and blue, covered armchairs and sofas. A wonderful and rich aroma permeated the house as we were led to our designated room for the night. I turned to Irma, slightly embarrassed.

"Irma, do your parents know we are not married? This room with one big bed is for a couple."

Irma started to laugh at my embarrassment.

"Anit, don't worry, my parents don't mind at all. Jacques has been sleeping in my room for two months now. It is the custom in Sweden to try things out before the marriage, so we know if we are made for each other. If it does not work we try again until we find the right fellow or the right girl."

I was shocked beyond belief, immediately thinking about Morocco and our archaic ways of dealing with girls about to be married. Was it possible this country was so advanced in their behavior as to permit a future bride to sleep with her fiancee? Well, the proof was there in front of my eyes. Charlie and I looked at each other with amazement.

Where were Irma's mother and father? I was anxious to meet them now, such wondrous people that permitted such things to happen under their roof. Running down a flight of stairs, we almost collided with Mrs. Olson, Irma's mother. The meal was ready. She gave us a big smile and said the traditional word.

"Vashogood."

Irma looked a lot like her mother. Mrs. Olson had white hair mixed in her pale golden mane, all of it tied in a knot. She was tall and strong with an impressive bust and was dressed almost severely in a dark red dress that reached her ankles, so conservative in her attire and yet so free. Leading us along, she gave orders to two servants dressed in local costumes for the occasion to open the heavy doors to the dining room.

What a sight! A very long table that ran the length of the room was laden with food, with not a square inch of space between the tantalizing dishes covering the red damask table cloth. Candles were everywhere –– some in tall candelabras glowing over the richness of the table, others in niches and on dressers lighting the white lace doilies and holly bouquets placed in scintillating crystal vases. On the paneled walls antique porcelain dishes of various sizes caught our attention with their intricate designs and colors. Mr. Olson was facing the fireplace, where huge logs were burning. Turning around to greet us, he gave us a handshake that could have broken a tree. What a giant of a man! He seemed to have been cut from the rock of a mountain, but his blue eyes were soft and smiling. Other people were there too: a brother and his wife and their unruly children running around, totally free to make all the noise they wanted. Two older ladies were sitting on a sofa wrapped in their shawls. One was Mrs. Olson's mother and the other was an aunt.

When all the introductions were made, we were given glasses of Aquavit, and onto the food. Where to start? What to choose? Most of the dishes were foreign to us. Guests were filling their plates with a beef liver pâté that contained, of all things, anchovies. Then there was jellied veal in slices, and near it a platter of homemade head cheese. There were boiled pork sausages, smoked Christmas sausages, and many other tantalizing dishes beside a Christmas porridge made with rice, milk, and eggs. The centerpiece was an enormous home-cured ham, all rosy from the brine it had soaked in since the Day of Anna, which was December ninth. But there was still more. There were plates of herring in different sauces–cream and dill, or wine– accompanied by sweet beet salad, and little meat balls with a big pot of red beans that had been cooked with molasses. Several large round loaves of bread that were made with pig's blood completed the gargantuan display of food. The pig's blood gave the bread an unappealing black color, but the taste was delicious.

We were almost full to the brim when a strange awful smell invaded the room. Two maids carrying long silver platters above their heads were bringing in steaming Lutefisk, a Swedish specialty made with ling cod. The thing had been placed in lye, I was told, since November thirtieth. This was supposed to be the *piece de resistance* and they all applauded when it appeared. It looked terrible, a mass of white, stinking, trembling gelatin. Charlie and I were repulsed by the smell and the appearance, but then we were offered two plates of it and asked to eat it. This was the Christmas tradition. My stomach went upside down, I thought I was going to faint. As for Charlie, who had wolfed down all these heavy pork dishes with great appetite, this was too much. He felt sick and excused himself, almost running out of the room. Nobody paid much attention; everybody in the room was tipsy with all the Aquavit they had drunk.

Later, going upstairs, my head spun as if riding a giant Ferris wheel. I could not even grab the bannister, it was wavering. The flowers on the stair runner seemed to dissolve under my feet. Awful, I would never drink again, was my only thought as I painfully reached the bedroom. That night was one to be remembered; neither Charlie nor I slept, taking turns in the bathroom almost without interruption. As the very dim light of a December dawn in Sweden spread its aura on that white and frozen Christmas morning, we came down the stairs cautiously, not wanting to disturb the deep silence. I went looking in the kitchen, opening cupboards, trying to find the coffee tin and a pot to boil water. Remnants of last night's revelry were everywhere; unwashed plates and glasses filled the sink with a stale smell from what had been a sumptuous dinner. Napkins and wrapping paper were strewn all over the floor and in a corner of the living room the once glorious Christmas tree was askew, its ornaments in disorderly rows. Charlie and I were sipping our very hot dark coffee with delight when Irma's mother showed up at the kitchen door.

"My God, you are early! I'm happy you found the coffee. I need some myself. But children, you cannot have coffee alone! There is a special treat I make for Christmas breakfast. You have to eat some."

She went to the pantry and came back with what looked like an enormous round cake. Frankly, the sight of food was not appealing this morning.

"Here it is," she said with pride. "I make it with the first milk of a cow that has just given birth. It's like cheese ,it is so thick, and I add lots of egg yolks and sugar."

Saying so she sliced two big portions for us to eat. Charlie looked at me and I looked at him. The sight of that yellow cheese cake was nauseating, but we ate a little spoonful under her watchful eyes. Very good, we said together, can we keep the rest for later? As soon as she left I gathered the slices, wrapped them, opened the kitchen door and buried the stuff under a mound of snow. It would be quite a while before she discovered the deed. Summer was far away.

In only a few days it would be a new year. What it had in store for us we did not know and we did not think about. For the time being our minds were on festivities and joyous events. We were getting ready for the big New Year's Eve bash at my amorous friend Leif's house. I had convinced him to invite Serge, Micheline, and Claude.

We decided to have dinner first at the finest restaurant, situated in the five star Hotel Billigen, the most elegant in town. We all had hard-earned money to spend and were going to splurge on fancy foods and wine. For that occasion I had to look stunning. I wore a very elegant navy blue wool dress, and the gold chain studded with emeralds and pearls Grandmother Nejma had given me before she died, and to top it off, very high-heeled shoes and nylon stockings. All of the finery had been made possible because we had finally received our trunk from Paris. Charlie was also dressed to the hilt in an elegant dark grey suit and superb silk tie. We felt like princes as we entered the Billingen. It had been a long time since we had worn these clothes and looked that good. After a fine meal, we made our way to the party.

Leif's parents owned a town house. Its architecture, the fancy wrought iron on doors and windows, spelled money. We climbed plush red-carpeted stairs and arrived in a large marbled hall where a maid in uniform took our coats and hats. Leif's mother was there to greet us. A small, fat lady in a tight flashy sequined dress, she oppened her arms, directing us toward the living room saying the magic word,

"Vashogood."

A thought came to my mind as I remembered Erik and Ingrid's dreary little house, the first set of stairs we had climbed the night we arrived in Skövde, cold, hungry, and utterly broke.

The atmosphere in this fancy living room was far from the warmth we had experienced in Erik's house. Here, sitting all around, were well-dressed men and women smoking English cigarettes, eating dainty little catered sandwiches and petits fours. Very different also from the big farm where we had spent Christmas and stuffed ourselves silly with lush home-made dishes.

The only similarity was the drinking, although tonight we had an infinity of choices, from various brands of Scotch to vodkas, wine, and sweet liqueurs. At first the conversation was cool and polite. As the evening proceeded, the stiff guests started to loosen up; how many drinks it took them to get to that stage I could only guess, but it was a tremendous lot. This was the upper echelon of Swedish society. Their upbringing was so conservative, they could not impart their true feelings without being drowned in alcohol. Leif's mother was very drunk, she kept laughing without stop, saying to everybody around, "*Roolit, roolit.*" Funny, funny. "You are all so funny."

By this time Leif's father was snoring loudly, sprawled in a Louis XV gilded armchair. Some younger guests, totally oblivious to their surroundings, were necking hard on various couches, and my amorous friend was completely knocked out, sitting on the floor looking into the void. Needless to say, we also had had too many drinks to know exactly what we were doing.

Not wanting to lose face in front of our hosts, we all left together, almost falling down the stairs. Hot and sweaty, we burst outside in the frigid thirty-below icy white night, not even feeling the cold. The difference in temperature in combination with the alcohol made us very very drunk. We decided to dance a ballet, singing a tune at the top of our lungs while trying to dance on the tips of our toes. That ballet was a mess as many of us slipped on the ice. We were making so much noise that some windows above us opened and we heard people yell that it was two o'clock in the morning, to please shut up. We paid no heed and continued singing loudly and dancing as if possessed. Crossing a small city park, Charlie spotted some very high parallel bars and decided against everybody's advice that he was going to jump up and show us a few tricks on the bars. He could not make it that high; he had to climb on Serge's shoulders to reach. Once up there he was actually amazing, doing all kinds of twists and pirouettes.

Then we heard him say, "And now Ladies and Gentlemen watch this. I am going to fly and land on the snow."

I said, "Charlie, no!" but with a grand gesture he threw himself up in the air, his arms stretched out, yelling.

"I am flying, Anit, I am flying."

We saw him fall and we ran, fearing the worst. He was buried in knee-high snow and did not move. Paralyzed with fear, nobody moved. Then I bent down and tried to shake him free calling for him to wake up, I was crying. At last we grabbed him and turned him over. He was breathing, thank God, but he had a big gash running down his nose and was bleeding profusely. In the meantime some of the window people had called the police because of the noise we were making. The accident and the police had an instant sobering effect on us all. The officers admonished us severely for disturbing the peace but they let us go. Next time they said we would be arrested. I was feeling the tremendous cold reaching to my very bones; we had to walk all the way home, no taxis at this time. I was holding Charlie by the shoulders with one arm trying to comfort him, while with the other arm I was holding a handkerchief to his still-bleeding nose.

We slept most of that New Years Day 1950. Charlie's nose was double its normal size and hurting very much. The night before as I was undressing I realized that my nylon stockings were glued to my skin; they had frozen on me while dancing on the ice. I could not take them off and went to sleep with them on. When I woke up my legs were burning; the stockings had literally shattered like pieces of glass, leaving my legs studded with tiny shards. It took many days and a lot of patience and suffering to get rid of them all. So much for alcohol. Charlie and I once again swore it would be a long time before we indulged again, but with no hard feelings for the wonderful holidays we had spent.

In January, Serge, Micheline and Claude left us, returning to Paris. It created a big void in that room of ours, even though we were happy to have all the space for ourselves. These walls had seen a lot, from boisterous feasting reunions to bizarre events. I remembered that one of the nights I was in bed sick with bronchitis. Serge and Charlie played doctor, putting suction cups on my naked back to relieve the congestion. For lack of the real thing they were using empty yogurt glasses that they heated with a torch made of rags dipped in gasoline. They had put the lights out to keep Miss Johanson from coming in. Micheline sat on my back to keep me still. It looked like a scene from hell. Two big flaming torches sent fantastic shadows onto the walls, while I, the victim, was sweating and screaming because they were literally burning me. Today, sixty-odd years later I still have a scar or two on my back from the ordeal.

After the holidays we went back to work, saving every penny for an eventual trip to Stockholm and maybe as far up north as Kiruna in Lapland. Snow was falling day and night; the thermometer went down to thirty-eight below. Charlie, always bragging, made a bet that he would run around the block bare-headed one freezing Sunday morning. Irma and Jacques were there having breakfast with us. We tried in vain to dissuade him from doing such a foolish thing.

"I bet you ten kroners I'll do it," he said, and rushed out like a madman wearing only a sweater and slacks. Anxious, we counted the minutes and before long he was back, shivering, his whole head encased in a half inch thick helmet of solid ice. We felt like laughing at his look of distress, but the matter was serious. We had to break the ice with a hammer and when it was all done Charlie ended up with a tremendous headache which spoiled the rest of the day for all of us. Foolish, foolish Charlie.

Shortly after that memorable Sunday we received a summons from the Criminal Police of Skövde. Literally terrified at what could be the reason, we racked our brains with no results. What could we possibly have done?

A few days later, answering the summons, we dragged ourselves to the Skövde police building wearing our best clothes and our most conservative looks. We were asked many questions. Our full names and address, where we worked, etc. Then the investigator asked us about our country of origin, who our parents were and what kind of income bracket they belonged in.

This seemed very bizarre, for we were not charged with anything. Finally the officer told us that an influential person in the city had asked for this inquiry. It was all very puzzling. Before we left we were told that as tourists we were only allowed three months in the country, and that we should renew our visas for three more months if we decided to stay. This was something we had not thought of at all. Taking us to the door, the officer told us that the limit of our stay was six months. They had lots of problems with refugees that did not respect the law, living clandestinely in the city; some even slept in buses to evade the police. We got out of there still wondering who had inquired about us and why? As for the other matter we now knew that our time in Sweden was limited and that we had to make the most of it.

It was about that time that Mr Brehm, the general manager at Volvo, invited us to his home. We were formally received one evening for dinner at a beautiful residence whose Greek revival architecture graced the vast park around it. As we dined in the company of Mr Brehm, his elegant wife and his daughters, two ravishing blonde teenagers, I was told that Charlie had earned the highest marks in the Volvo company for swiftness and inventivness, which was the reason why we had been invited tonight.

After dessert and liquors, the oldest daughter Gunilla took us around the house for a visit. She was really lovely, slim as a reed, her long heavy flaxen hair a shimmering wave. At one point I had to excuse myself to go to the bathroom. When I came out, Charlie and Gunilla were nowhere to be seen. Going back down to the living room I stopped suddenly, finding the two kissing passionately against a marble column. I stood there speechless, not comprehending. Then they saw me standing there petrified. Charlie jumped back and they both came to me as if nothing had taken place. I was very hurt and tried to conceal my pain as best I could. Then I told Charlie that I wanted to leave immediately. Mr Brehm and his wife could not understand why we were leaving so soon.

We walked home in silence at first. Tears were running down my face, leaving a salty taste on my lips. At last Charlie spoke.

"Don't cry like this, it's not a big deal. So I kissed a girl, I was just having a little fun, nothing serious, and actually she started the whole thing. Tomorrow it will be forgotten, come on, be a good sport."

This should have been a warning, but I was in love and did not want to believe that it could happen again. So I dried my tears and was a good sport. The morning after, Gunilla called; Charlie declined the invitation. There were several more calls that week. I really did not know if they had met again, but I warned Charlie that if I found them together once more, or heard that they had met, I would leave immediately and it would be over for good. Nothing more was said; I really wanted to believe that he would be true to me. Since I had made that deal with him in a taxi so long ago, I considered him my man. I had chosen him and I wanted him for life. Up to now there had been only honesty between us, and I truly thought it could be so. Two friends in love forever. In later years I paid very dearly for so much trust.

We met with Jacques and Irma that week and recounted the invitation to them, omitting the portion that dealt with Charlie and Gunilla. We also told them about our being called to the Criminal Police a week earlier. Did they know what it meant?

Irma produced a conservative little laugh and said,

"Oh, I know why. You see, in our country we do not ask people into our houses unless we know exactly who they are and where they really come from. This type of investigation is usually not done by common everyday people, but mainly by the rich and powerful. I am sorry you had to go through that. It must surely be the Volvo general manager."

"I'll be damned," said Charlie, "if I had known, I would not have set a foot into his house."

"That would have been very wise." The words just jumped out of my mouth, referring of course to the blonde Gunilla.

At the beginning of March the paralyzing cold let up a bit. On a sunny Sunday Charlie and I decided to go for a walk in the woods around town. As we walked hand in hand among the tall firs, big gray clouds started to obscure the sky and in no time it was snowing again. Charlie had seen some large fir cones on the ground and wanted to gather some to bring home.

"Anit, continue walking so you won't get cold, I'll join you in a little bit."

Now the snow was really falling, I had not walked too far when I turned around to see if Charlie was following. No Charlie in sight. I called once, twice, no answer. I could not see the path anymore, it was like being in the middle of a big cotton wad. I had no idea of how to get back home and started one way only to change direction again and again. The snow was relentlessly falling thicker and thicker, whiter and whiter, a paralyzing opaque curtain that erased everything. All that white was blinding. I started to panic with a very strange feeling in the pit of my stomach. My thoughts became confused, I felt faint. What was happening to me, was I losing my mind? I had to get out of this in a hurry. Summoning all my strengh I yelled, "Chaaarlie!" and closed my eyes for an instant, dizzy, ready to drop to the ground.

"Where were you? I have been looking for an hour at least, thank God I heard your scream."

Opening my eyes I saw Charlie between two trees, his arms full of pine cones. I threw myself against him, spilling his precious cargo.

"I thought I was lost for good, Oh Charlie, what a horrible sensation."

"Yes, it is very easy to get lost when so much snow is falling and the silence is so thick it is frightening. I was uneasy myself. Come and warm up in my arms." He held me for a while against his chest and all was well. It was quite an experience, something I hoped would never happen again.

The work at Libo was getting really boring. I asked Charlie how he felt about quitting his job at Volvo. We now had a little money put aside and still dreamed of travelling north. Stockholm was like a mirage unfullfilled, and further north the Arctic Circle was a dream that we did not dare anticipate, but secretly wished for. Charlie told me that he couldn't just leave his job like that. He would give them notice right away, but expected to work two more weeks. "And this goes for you too I am sure," he added.

We were already in the middle of our two weeks notice, almost ready for our trip when one morning I got a call from someone at Volvo telling me that Charlie had been transported to the hospital with a possible hernia; this after having lifted some very heavy object at the factory. I rushed to the hospital and sure enough it was a bad hernia. Charlie was already on the operating table. I waited what seemed a very long time in a sort of living room furnished with wicker armchairs and flowered sofas, all immaculatly clean and cheery. The weirdest thing was a potted banana tree in a corner of the room. All this exotic stuff was probably meant for the recovery of patients, imagining themselves on some island instead of in cold and snowy Skövde.

Charlie recovered in no time. He seemed very happy in that hospital staffed with beautiful blonde nurses that he courted openly from his bed. Thank God he was home after a week, and I just closed my eyes to all his flirting at the hospital.

Half a month had passed. We were now in mid-April, and snow was melting everywhere. I had borrowed Mrs. Yohanson's bike to do my errands, sloshing through muddy streets and almost getting killed as I rode on the right side of the street while cars were driving on the left like in England. It was getting considerably warmer. One morning, opening the window, I saw a package on the window sill and suddenly remembered. Last December I had put a wrapped steak at that very spot to keep it fresh for the next day and had forgotten it. It had lain all these months under a thick coat of icy snow and it was still very fresh.

Mr. Brehm at Volvo had kept in touch. Several times he had taken us for sleigh rides across miles of crystallized white forests, always bringing fur coats for Charlie and me. He mentioned several times how free he felt with us two, away from the burden of family and work. It was obvious though that he was attracted to me, always asking me to sit close to him in the sleigh, for safety, he said with a curious smile.

Chapter 19: 1950

The Great North

At the end of April we had packed our belongings and left them with Jacques, ready for the trip to Stockholm. We had planned to take the fast train, the same one that by a bizarre twist of fate we had missed that past November. It seemed we were not fated to take that train. Before we bought the tickets, Mr. Brehm called Charlie one morning saying he was going to Stockholm on business, and would we like to ride with him. What a good surprise that was, the money saved and the pleasure of a fast ride in a comfortable car.

We arrived at nightfall at "Af Chapman," the new youth hostel opened the previous year. It was a full rigger ship moored along Skeppsolmen Island. It was too dark to see much around us, but the ship's masts were illuminated, casting spots of light on the long elegant hull. For the first three nights we had booked a berth with two beds, expensive for our purse, but we wanted the luxury to make love all night if we so desired. For the rest of our stay it would have to be a dormitory with ten beds. Too bad, but we had to economize somewhere.

The cry of seagulls woke me up in the morning. Through the porthole I could see hundreds of them flapping their white wings over the choppy green waters. Charlie did not want to get up. he felt too good in his berth rocking gently with the ship's sway.

When we emerged on deck we were stunned by the beauty around us. Islands and water as far as the eye could see. The morning was crisp with a sharp north wind that made us shiver. Ribbons of white clouds were racing across the pale blue sky almost in unison with the many ferries crisscrossing the channels. Facing us, the superb architecture of the Royal Palace sparkled in the morning sun.

Taking a bus was the cheapest mode of transportation. We bought a pass for the week and started to discover this unusual and beautiful city scattered over so many islands. Our first thought was how lucky we had been not to have come directly here in November. This was a very large city indeed. As Erik, our rescuer friend from Skövde, had mentioned, we would have starved to death begging in the streets. Very soon we found out how expensive everything was here, much more than in the provincial town where we had lived. The afternoon was spent walking the old neighborhood of Gamla Stan, dating from the middle ages. Crooked streets, medieval houses, little shops were a delight. As we were discussing the price of a possible purchase with difficulty, a young man approached us to help.

"My name is Börje" – he pronounced it Burryay – he said, and I started laughing. He looked at me, vexed, not understanding.

"Beurrier," I said, covering my mouth with my hand so as not to laugh again. "In French it means butter dish, how funny."

In no time we became the best of friends. He was studying at Uppsala, the great University, and was willing to be our guide for the duration of our stay. Once more we were lucky in finding a total stranger wanting to help. We did not realize at the time how very exotic we seemed to people of other lands. For them Morocco was still a strange and distant place. Whatever they had read or seen at the movies was enough to trigger their imagination.

Börje, alias beurrier, took us to visit impressive sites like the Parliament that covered the island of Helgeanshomen; the name itself seemed long enough to cover the land.

Charlie and I had brought our bathing suits in the hope of a good swim in the waters around Stockholm, but it was still icy cold. Börje told us of a large swimming pool downtown that also had a sauna, showers and cafe.

That same afternoon we trekked to the place. After paying to enter Charlie was directed to one section of changing rooms and I to another. In mine, women were in various states of undressing or getting ready to leave. I saw nothing out of the ordinary. I went out to meet Charlie in the corridor; no one was there but him. Hand in hand we walked the short distance to the pool, relishing the moment we were going to plunge in the water. It had been a long time since that day in September when we swam across

Copenhagen's harbor to the feet of the Little Mermaid. We were in for quite a surprise. The pool was full of people, men and women, naked!

We froze on the spot, feeling quite silly standing there in our bathing suits; some bathers were looking at us with an expression of amusement on their faces. To us all these naked people cavorting in the pool was outrageous. We had been brought up so differently in Morocco that even with our free way of thinking it was very difficult to swallow what we were seeing. It took us a moment to decide whether we would go in with all these lunatics or flee to a safer place. Our desire to swim was too strong, and besides we both were good divers; we had to show off.

I must say that our swim was very agreeable. We had to temporarily dismiss the fact that we were among naked people and probably looked as strange to them as they did to us. Nevertheless we both decided to avoid the sauna. As we sat at the pool's cafe where everybody was dressed, thank God, I reflected on the Swedish free mode of life. I kept wondering what attraction could men and women alike have toward each other when there was nothing to hide anymore, no taboos to be violated, no secrets to unveil. Was the art of making love only a sport to them?

Our week in Stockholm was coming to an end; it had been exhausting running around every day from sun-up to past sundown, hopping from one island to the next, but the sights were worth the trouble. The Churches were magnificent and so different from the ones we had seen in France and Germany. Their shapes were in a way simpler, more severe and many of the structures were made of wood. Börje took us up a hill to view the Obelisk, known as the toothpick by Stockholm residents. From up there the view was unparalleled, as far as the eye could see were the islands, the shimmering water and the city spread at our feet. The streets were full of people on foot or driving honking their car horns in busy streets. The last days were frantic trying to cram as much as possible in a very short time. We visited the Isle of Knights and ran from one palace to the next, until at last I said, "No more Charlie, I cannot see another painting or another gilded salon. Let's get out of the city."

Our last day was spent in Uppsala, seventy kilometers north of the city. The university was impressive; we were told that it dated from 1477, and that it had been the main focus of the town for centuries. And we knew about the Nobel Prizes that had been awarded here for science, literature and humanitarian achievements. After that long walk across the campus,

Börje insisted on showing us the Rosersberg Slott, a seventeenth-century palace built by Gustave Vasa, a Swedish hero. By now Charlie and I were dragging our feet, but it was our last day with our friend. He had to go back to school after playing hooky for a week, so we agreed to see our last palace. It was stunning, a huge renaissance-style wedding cake sitting in the middle of a beautiful park.

Afterward, sitting in a small restaurant, the three of us ordered a hearty lunch of split pea soup and pancakes smothered in lingonberry sauce. It was difficult to walk after that. The three of us stayed a long while slumped on a bench facing the Fyrisan river, letting its beautiful silver water soothe our tired minds. Börje said good-bye to us. We promised to write and to keep in touch and so did he. Leaving, he waved back at us for a long time. We never saw or heard from him again. Sometimes I wonder what became of so many lost friends, and I dream of different futures for each one of them.

We had thought and turned the question over a hundred times in our minds: would we go as far as Kiruna? Looking at a map, it seemed so far away, the last city in the very north of Sweden, very close to the Finnish and Russian borders. It was going to be a long, long train ride. Was it worth it? For once I was less enthusiastic than Charlie. Would we have enough money then to go back all the way to Morocco? I did not feel that I could stay another six months working in a factory to make some money. At this point even Charlie had started to become homesick, but he argued that having come this far it would be silly not to make it above the Arctic Circle.

"Imagine," he said with a flourish, "coming back home to Casablanca like heroes."

It did not take much more to convince me. Charlie had such charisma, he described things so well. Once again I was under his spell.

Twelve hundred and thirty nine kilometers north! Seven hundred and ten miles, that's how far Kiruna was from Stockholm. Until the last moment we debated 'Go, or no go', and counted our money again and again. In the end we had to make up our minds and finally bought the train tickets, round trip from Stockholm to Kiruna and also a one way ticket from there back to Skövde, where we had left most of our stuff. We boarded the train early one morning, leaving behind us a gray and sleepy Stockholm. Once more we were going to live a great adventure. As the train jerked, whistled and rattled its way out of the station, both Charlie and I said, "*Ala bab Allah*" an Arabic sentence that could be translated as "At the mercy of God."

There was a stop in Mora where there was a switch of trains. I realized I had slept all the way from Stockholm and was surprised to see a beautiful lake as I opened my eyes.

"Lake Siljian," said a fellow passenger. "Good fishing," he confided.

We were now traveling on the Inlandsbanan train to the great North and Lapland. Inching our way north toward the mountains, the landscape became more rugged. There seemed to be water everywhere, swift rivers, white tumbling falls and crystal clear lakes, some iced over like mirrors. Green grass was pushing its way through patches of snow on the ground surrounded by pale birch trees and dark tongues of tall firs. Not a soul to be seen, not even animals. The feeling was of remoteness; the land was virgin, still untouched by humans and thus a little frightening in its cold beauty.

Toward evening the train slowed down along a huge lake. For some time now we had seen farms with their typical dark red painted barns and a few animals: horses, cows, dogs. The landscape was now alive and reassuring. The train stopped completely as we entered the town of Östersund. We were told to get off the train; nobody had warned us of this. Perhaps we had not understood what the ticket man was telling us in Stockholm. My Swedish was very basic. Though Charlie could make people believe his speech was fluent, he was not much better than I was. It seemed we had to spend the night here, a regular stop for the Inlandsbanan. After asking the controller, we were told that we could leave our stuff on the train; we would have the same seats tomorrow for the rest the trip. To us it seemed incongruous, we had no confidence at all in the honesty of the people around us, and coming from Morocco we were naturally suspicious. Nobody would do such a foolish thing in our country.

The first thing we were told coming down from the train was about the local monster. This was enough to spur our interest. Students coming out of school had attached themselves to us. In their faulty English they tried to tell us what was appealing in their city. It seemed the lake monster, which they called "Storsjöodjuret" was maybe a distant cousin of the well known Loch Ness monster. The youngsters dragged us down to the very edge of the lake telling us that if we looked intensely over the water we could get a glimpse of him. It was at the hour of sunset when the monster usually appeared and they added,

"You will recognize him immediately because he has a dog's head."

They left, running and laughing, and I wondered if they were pulling our leg. With a name like this he must really be terrible, Charlie said, not believing. In my halting Swedish I asked an old man who was there near us, staring at the lake.

"Yo, yo," he said, "it is true, we even have boat tours to see Störsjöodjuret."

The town was surely a vacation spot. There were bungalows dispersed here and there along the shore framed by a sinuous line of dark green firs. Other trees and bushes that bordered the lake were barely budding. flocks of birds followed the soft ripples on the pink-tinted water as the sun slowly sank into the lake. On the opposite side was a steep hill with an old church that was now barely visible in the invading cold blue dusk. We stared at all this beauty, mesmerized, holding ourselves tenderly by the shoulders. But no monster showed up. Too bad, it would have made our day.

There were no tourists in the streets. We had arrived out of season. Most of the attractions of that city were closed and would only reopen in mid June. The closest hotel was the Nyapensionatet, up a hill. It proved to be a good choice; the rooms were tastefully decorated if a bit old fashioned and the price was right.

We ate whatever we found in a konditory which sold coffee, cakes and sandwiches. It was a great pleasure to sink into that soft bed, after a long, hard day shaking on the seats of the Inlandbanan. Early morning we regretfully got out of bed, dressed promptly and had coffee and pastries at the station restaurant. Our train was there waiting, white steam from the engine billowing in flowery puffs. One more day and we would be in Kiruna.

It did not happen the way we had planned. Three Sami men came into our compartment dressed in their fantastic costumes of blue, red, and yellow embroidered felt, their bonnets adorned with tassels and pompons. The men were short and stocky, with red tanned faces and hands, small blue eyes and black hair. We kept staring at them and smiling to make it less obvious. Sure we had seen some Sami people before in Skövde, but they were dressed in regular clothes and it was not the same.

Charlie tried to engage them in a conversation. It was not easy, for these particular people spoke little Swedish and therefore they were difficult to understand. Their Sami language was more like Finnish, something totally foreign to us. As usual we used our hands and eyes, besides the little Swedish we spoke and all was well; in no time we made new friends.

Everyone on board seemed excited by the approach of the Arctic Circle and so were we. We made a stop in Storuman, a one-street town, and another one in Sorsele. Later on we stopped on average once every twenty minutes; reindeer were everywhere around us, but mostly on the tracks, and they had to be removed. There were also other reasons for stopping without warning; the conductor came to a halt just to jump down and pick up some spring flowers or some herbs. It seemed in full summertime it was even worse when there were many ripe berries to be had.

"Avidjaur, that's where we are going," said one of our Sami friends. "Big town, you should come with us."

"No, no," said the second man, "the place they absolutely have to see is Jokkmokk." And turning to us, "It is the capital of Samiland and it is also a trade market and a center for arts and crafts, very good, very good and so beautiful, the valley of the Lilla Luleälven, a little paradise, you go there, you see."

He looked so enthusiastic. I turned to Charlie with a question in my eyes.

"Well," he said. "I don't really know, I thought Kiruna was the place, but we could spend a night in Jokkmokk and see what it's all about. What do you think?"

It was OK with me, I was eager to see more of the Sami people in their superb costumes, and besides we could perhaps buy some souvenirs for the family. Secretly I thought it was a wonderful occasion to buy something striking for myself.

Passengers were all at the train windows; the conductor had slowed down to a snail's pace and the whistle blowing full blast was rending the cold air outside. At last we came to a full stop. The Arctic Circle! We scrambling down with the rest of the passengers like a herd of wild goats jumping here and there, putting earth in our pockets, even breaking off pieces of the white painted rocks that marked the place all the way over the distant hills. It was pure madness! Charlie and I were dancing around with total strangers, kissing and congratulating each other. We had made it in spite of everything; too bad our French friends had had to return to France so soon. I stopped a minute to think about them. Serge, Micheline, Claude. Where were they? probably in Paris and working, poor guys.

Soon after we were in Jokkmokk. The town was nestled in a very green valley, and tall trees lined the streets. Most of the houses were built of wood and painted in heavy varnished bright paint to ward off the cold. Their colors were bright yellows, greens, whites and even pinks. I was surprised at how mild the weather was compared to the towns we had passed further south. In a restaurant I inquired about this phenomenon and was told that the mild climate in Lapland was due to the gulfstream effect. Even during winter the temperatures would be higher in this northern region than in Stockholm. The town was full of Sami people in their very colorful costumes going about their business, which all centered around reindeer.

Soon we found stores where they sold their magnificent crafts. Charlie was fascinated by a long dagger with an intricately carved antler sheath. My eyes went to a pair of boots made of thick reindeer leather. Their shape was strange and appealing with an upturned tip, a red star inlay on the side of the boots, and to finish a leather tassel hanging from the top. It was too much, they were a little too expensive, but I told Charlie, who was eyeing me with disapproval, that they would last for years, and I bought them. In the end he also cracked for the dagger. Unfortunately our thought of buying whole Sami costumes was out of the question, much too expensive

The rest of our purchases consisted of souvenirs for the family and two Sami embroidered felt bonnets adorned with huge pompoms. Those we wore right away, to the delight of the passers-by. We spent two days in that fairy-tale town. We ran around as usual, trying to see as much as we could, from old Sami dwellings in the shape of truncated wooden triangles, to a morning on their lake with a local fisherman and a meal of grouse cooked with unknown dried berries, while mosquitoes were eating us alive.

Deciding to take another route to the next town, we climbed on one of their yellow buses for Gällivare. This turned out to be a larger industrial city with some very important iron and copper mines, but for us there was no good reason to stop here. It was raining when we got there. Everything was in shades of grey: the buildings, the trees, the road, even the people looked gray. After a brief stop at the bus station, we boarded another bus en route for Kiruna.

On the bus were a few young men and women on early vacations. They were naturally curious about us and we soon were chatting together as well as we could. They told us about the immensity of the Kiruna community and we could not believe it. Twenty thousand square miles, six thousand lakes, seven virgin rivers, and the highest mountain summit in Sweden, called Kebnekaise. To add to that astonishing fact, one of the women in the group added proudly, looking very serious,

"Statistically if all the inhabitants of the world were confined inside the border of Kiruna, each person would have four square meters to stand on."

She looked at us to see the effect. Charlie's eyes were rounded into wide saucer-like shapes and my mouth was open and hanging in disbelief. As we were nearing our destination, a glorious sun came out chasing the clouds away, welcoming us to our last northern city.

The first striking thing we saw upon arriving in Kiruna were two big black shapes barring the sky, one on each side of town. The sun was shining just behind the tip of one of these curious mountains, where steps had been carved all along one side, cutting a very strange profile against the bright sky. It was really bizarre to see the sun shining so late in the evening, that strange phenomenon, the midnight sun. We were facing one of the most important iron ore mines in the world.

Once more we lodged in a very old hotel near the train station, the "Fyra Vindar." Small, but cheap. The official summer season was starting only at the end of the month. For that reason rooms were still inexpensive. The youth hostel was still closed. The coming days were going to be exciting and surprise us both. In the morning, we found out the town itself was at the eastern end of the magnificent Luossajarvi lake. It was Sunday, and boats were already gliding on the glass-like water reflecting a pale blue sky and the dark mountains.

Later that same day we met a group of young Finns, all of whom worked in the iron ore mines. They were difficult to understand, only one of them spoke a little English, so everything had to be translated back and forth. They could not believe we had come from so far away, Africa.

"We are very proud to know you," they said, dragging us all around town to meet their friends. Charlie and I were letting ourselves be pampered. Free meals, where we sampled more of the the local fare, including some hot salted tea in which swam a piece of reindeer butter, and a dry flatbread accompanied with sweet reindeer "ost," a brownish cheese which was less than appetizing to my palate. Now I was beginning to seriously miss our good, spicy, aromatic Moroccan food.

For my part I had accomplished what I had set out to do, and I felt the pull of home – it was really time to go back. For almost a year I had tramped around without so much as a thought for my parents, my little sister Glad, and the only life I had known so far. Pangs of guilt were invading me for the first time in my life. I did not mention that spell of blues to Charlie, but he was no fool and he could sense my general mental fatigue.

Our new friends insisted on taking us around in an old jalopy that belonged to one of them; Ekki Mikkonen was his name. To us a name like that was as foreign as it could get. The first outing was an eighty-five kilometer ride to Kebnekaise mountain where we trekked all day looking at its curious lopsided snow-covered summit and got cold and exhausted. The next day I felt really very tired, but followed the group for a tour of the fabulous Kirunavaara, the world's largest iron mine. It was very impressive. The mine is almost five kilometers long and two kilometers deep.

Charlie was oppressed by the fact that we had gone so far underground, and I also was feeling queasy. It was good to get out of there. I could not imagine working day after day in that enormous black pit. We went for drinks in a nearby pub to chase the thought of all that darkness. Sitting on our bed that evening, I told Charlie that it was time to return home.

"I am not ready yet," he replied. "I understand how you feel, but we may never again come back to this part of the world. I didn't tell you before, but my plan is to go to Russia; we are very close to the frontier. It will be a cinch." He looked at me sideways to see my reaction. I exploded.

"Are you crazy or what? Russia? You can't mean it. You'll be taken prisoner immediately by Stalin's patrols and thrown into a Siberian jail to rot until the end of your days. What's gotten into you? You want me to go with you? No way. I will not enter the mouth of the dragon to be swallowed alive."

Charlie sulked all night, smoking cigarette upon cigarette, I was trying to find a way to dissuade him from going on that foolish trip. No love-making, no kisses and sweetness all that terrible night. The day after we were to go fishing on the big lake with Ekki and his friends. I told Charlie I could not go, I was coming down with a cold probably caught the day we climbed Kebnekaise. In reality I needed time to think out Charlie's monstrous idea of us going into Russia.

Eight o'clock in the evening and Charlie had not returned from the fishing outing. He was probably eating some dinner with our friends. I was tired after a long boring day of twisting my mind trying to find a solution to the problem. I fell asleep all dressed up on the couch. A honking car woke me up. The room was drenched in sunlight. Where was I? How late was it?

240

Looking around dizzily, I realized Charlie was not in the room. A sudden sharp thought tore through me; they had drowned in the lake. No, no this was impossible. Yesterday had been a beautiful day, just a little too breezy perhaps. While taking a warm shower, trying to calm down, I said aloud, 'He just went out early to get some hot coffee and pastries, to surprise me.' I waited an hour, no Charlie. Leaving a note on the night table, I ran down the stairs and asked the old man at the reception desk if had he seen Charlie.

"No," he said, "not this morning."

I was really at a loss as to where to go or who to ask. The natural thing would be to ask our friends the Finns, but they were working, far down in the iron mine. There was no way to get to them until they came out.

My decision then was to head straight to the lake and the boat shed. To see what? I did not know, but I would perhaps find somebody who had seen Ekki and Charlie yesterday. The boats were there, drying in the sun, drawn together, in mutual silence, keeping their secrets. Nobody in sight, only the immense shiny lake whose little waves spoke a language I could not understand. The void was immense; I realized how much I missed him. Charlie had become the other half of myself. For hours I walked, first along the water then back to town. Almost automatically I entered a nearby church, a wooden structure built half in Swedish and half in Sami architecture, a bizarre truncated triangle with two roofs. Inside I sat on one of the benches and thought very hard, closing my eyes. "Come back, Charlie."

Our room in the hotel was still empty when I returned. I started crying. could Charlie have really abandoned me, or was he dead somewhere at the bottom of the silent lake? Later I called on our friends; two of them shared a room in a small building. Ekki had not shown up at work today, they said; nobody knew where he was. They asked me to come for dinner, but I was not hungry. I went back to walking around town to sort things out. I felt very strange in that remote unfamiliar place, and the sun over my head so late in the evening made it even more alien.

One more sleepless night alone. I thought of going to the police the next day to report Charlie and Ekki's disappearance, but then thought better of it. It would certainly create more problems than solutions.

In the morning the truth hit me like a stone: Charlie had gone to Russia! Oh my God! I would never see him again. So he had gone without telling me, for fear I would stop him. What a fool, what a silly fool! I kept walking round and round the small room repeating these two sentences again and again. Late in the afternoon I made up my mind; I would wait two more days, which was actually the time we had set to go back to Skövde to get the rest of our gear before starting the long journey home.

Where was the money to pay for the hotel and the train tickets? A pang of panic caught at my stomach. Fumbling nervously through our bags I finally retrieved a yellowed envelope, opened it, counted it. Thank God most of the money was there. I fell in a lump on the floor and stayed there totally numbed by the sheer enormity of it all.

The last night was terrible; I was torn between wanting to stay and wait for Charlie to return (if he did return), and the decision I had made to leave in the morning. The bags were packed, my ticket was bought, I had already contacted the hotel with instructions; they were to keep Charlie's rucksack and some money from the envelope. At midnight sleep overcame me blissfully. I would take the morning train to Skövde.

I dreamed of water dripping on my head, running cold down my hair in rivulets and reaching my cheeks and lips; it woke me up. In the darkened room, at the far corner I heard the water running out of the wash basin. That was impossible, the faucet had been turned off all evening! Sliding out of bed barefoot I sleepily walked to the corner where the noise was coming from. I saw a shadow moving next to the sink and screamed at the top of my lungs with all the anguish that had built up during these last days.

"Anit, Anit, it's me Charlie, I did not want to wake you up, I just came back and wanted to wash up before going to bed."

At first I could not utter a word and stayed there rigid as an ice carving. Then I spoke.

"Do you realize what I went through while you were gone? Probably not, otherwise you would not have left me without a word of your plans."

I felt miserable, but at the same time so relieved that I decided on the spot to say nothing more and let him do the talking. He took both my hands and kissed them.

"Anit, Anit, yes I tried to do what I had in mind, that is, enter Russia. Ekki drove me to Munio, a small frontier town between Sweden and Finland. His parents live in a nearby community, that's where we slept. I knew that for the rest of the trip I would be on my own. We had driven about one hundred and fifty kilometers, but I still had almost three hundred left to the Russian border and no money to speak of. Ekki's father took me aside and told me how foolish I was to attempt such a ridiculous adventure.

'You will not find a ride that far north,' he said. There are numbers of lakes to cross, bogs, millions of mosquitoes, you'll get lost and then what? Let's say that you reach your destination. You do not stand a chance, you'll be picked up immediately by the Russian border patrols.'

I could hear the echo of your voice, Anit, and how right you were, please forgive me. I never intended to leave you, I would have contacted you somehow if I could. I realize now that you are a true friend and that I care very much for you."

I got up two hours later, hopped to the train station, and changed my ticket for the following day, at the same time buying one for Charlie. He was fast asleep when I came back. I slipped into the warm bed snuggling against him. The rest of the day was spent in a bliss of lovemaking. We forgot about Lapland, about the midnight sun, and everything around us. We could have been anywhere. That bed was the center of the world as far as we were concerned.

Chapter 20: 1950

The Return Home

That was it, we were leaving Lapland for good, perhaps never to come back. Charlie and I were glued to the train window for hours trying to absorb as much as we could of that strange land we had discovered and loved. Rolling steadily across mountains, rivers and plains, the train's motion finally put us to sleep.

With all that had happened before our departure, I had totally forgotten about bringing some food for the trip and found out to our dismay how expensive the restaurant was on board. Looking at our meager funds we decided to bypass Skövde and go directly to Göteborg; the things we had left in Skövde were really of no great value. We would write to our friends Gustav, Jacques, Irma, and the Eckarts to say our goodbyes.

Totally numbed by so many hours riding the train, we stepped out on the platform of the station at Göteborg stumbling, not knowing where to turn first in that big busy harbor city. Before going anywhere I suggested finding out about the fare from Sweden to the south of Spain. From there we would take the ferry to Tangier. The price quoted was staggering. Sure it was thousands of miles, but we had never imagined it to be so high. This was way beyond our means; what were we going to do now?

Finding a youth hostel came first; unfortunately the only one around was closed for repairs and the others were too far. Dragging our sacks out of the station we asked a porter if he knew of a cheap hotel nearby. He obliged, showing us where to go, pointing with his index finger as to which street and what turns to take. Before going to the hotel it was imperative to find some food. We only bought bread and milk to feed our ravenous appetite, when we could have devoured a whole side of beef after the very meager food we had eaten during the long train ride.

The hotel room we rented looked like a monastery cell, small and painted all white. Sitting on the tiny bed, the black iron frame creaked under our weight. Charlie said matter of factly:

"We have to sell something. Otherwise we're not going anywhere, we're trapped here."

"What do I have that I could sell?" I said fingering the chain that was hanging from my neck, "I really don't know."

"The chain!" Charlie yelled. "That's what we are going to sell."

My beautiful heavy gold chain with all the pearls, emeralds and priceless enamels, the very one Grandmother Nejma had given me before she died. How could I sell this princely jewel? I had worn it for two years now without ever taking it off my neck. I looked at Charlie with despair.

"I know, I know," he repeated, "but what else? I have nothing worth selling myself and we can't stay here, we will starve in the streets."

I looked at this beautiful city with horror as we walked the large boulevards the next day in search of a store that would buy my necklace. Asking questions here and there we were put back on the right track or so we thought, but it was hours of tramping around before we found ourselves in the fashionable neighborhood on Kungsporsavenyn where all the elegant stores were located. Entering jewelry stores and showing the necklace did not get us anywhere. The merchants looked at us with suspicion, thinking we had probably stolen the piece. I must say that our accoutrements were less than elegant, but our clothes were clean and neat. Nevertheless, to these people, we were suspect.

Three days had passed and nobody was buying. We had paid for only two nights of hotel; the whole thing now was getting to be frightening. At the end of these exhausting days, we fell on the bed like two logs thrown together on the creaking mattress. At least for the night we were free of worries, slumbering in a deep dreamless sleep. The morning saw us numb, not yet realizing what was ahead for that day, but after some dark coffee and a cold shower we were fully awake, and gave each other renewed courage.

The fourth day found us on the Götaplatsen south of the Avenyn, a large square with a sculpture of Poseidon strangling a shark. There we sat around noon, eating some black bread and herring, after having tried every jewelry store on our way that morning, but to no avail. In one of the stores a charitable lady gave us a lead, telling us to go to the old Göteborg neighborhood where they sold antiques. Too tired to walk the distance, we took a tram, crossed the Rosamund Canal and emerged in that old neighborhood. Some beautifully restored nineteenth-century houses seemed to be sleeping in their vast sunny gardens. The tree-lined streets were silent, as if they wanted to keep their secrets from passers-by. We only glanced rapidly at this tranquil place, not having the heart to stop and admire the sight. Neither did we visit any museums or churches we found on the way.

At the end of the afternoon, totally demoralized, we entered a somber little antique store and repeated to the merchant sitting behind his counter the same story for the hundredth time. He took the necklace and I saw his eyes light up in surprise; lifting his face, he said,

"This is a very fine piece. Where did you say it came from?"

"It was a present from my grandmother. At the time, she told me the necklace was rare. Eighteenth-century Florentine, and the chain is made with twenty-four carat gold." I spoke without stopping, afraid that he would change his mind. "As you can see it also has twelve round emeralds and as many pearls, not counting the enamels." I waited breathless for his answer.

"Young lady, I can see how valuable it is, but I could not in the world give the amount it is worth. I can only give you four hundred crowns, take it or leave it." He held the necklace high in front of my eyes, making the gold shine softly between the green lights cast by the emeralds and the iridescence of the lovely pearls.

Silent tears fell on my cheeks. I swallowed hard before I said in a strangled little voice,

"Alright, we will take the four hundred."

Charlie stood near me feeling uncomfortable, but said nothing.

That was it, the necklace was gone forever, but in reality there was nothing else we could have done. We had to get out of this town as fast as we could. Back in our miserable hotel we took great pleasure in packing as fast as we could. Thank God we were leaving this town.

The ferry trip From Göteborg was not very long, but for us it was memorable. As soon as we boarded the wind started blowing. At first there were short gray waves running tight together spewing angry white crests. The sky became darker and darker, the color of diluted ink. Our small boat was swaying dangerously in a fierce wind that tore at everything.

From inside the cabin, my face against a window, I witnessed a deluge of water running down the panes, when suddenly we pitched forward in an abrupt plunge, the passengers falling one on top of one another with loud screams.Fortunately, nobody was really hurt. We sat down on the floor and held each other to prevent injuries. Now we could see enormous waves riding above the ferry like liquid monsters trying to swallow us. It was very frightening; I wondered if this was an omen for the rest of our trip? No, these thoughts only came because I was tired with the tensions of the past days. I looked at Charlie; he also was very pale and tired from all we had gone through. Suddenly the motion on the boat was too much for him, he got sick and vomited, but so did many other passengers; it was a real mess.

Disembarking was not easy because the gangplank was dancing between its ropes and all of us travellers were weak in the legs after that rough crossing. Reaching firm soil felt good. Once again we were in Helsingør, but this time there were no thoughts of Hamlet's castle. Our only preoccupation was to get to Copenhagen and take the train back home.

In a half dream, the same landscapes we had seen more than six months ago filed in front of our tired eyes, reminding us of all we had experienced, the good and the bad. The only difference was that now the fields and the mountains were green with summer grasses and almost everywhere the ground was covered with lovely flowers. I had anticipated a stop in Amsterdam for its Rembrandt museum and another in Bruges for its medieval beauty and its beautiful handmade laces, but we couldn't go; it was too risky with so little money in our pockets and still a very long way to go.

Nearing Paris one late afternoon, the sun was casting bright orange light on the old gray buildings. I sighed, we would not revisit this magnificent city either, having just a limited time to catch a cab from the Gare du Nord to the Gare de Lyon, our train station going south, and then our connection to the Spanish border.

We passed more exhausting hours sitting in our second-class compartment. Having to deal with passengers climbing in and out at various stations did not help. To rest, I often closed my eyes, visualizing the beautiful open spaces we had walked, and mentally breathed the fresh and clean air of these wonderful places. By the time we reached Irun none of us could stand another hour in a train. During the long hours of traveling, Charlie and I had decided to walk a portion of Spain to remove the cramps from our legs.

From the station we went to the nearest grocery to buy huge Basque salami sandwiches, and walked to the nearby beach. There on the black rocks we undressed to a minimum and ran to plunge our tired bodies in the huge green waves. It felt so good to be washed by the powerful sea, I shouted with joy. Drying up on the sand was not too rewarding, for the breeze was cool on our wet bodies. It was impossible to dry completely and by now we were ravenous.

Time was running out. We ate our meal in a hurry, but with a lot of relish, before hitting the road. Our plan was to hop on a train again on our way to Algeciras. As we left the beach I turned around to look at the waves and remember their thunderous symphony.

All afternoon we walked. The sun was hot; it had been a long time, it seemed, since we had walked such a long trek. We passed villages and small towns, Deva, Motrica. Late in the evening our feet gave up; we stopped for the night in Elgoibar, a place with a strange name. It took two more days to reach Tolosa, where the next train would take us south. I swore I would not walk a step more.

Coming down the mountain passes had been beautiful. Up there summer was in full swing, shepherds and their flocks were seen in flowered meadows; occasionally we heard the sound of flutes in the distance. It was a wild and free part of the country.

The train we took in Tolosa was bound for Madrid. There again we had to change trains to go all the way to Algeciras at the very southern tip of Spain. To economize, we bought third class tickets and had to share quarters with peasants going to or returning from local markets. Fortunately they sang, played guitar and shared their food with us. They were such a lively and generous people, we almost forgot the unpleasant odors.

Passing through Seville, the weather became unpleasantly hot; already we could feel Africa was nearing. Both of us were wilting with heat and with fatigue. When the train controller announced Jerez de la Frontera I realized we were on the wrong train; the terminal on this line was Cadiz instead of Algeciras. Spontaneously we decided to get off in Jerez, go to the nearest winery and sample a glass or two of their famous sherry wine. Algeciras would have to wait. It was imperative, we thought, to enjoy the rest of our time in Spain.

Walking in the blinding sun we rounded the tower of a white ancient Moorish Alcazar; on the sidewalk tall palm trees rose to the indigo sky, their huge heavy leaves swaying in the hot breeze. The houses in Jerez de la Frontera looked like pieces of pink and white frilly candy ready to eat, giving the feel the town was always on holiday.

Finally after tramping half the town we found a recommended bodega not too far from the river Guadalquivir. It was an establishment locally renowned for their Jerez wines.

Noise and music drew us to a lush covered garden; a number of people were standing there drinking and laughing. As we hesitated to come in, they called to us. "Come in, Bienvenidos, come and drink with us." So we were invited in, and cheering with them drank their wonderful cold wine.

Servers brought tapas to the wooden tables, wonderful foods, olives, manchego cheese accompanied by big round breads, jamon serrano and linguisa to tempt any palate. We were in a bodega, but this was a private party; how lucky for us to have been invited in. Soon a wonderful feeling of relaxation invaded me. My stomach was full, I was finishing my third or fourth glass of wine and all that for free. Hooray for the Spaniards! Charlie was feeling so good he refused to leave; I almost had to drag him out of the place to catch our train.

In reality we had a little more time than I had told him. It was too hot to stay outside, so to keep cool we entered the gothic church of San Miguel de Santiago and there we sat in silence cooling off.

It was late evening before we entered Algeciras. A crescent moon painted the bay in soft silver; on the other side of the water was Morocco. It had taken us a long time, but we had made it. Tomorrow morning taking the ferry across the strait of Gibraltar to Tangier would be a cinch. Almost home, I beamed with joy.

Algeciras was a busy town, teeming with people. At this late time they were still sitting at cafe terraces, drinking wine or anise liqueur. Every little store was still open and business was going strong. Throngs of young girls arm-in-arm in rows of four or six were walking up and down the main street giggling, trying to attract the attention of boys talking in small groups. There was joy everywhere, it seemed.

We found a room in a seedy hotel, but so what, it was only for one night. Our money was almost gone, just enough to eat a meal tonight, buy the ferry tickets tomorrow and get a cab in Tangier to my cousin Solomon's. There we would ask him for some money to finish our journey. It was all very simple.

In the night I woke up thinking I was having a nightmare. The room was pitch black, but still I could see the white curtains twisting with a sort of fury. The shutters rattled with violence as if some strong man was trying to break in. I woke up Charlie who reluctantly went to the window.

"It's the wind." he said. "By tomorrow it will be OK." We both fell back into a deep and sweaty sleep.

Howling noises woke us up early; it was the feared and terrible wind the Spaniards called Levante. Nearly impossible to even walk outside, it was so strong. Painfully we made it to the pier to hear that no boat was getting out of the harbor that day and that it could be several days before the Levante gave up. We were faced with a dilemma; how many days were we going to be delayed?

Counting every penny for the hundredth time didn't change the amount left. No more hot meals for us; this little money was only going to buy us bread and olives for about three days. As for the hotel, we'd have to come up with a bright idea as to how to pay for the extra days of our stay.

"It's easy," I said suddenly. "Let's take some of the money to call cousin Solomon in Tangier; I am sure he will wire us the money immediately."

The wind did not abate and the money did not come. Our time was spent at the local post office checking every hour for the awaited telegram. I had plenty of time to think of how foolish we both were. Not even capable of managing such an important thing as money during the many months of our trip, that is, after we had departed Skövde. The fact that we were so close to Morocco and unable to get there was more than frustrating.

Pangs of panic knocked at my door; what if we did not get an answer from Tangier? What if my cousin was out of town, on vacation, perhaps? I kept all this to myself; it was no use to get Charlie more nervous than he was. We certainly could have wired our parents in Casablanca, but no, we both had agreed that we were going to give them the surprise of their lives by showing up unexpectedly, and nothing was going to spoil the grand finale of our fabulous trip. On the other hand, the real reason was that asking our parents for money would make us lose face, and we had to come back as heroes.

The third day toward evening the wind stopped, but still no telegram; I felt like crying. Sitting at the edge of the pier our bare feet dangling in the water, we were looking with despair at the fishing fleet getting ready to sail. Tomorrow morning the ferry would leave for Tangier without us.

The whole town was covered with debris from the wind storm; small tree branches littered the streets, and everything was covered in a fine dust. We dragged our feet back in town to the post office again. I had put on my Lapp boots, the only shoes I had for the trip. Several street kids were following, shouting obscenities at me. It was true that in Spain at the time women did not wear slacks or boots. All this was getting on my nerves, but I could not help laughing when a toddler shouted in his drawling Andalus accent, *"Si me da una patada en el culo con la punta de las botas, me sacca las tripas."* 'If she kicks me in the ass with the tip of her boots, she'll drag my guts out.'

Back to the post office with our heads down, tired and disgusted, we waited standing outside the open doors. By now, everybody there knew us, they were understanding, smiling and comforting. We heard a scream; turning around we saw the woman behind the counter shaking a piece of paper high above her head. *"El telegramo, ya vino!"* 'The telegram, it has arrived.'

It was like being hit with a heavy stone, we could not move, our mouths open in disbelief. Then we shot as fast as an arrow across the room, our arms flailing wildly, and almost tore the telegram out of the woman's hands.

All was secure, the money had come. We bought our tickets for the next morning's departure. That evening had no end, it seemed. Charlie bought a bottle of wine in a café. We sat there for hours discussing the return home and all it implied.

Only now that we were so close did we think of the reception we were going to get from our parents. After all, we had abandoned them selfishly for our own satisfaction. Now I realized what the impact of my departure had meant for them. Torment, no doubt, sleepless nights, and worries galore. Would I be welcome? I had to chase my somber thoughts in a hurry; nothing was going to mar our arrival home.

Stepping onto the soil of Morocco was an indescribable joy. We were splashed with vivid colors, the smell of spices, the green of palms and the multitude of flowers hanging over garden walls.

Cousin Solomon was there waiting for us in one of his many sports cars. What a wonderful guy he was, always acquiescing to my every whim. He was still in love with me, since I had seen him on my first vacation alone in Tangier in 1946. He offered to drive us to Casablanca the next day; he had business to do there. We were lucky that we did not have to

251

take another train for the rest of the trip. Driving through Tangier's narrow crooked streets, honking the car horn without stop, for the slow walking pedestrians never moved, I felt as if I had never left this land.

Speeding on the roads of Spanish Morocco was impossible. No repairs had been made for years, leaving gaping holes all over. By mid-morning the heat and dust took their toll; we stopped in a village and refreshed ourselves with cold Orangina sodas. Now entering French Morocco, we found ourselves driving on the good roads they had built along their portion of the country. Pushing the pedal all the way down, Solomon drove like a madman, literally flying. The towns of Souk el arba, Kenitra, and Rabat zoomed by and at three in the afternoon we entered Casablanca.

Emotions overwhelmed me. I felt a big lump in my throat and tears rolled down my dusty cheeks. Charlie took my hand and pressed it against his chest. It was his way to tell me how deep his feelings were. Neither of us could utter a word. What would happen next was like a big empty place to be filled. It depended a lot on how our parents would take the fact that we had lived together for a whole year. Certainly it would create a stir, and not a pleasant one for sure.

We dropped Charlie at the Place de Verdun near his home; his street was too narrow for a car to pass. I barely had time to say goodbye, but as he stepped out of the car he yelled:

"Tomorrow morning 10 AM at the Milk Bar" and he was gone. I had been with him every day for so long, it seemed inconceivable to be separated. He was going to his parents' home and I was going to mine and for the moment that was that. I had a dreadful moment of inner panic when Solomon left me at Place Edmond Doute in front of the building where father had his office.

"You are on your own now," he told me. "Good luck with your parents, I shall see them later."

Before I went up, I had a look at myself in the window of an adjacent store. I was shocked at my appearance, I looked like a wild man rather than a young lady. Disheveled short dusty hair, a wrinkled shirt, riding pants and my famous Lapp boots. The heavy rucksack I was carrying on my back made me look like one of the market's porters. Where was the fashionable young lady I had been? Gone forever? No, I did not think so. For the moment the only thing I could do was to run my fingers through my hair and wish for the best.

Climbing the dark staircase of the old building, my heart was beating a hundred kilometers an hour. I stopped in front of the frosted glass door, frozen, incapable of ringing the bell. Swallowing hard, I knocked. Father's secretary opened the door and her jaw fell.

"Oh! Mademoiselle Anit, ce n'est pas possible!"

The sun was drenching the sparsely furnished room through wide-open windows. Father's old Remington typewriter sat on a plain wooden table and reminded me how sober he was. The only luxury was a beautiful oil painting of a majestic sailing ship riding on dark green waves. Father always said, "This boat is coming home to bring my good fortune," and he really believed it would happen.

I could hear the noises coming up from the street, cars honking, the voice of an old peddler shouting his ware, children playing in the small nearby park.

"Where is Father?" I asked.

"Your father is coming back from lunch in about fifteen minutes and your mother called saying she was coming a little later."

"I am going to hide in your office," I told the secretary. "I want to surprise them."

The minutes passed very slowly. I couldn't stand it anymore, I was getting very nervous, my hands sweating. All of a sudden I heard his voice and could not contain myself anymore. Flinging the door open, I burst in yelling.

"Dad, Dad, it's me! I have come back!" and I threw myself in his arms. He was stunned, his mouth wide open, but no sounds came out for a whole minute. To me it seemed an eternity. Then he cried and hugged me again and again saying,

"Darling, darling let me look at you. You are fine I can see, you look stronger."

He then sat down as if exhausted. Fifteen minutes had not passed when I heard mother's steps coming down the hall on her high heels.

Father got up suddenly, very agitated, saying,

"How are we going to tell your mother? Please go into the other room and wait, I have to prepare her."

How sweet was her voice was when she entered the room. I heard Father telling her to sit down because he had some very good news to tell her. By then I could not wait anymore; I opened the door, and as I said,

"Maman," she fainted right where she stood, sliding slowly to the floor. I felt silly and shameful; it never dawned on me that I could have killed them both. After drinking some sugared water Maman smiled through the tears that were drowning her face. I put my arms around both of them and we started whirling around the office kissing, talking and singing all at once, while the secretary stood there watching us, totally flabbergasted.

My sister Glad and her husband Gabriel came home in the evening; more emotions. Then for hours into the night I told of my adventures. They were spellbound and could not believe all I had gone through. I was careful not to mention Charlie. I thought it not the right moment to speak about him. It would come soon enough, no use to spoil their joy at the moment.

The next morning at ten AM on the dot I entered the Milk Bar. Charlie was already there with all our friends. As I came in they lifted me up in the air as if I was some kind of trophy, and walked between tables shouting, 'She did it, they did it. They had the guts'. In the middle of applause and hip-hip hoorays we sat at a table and were invited to eat and drink anything we desired.

During the last portion of our trip Charlie and I had discussed several times the unpleasant fact that he had no job, that I was four years older than him, and that in Morocco fathers did not give their daughters in marriage to a penniless fellow. There was no way we could live together in Casablanca without being married. The thought was intolerable, but we had to deal with it. That morning after all the friends had gone home for some lunch, Charlie and I stayed at the Milk Bar. We sat at a little round table in the back, holding hands and looking deeply into each other's eyes. There was no need to speak; we knew instinctively that the moment had come. We had to separate. Where were all the future joys we had dreamt of together? It was a very heavy moment to swallow. We then decided to try not to see each other for one whole week and analyze our mutual feelings.

Summoning all the courage I could muster, I got up and said, "Goodbye Charlie," and left in a hurry, no longer able to hold back my tears.

Every hour of that first day was torture. At home nobody could understand why suddenly I looked so sad. I dared not speak to father about Charlie, knowing very well what would ensue. The second day was even worse; I went out and walked for hours trying to sort things out, but nothing made sense anymore. The third morning I could not stand it anymore and went straight to the Milk Bar. Would he be there perhaps?

As I rounded the Rue Poincaré, I saw him on the opposite sidewalk pacing like mad in front of the establishment. He then lifted his head and saw me.

"Anit, Anit," he shouted.

We flew to each other across the busy street, oblivious of the honking cars and collided like two trains at full speed. Together, we were back together. Charlie almost carried me to the sidewalk.

"I was about to go and brave your father when I saw you."

We saw each other every day after that, but we could not make love, except furtively on a deserted beach or in the Mimosa forest of Sidi Abderhaman under the heavy branches of yellow flowers. We could have been arrested and gone to jail if we were caught. These moments of passion were marred by the constant fright of being discovered.

Chapter 21: 1950

A Married Woman

It was around this time that I ran into Maurice, a distant cousin. He was accompanied by a lovely French girl that he introduced as his fiancee. When he asked why he had not seen me in such a long time, I told him my story. Maurice was a thirty five year old dandy, spoiled by the aunt that had raised him. I never thought he would be really interested in what I was telling him, but after hearing me, I was surprised to hear him say that he would do the utmost to help.

"First, I have to meet with Charlie," he said.

Things did not go exactly as planned. Before Maurice could do anything, Father received an anonymous letter saying that I was Charlie's mistress and that he had gone to Sweden with me. A long time after, I found out who had written that nasty letter to discredit me with my father. It was the same insane, jealous, unfulfilled young man that had years ago tried sorcery on me. He had spied on Charlie and me when we had spent some weekends together while my parents were on vacation.

Mother was waiting for me to come home that afternoon. She told me about the letter and warned me that father was in a madman's rage; he had taken his revolver and was going after Charlie to kill him. How I was going to confront him I had no idea. Here I was again in a cage, not able to move without parental approval, and I was almost twenty seven years old.

That evening father did not speak a word to me, only addressing Mother in brief sentences. His eyes were of steel, his lips retracted into a thin line. I could see his determination and got very scared. After dinner, in desperation I slipped away and called Maurice. He reassured me, saying he would phone tonight and request a meeting the next day in Father's office for some very important business.

In the days that had preceded the catastrophic letter, Maurice had met with Charlie and had found him to be a very charming, well-educated young man, quite suitable to marry the daughter of my snobbish father. He decided to contact Charlie immediately and bring him to the appointment.

The meeting between Father and cousin Maurice was set at two o'clock the next day. Mother was as anxious as I was. No use staying at home; we went out and walked rapidly for two hours without stopping.

I kept repeating, "It has to work."

And Mother kept replying, "I am sure it will turn out all right."

That night I saw my father beaming with joy. He kissed me as I came in. He said,

"I met Charlie today, what a charming lad, I had no idea! He will be working for me in the real estate business. He will do well, he is extremely intelligent. He asked for your hand in marriage, and everything is set. You are getting married this very December. You have little time to get ready."

I sat down, drained of all my strength. It was difficult to realize that my troubles were over.

We got married on December 20, 1950, after two months of frantic preparations. Mother went crazy to have my trousseau ready in time, hiring a number of dressmakers, tailors and embroiderers. My time was spent running around with Mother trying to find the best fabrics, from silk, satin and laces for the lingerie, to wool, velvets and more silks for dresses. After countless fittings the trousseau was finally finished.

Before the big day, there were several ceremonies. First, the reading of the marriage contract, the Ketouba, by two high ranking Rabbis, and the traditional Sephardic Jewish wedding at home, where I wore my grandmother's beautiful gown. This outfit had been passed down from generation to generation and was actually a ceremonial costume similar to ones ladies wore in fifteenth-century Spain. Such fineries as the long violet velvet skirt covered in heavy gold embroideries and the matching bolero made me look like the Queen of Sheba. My veiled head and my throat were covered with all the jewels in the family. That ceremony was called the Henna night. All the guests were anointed in the palm of their hands with a red henna paste for good luck.

Then came the civil wedding; it took place on December 16th at the Casablanca town hall. All the immediate family was there, my in-laws, Charlie's sisters and little brother, Lucien. On my side, there was Father and Mother, Glad and Gabriel and their twin children, my father's sister Mazaltob and my cousins, all six of them. All this was very formal. I did not feel totally at ease dressed in a strict pin-striped navy blue suit, nor did Charlie, who looked stiff in his expensive new clothes.

The night before the big day – the formal religious wedding – I was forced to go to the Hammam, a public bath, for a ritual cleansing. In this ordeal I was accompanied by my mother-in-law Gracia and her daughters. I thought of the irony of it all. It had been quite a while since I had lost my virginity. I would have to scrub down to the bones of my body in order to wash all my sins away.

The twentieth was a Wednesday and it was raining hard. The skies were lead gray, but the mood in our household was ebullient. The hairdresser was ready for me and the dressmaker was there waiting to fix or to stitch a last minute pleat in my magnificent pearled white satin dress. It had been made by Maurice's girlfriend, Jacqueline, who worked at Christian Dior, the fashionable couturier. She had risked a lot when she had smuggled a cloth pattern out of Dior's workshop to make the dress.

I came out of the shower and stood naked in front of the tall mirror in my bedroom, I had a good look at myself and thought that the minute I clothed myself in that beautiful white gown I would belong to another person. The thought was annoying, even disturbing. I was giving up a freedom that I cherished above all, to live my life with the man of my choice, but it also meant many more ties.

Glad, Maman, and two of my first cousins came to dress me, from the delicate lingerie to the final touch, the veil and a crown of fresh orange blossoms. A cascading bouquet of lilies in my gloved hands, I came down the marble stairs, the bridesmaids helping with the long train. Father, decked out in tails, was waiting downstairs. He scooped me up across the sidewalk in the pouring rain into the flowered limousine. All the neighbors had assembled on each side of our entrance door and were applauding. Before reaching the synagogue the whole retinue stopped at the photographer, where Charlie was waiting. This was an ordeal, but in those days photographers could not carry their heavy equipment around, at least in Morocco.

When the big doors of the synagogue opened I was stunned by the magnificence. The place was packed with friends and relatives, the women wearing long shimmering gowns and precious jewels, the men in dark elegant suits. Flowers were everywhere. As I entered with father holding my arm the choir started. I had requested a portion of the Peer Gynt opera by Grieg.

My new sister-in-law Helene sang a soprano solo. She had a beautiful voice. It all seemed so unreal. I felt I was acting on a stage, which was not completely untrue. Charlie, in tails and top hat, was waiting at the altar. He looked uncomfortable in the attire father had insisted he wear, and he looked agitated, perhaps because of the fright of such a commitment.

The glass was broken, we were officially married and walked down the aisle to the sound of Mendelsohn's Wedding March. The guests and family were congratulating, kissing, laughing; sugared almonds were distributed at the door in fancy white satin bags monogrammed A.C.

The wedding reception, a grand luncheon, was held at my mother-in-law Gracia's. She had outdone herself for the occasion by preparing Moroccan dishes fit for a king's table – a veritable mountain of delicious food. But neither Charlie nor I were hungry; we just wanted to get out of there and be on our own.

Our honeymoon destination was Spain. For the first night, Father had booked us a suite at the superb Balima Hotel in Rabat, the capital; he had also loaned us his second car, a small Citroen. Maurice and Jacqueline accompanied us all the way to Tangier and were going to return with the car. Rabat was not far, only one hundred kilometers from Casablanca. We had loaded the car with champagne bottles and other goodies for the road. It was about six o'clock in the evening when we left. I had changed my wedding dress for a suit and all our bags were ready for our honeymoon journey to Spain.

We drove recklessly and at frightening speeds, drinking champagne all the way even through dangerous curves on the road. We made it in about forty-five minutes; all of us were tipsy and in a tremendous good mood. The royal suite at the hotel was more luxurious than I expected, with all kinds of amenities. Father had sent an impressive bouquet of flowers.

The four of us sat on the huge ornate bed and continued drinking and nibbling on some petits-fours we had brought with us from the dessert table at the wedding. When the last bottle had been gulped we were very drunk and forgot everything.

The next morning, to my surprise I found myself all dressed up and lying on the wedding bed with Charlie, Maurice and Jacqueline all mingled together; certainly not a pretty sight. To top it all, as we left the hotel the manager ran after us to tell us that Father had not paid for the flowers, and the price was staggering, but after all it did not really matter; Charlie had already made a lot of money working with father in the real estate business. We were happy, free at last from the family and leaving for a fabulous trip.

It took several cups of very strong black coffee before we could drive to Tangier. We arrived at the pier just in time to catch the ferry, two hours to Algeciras in Spain where we were taking a fast train to Seville. Even though we arrived in Seville only a few days before Christmas, the weather was mild and sunny. We decided to really live it up and hired a young guitarist full time. He followed us everywhere, walking behind us in the streets playing Flamenco, sitting with us for hours at café terraces while we sipped a glass of Jeres with not a care in the world.

Christmas night was a somber affair in Seville; the streets were empty and the restaurants closed. We decided to walk to the ancient La Jiralda cathedral. Inside, the vibrating sounds of liturgical music on the powerful organ filled the high arches; the midnight mass was starting with all its pageantry. The high clergy wore vestments of gold and rich brocades in reds and purples as they walked solemnly down the aisle in a cloud of incense, while the choir in white lace and red robes sang heavenly psalms. In contrast to all this were the people, entering the church humbly, some crawling on their stomachs face down against the cold stone.

From Seville, we continued on to Madrid, where my cousin Jacobo received us like royalty. He lived here in grand style, having made a bundle in real estate. He gave us a chauffeured limousine for the duration of our stay, and as if this extravagance was not enough, he threw a Thousand and One Nights party to welcome us and to introduce us to his aristocratic friends. For the occasion, the stairs of his townhouse were lined with a double row of superb men holding torches and wearing turbans. The enormous living room had been fitted with a silk tent stuffed with rich cushions. Here and there lamps and statues wore precious necklaces, some with rare pearls, others with priceless emeralds and gold; the epitome of luxury. Looking at all this wealth, I could not help remembering father, who a few years back had loaned him twenty thousand francs to start a business; money Jacopo had never repaid.

Then came a fabulous New Year's Eve, where we milled in the streets among hundreds of merry people while eating the twelve grapes and counting the midnight hours, as was the custom in Madrid. We finished the night as Jacobo's guests in one of the grand hotels, eating, drinking hard and dancing crazily till the early hours of morning.

The next afternoon, sobered up, we realized how costly our honeymoon had been; we had splurged and spent all the fast money Charlie had made in the brief time between father's consent to our marriage and our honeymoon. It was time to return home. Nevertheless Charlie was confident the money would continue flowing when he started work again.

It was snowing and quite cold in Madrid the day we took a plane bound for Casablanca. All was fine for a while, but then fierce winds and a snowstorm buffeted our little two-engine plane. Shaken up, down, and sideways, it seemed the plane was going to disintegrate at any time. Passengers started to panic; a priest stood up holding the back of a seat. He started reading the prayers from his open breviary. I was deadly afraid and so was Charlie; we held hands tight, not believing that after that sumptuous honeymoon we were going to die just like that. At that moment the pilot's voice was heard.

"I promise to bring you safely to the ground. We will have to land somewhere around Seville. Pray for me."

We were going down fast, ripping through menacing gray clouds and deadly lightning, just above the trees now and then ripping through branches. Breathless, I squeezed Charlie's hand so hard his knuckles turned white. We did not look at each other any more, each of us contemplating death privately.

"Hold tight," came the shrill pilot's voice. "We're landing."

Eyes wide open I watched the earth nearing so fast it seemed an enormous wall was ready to crush us. We hit the ground with a tremendous bang, bang, bang. Screams filled the trembling cockpit. The evacuation was swift, and we found ourselves shaking in a muddy field under pouring rain, not believing we were still alive. An hour later we were driven into Seville where we drank ourselves silly in a downtown café. It wasn't our fate to die, and we were glad to be alive, but neither was it how I had imagined the beginning of our marriage.

The next day, shaken, but still wanting to get home, with some trepidation we boarded another plane for Casablanca.

Chapter 22: 1951-1953

America

In Casablanca the mood had changed abruptly during the short absence of our honeymoon. The political duel that had started a few years ago between the Nationalistic party led by the Sultan, Mohammed V, and the French Resident, General Juin, was getting worse. There were sporadic terrorist killings in the countryside and in most cities, creating panic among the non-Moslem population.

The price of property had dropped alarmingly; it had become difficult to sell the least parcel of land. To make things worse, the past summer drought and the recent winter floods in the south were complicating the economy even more. Country people were flocking to the big city to find work and survive. Casablanca was in a state of confusion, and with it came a shortage of apartments.

Charles decided we would stay at his parents for the time being, which was not to my liking at all. My in-laws were old fashioned and did not make life easy for us newlyweds. After a short while even Charlie could not stand it anymore. We left when Charlie had words with his father about the way we should conduct our lives.

Then started the apartment chase. The only available flats were sublets. One month here, three months there, and in between one night stands in hotels of all kinds. We were living like nomads and not too happy about it.

At the office, things were no better. Father could not keep Charlie as a partner. There was simply not enough work or money to be made. Suddenly we were poor and could not even afford a decent meal. To calm his nerves,

Charlie took up the bad habit of going out every night with his old buddies, leaving me alone to worry most of the night. I often cried, waiting for him at the window. This was not at all the married life I had imagined. Things had to change.

The summer of 1951 came and with it a new job for Charlie at the American air base in Nouasseur, at the outskirts of Casablanca. Our life became normal again, except that our parents meddled too much in our affairs. It had to be lunch every day at my folks, and lunch was the principal meal of the day. It was always a formal affair. Hors-d'oeuvres of all kinds covered the table, followed by an entrée, like a superbly spiced leg of lamb, roast potatoes, and vegetables, or a large fish cooked in a sauce, or grilled with various garnishes. For dessert, a basket of oranges, raw artichokes and in-season fresh almonds in their tender green robes. This was food fit for kings, but too much is too much. Lunch was at least a two hour affair, after which our only thought was to slumber on a couch.

Every evening, we had to have dinner at my in–laws. Same ritual, the food was rich, spicy, and plentiful. On Friday nights Charlie's entire family would be there. His eldest sister Nenette and her husband Simon, who eventually moved to Marseilles, were regulars. Nenette had been a straight A student at school, and she had a very sharp mind – and a sharp tongue to match. Next came Rosette, Charlie's middle sister, and her husband Charles. Rosette could always be counted on to liven things up – she was also the prettiest of the sisters and had a radiant smile and an infectious laugh. Helene, Charlie's youngest sister, was already my friend. She was also the most modern, much less traditional than her sisters. She had a beautiful body and a fabulous voice. The baby of the family was Lucien, whom we all called Lulu. At that time he was not quite ten years old. Lulu was a shy little boy, but already displayed an amazing talent for drawing and painting.

Charlie's grandmother Ima Zohra was there as well, a very soft spoken old lady, she must have been a great beauty in her youth. She had been married very young to a man who was a hero to the Jews of Meknes; he had led the defense of the community in several pogroms by Moslem terrorists against the Jews. She was herself a true warrior, making bullets for her husband. When he was murdered in one of the pogroms, she raised three daughters on her own.

Presiding over all of it were Charlie's parents. His father, Abraham, was all powerful in his household, strict, but not without a certain sense of humor. And his mother, Gracia, always busy serving her family, was a remarkable woman. She came from a family of scholars, and it was she who had insisted that all of her children not only go to school, but excel. Above everything, she was a master cook and baker, who taught me much of what I know about Moroccan cooking.

These dinners were also hours-long affairs. And we could not leave immediately after. and often fell asleep sitting at the table. It reached a point where, as much as we loved them, we felt were were being not so slowly suffocated by family. Around that time, I began thinking we should perhaps move out of Morocco, but where? France? England? America?

We had to make a decision to leave sooner or later, not only because of what was happening with our parents, but also for reasons of security. The country was in real turmoil; people were getting knifed in the streets almost every day now. Bombs were thrown under cars, killing families.

The Moroccan Moslems were hard against the French Colonialists, wanting their independence at any cost. In 1952, after Sultan Mohammed V reaffirmed his intention of independence, and bloody riots sprung up in Casablanca on the seventh and eighth of December, the crisis exploded like an overfilled balloon.

The presiding French authorities, with the help of a powerful man, Tami El Glaoui, the feudal master of Morocco's South and the Sultan's arch enemy, deposed the Sultan. He was exiled with his family first to Corsica, then to the far away island of Madagascar. His cousin Ibn Arafa, a puppet in the pay of the French, replaced him.

By the end of 1952, many Jewish families had emigrated, fearing the worst. The wealthy to France, Canada and the United States, the poor to Israel. Some French Christian families were also reluctantly returning to France. Contemplating the idea of emigration, we also had to weigh the pros and cons of leaving our country for good. Other than the political unrest and our little family affairs, we realized what a good life we had here.

The country was beautiful, our life had become easy, we had servants, we ate well and we had made good friends. My second cousin Maurice, who had made our wedding possible, had married his young fiancée Jacqueline. We saw each other almost daily. Another dear friend, David Levy, had married a German refugee, Mary. The six of us became inseparable. David was one of the rich young men in town. His mother owned a renowned hotel, restaurant and nightclub. On Sundays we all went on memorable picnics, and the evenings were spent at each other's homes, but also often in David's nightclub, where we stayed until the wee hours of morning dancing the fiery Bambas and the languid Tangos.

One evening at the nightclub, David and Mary announced they were taking a vacation to California, where her parents now lived.

California! Hollywood! What a dream. We envied our friends. How lucky they were to travel so far, to those fabulous places. While we were excitedly conversing on the subject, David turned to me and said,

"Why don't you and Charlie join us there? I haven't told mother, but we actually intend to stay in California and start a restaurant in the heart of Hollywood. The four of us could do it together."

I looked at Charlie, questioning him with my eyes. Suddenly the future seemed simple and new horizons opened before me, but Charlie seemed hesitant; he was not so sure about the whole venture.

"It's not a bad idea," Charlie said, "but we cannot decide just like that, you know. I have a good job now. Sure, the country is unstable, but still I have to think about it."

From that day on, I worked on Charlie, trying to convince him to go. We did not have the money to be equal partners in that future restaurant, but we were two very talented beings and could be real assets to our friends. Since before the war, we had been fed American movies with all their extravagances. Seriously, I thought that life in the United States was similar to the beautiful images seen on the screen. To me everything was possible in America.

Our friends left for the States in February 1953, after making us promise that we would join them. Charlie had finally been convinced to go, but we had no idea how difficult it was to emigrate to the United States. We had to have an affidavit from an American citizen, vouching that we would not be welfare cases, in case things went wrong. I wrote several letters to our friends, the soldiers that had come to dinner every Wednesday night after the Americans had landed here in 1942. They regularly corresponded with Father every Christmas, but so many years had passed since the war that I only had a faint idea of what their life was like today. Could they, or would they, help?

With a Moroccan passport, it was almost impossible to enter the U.S. Fortunately I had been born in England, and Charlie was employed by the U.S. Army. This seemed to soften the progression of our visas. What we did not know at the time was that American authorities were totally engulfed in McCarthyism, and were acting accordingly. We were interrogated again and again, to find out if we had any affiliations with the Communist party. They were so suspicious and made us feel so uncomfortable, even though we both had nothing to hide. Despite the continuous harassment at the American consulate, I did not despair; we were going to America no matter how long it took. While waiting for our papers, we had to think about how to raise the money for such a long journey.

Both Charlie's parents and my parents had refused to give us any funds for a trip they did not approve of. On the other hand, they said, "If you stay, we will buy you a house and a brand new car," but our minds were made up, we were going. No bribe was going to tempt us.

Selling my trousseau was one way I made money, but it created a scandal. Mother was crying almost every day; how could I do such a thing? It had cost father a small fortune to have all these beautiful tablecloths and towels hand embroidered, besides the countless pairs of silk underwear ornamented with the most expensive lace. The culmination came when Charlie and I sold our wedding presents; people in town said we were totally crazy. We had no respect for anything. All this did not matter to us at all, because in thought we were already far away, on the other side of the ocean.

Finally we had all our papers. The affidavit arrived from our soldier friend John Vergis, now a professor of history in Los Angeles. We had our visas and enough money for our travel. All seemed perfect. It was the beginning of April 1953. We had booked passage on the U.S.S. Constitution, a large ship leaving on the fourth of April from Gibraltar.

The bad news came days before our departure. It was a letter from our friends David and Mary. They were coming back to Casablanca. David's mother had threatened to disinherit him if they remained in California. What a blow. What were we to do now? Charles was somber.

"It's all your fault," he accused me. "These ideas of going to America were yours, and you finally convinced me. Look where we are now."

I thought for a moment.

"There are no real reasons for us not to go," I finally replied, trying to soothe him. "I have some family in the States, a great uncle and aunt and several cousins. Some of them live in New York and the rest of them In Los Angeles. I am sure they will be of some help. Anyway, we have our tickets. We cannot afford to lose that. Come on, smile."

A dreadful ten minutes passed before he answered,

"All right, we will go. I cannot afford to lose face with my parents and my friends. You are right, we will find a way; come here and give me a kiss."

The day of departure was dramatic. Tears came down the faces of our respective mothers, blessings came from our fathers. As we left the house, water and coins were thrown behind us. Turning our heads back at the sound meant that we would return one day – an old Moroccan custom.

Maurice and Jacqueline were accompanying us all the way to Gibraltar. We drove father's big Citroen to Tangier almost without stop. The weather was beautiful, the whole countryside wearing fresh spring green, and everywhere flowers were hanging from garden walls.

In Tangier, cousins and aunts went out of their way to make us feel welcome, treating us to banquets and long rides to the mountains and sparkling beaches. They wanted to show this young adventurous couple how beautiful life was in Morocco. They did not understand our thirst to discover and experience a new land. We went up to El Marshan, that rich old neighborhood up the mountain to say goodbye to Grandfather Leopold. His palace gates were closed. The new groundskeeper told us that grandfather was traveling in Italy. I had really wanted Charles to meet my very special grandfather. In New York we were going to meet his youngest brother Benjamin and his family.

At last we took the ferry to Gibraltar. Maurice and Jacqueline were encouraging us and kept us in high spirits during that short crossing. As we sailed, I remembered the time we had sailed the same waters last, coming back from Sweden. It was only three years ago, but it seemed eons.

Gibraltar was a curious town. Most of the inhabitants were Spaniards, with a good sprinkling of Jews, and of course the English. Everything here looked old and decrepit, including the hotel we stayed in; the type that had naked bulbs hanging precariously from a peeling ceiling. The streets were crowded with sailors of many nations and tourists in transit to America or to the French Riviera and Italy.

We followed the bizarre mix of people up the mountain, whose Arabic name is *Jebal Tarik*, mountain of Tarik. We emerged on a sort of wooded plateau and were bewildered by the hundreds of monkeys who dwelled there. They seemed used to the contact of tourists and were begging for food with loud cries. Things were different on the south side of the plateau; no monkeys there, but a stiff rifled British soldier walking his beat. Underneath

267

him was the mighty fortress the Britons had built in 1704, making them the masters of the Mediterranean.

April 4th - we boarded early in the morning. The Constitution was an imposing black-hulled ship. I felt small, insignificant in front of that mass; for a brief moment I fully realized that we were really going for good; there was no return now. Maurice and Jacqueline had only a few moments to say goodbye. Both were crying. We had gone through so many joys and hardships together. Were we ever going to see them again?

Slowly the ship moved away from the pier where our cousins were frantically waving little kerchiefs. They became smaller and smaller until they disappeared. We were at sea. I had never sailed on such a big ship. The smells of food drifting from the kitchens and the whiff of floor polish made me uncomfortable. Charlie was already sick with the slow movement of the ship; I saw him running to the rail in a hurry.

Six days of sailing. After passing the archipelago of the Azores there was nothing but water and sky. Each time I walked the bridge for exercise, anxiety set in; claustrophobia invaded me. The ship looked so small in that immense ocean. Perhaps I also had apprehensions about that new country we really knew so little about.

As a distraction, Charles and I engaged in all the activites on board, including the Captain's Night, a costume party, where some of the guests would appear in plays and dances. We were in line for their dance contest. We came dressed in seedy 'French Apache' fashion, where a pimp and a prostitute whirl together to a sad refrain. The dance finishes with a fight for the money the prostitute has stashed in her stocking. Nothing to do with the real Apaches though; to this day I have never found out why the French riffraff was called by the name of an American Indian tribe.

It was a great success, especially when Charlie threw me on the floor, sliding on the parquet across the room, as a finale. We won first prize for the costumes and the originality of the dance. From then to the rest of the trip, we became celebrities on board and forgot most of our worries.

Was I dreaming of a foghorn or was it real? I got up half asleep and walked to the porthole. Blinking through it, I saw black waters reflecting city lights. My God! We had arrived.

"Charlie wake up, we are in New York!"

Jumping into our clothes, we both rushed to the nearest railing where we found hundreds of people already there huddled together. The ship was gliding very slowly toward the pier. The sun was coming up at the horizon, a faint pale glow, trying hard to pierce the dying night. And then suddenly, there she was, torch in hand in the budding dawn, the Statue of Liberty. A goddess of promises standing in all her glory, lighting the way. Majestically the ship moved in front of her. I was speechless with emotion. Charlie had his arm around my shoulders, squeezing tight. What did the Statue of Liberty really mean to each of us immigrants? Turning around to look at other passengers' faces, I deduced it meant something different for each of us, depending on our origins and the culture we had been brought up in. Certainly a new life was beginning. It was as if we were born a second time.

As we approached the pier, the multitude of high-rise buildings grew larger and larger, a city of giants standing close to each other like an army. The power of it all was disquieting. Somewhere on the pier, mother's first cousin Harold was waiting for us, but I had no idea what he looked like; we had corresponded briefly in order to have his parents' correct address and had forgotten to ask for his description.

It took a long time to get our luggage. All the while we kept wandering through a crowd of disembarked passengers, looking for a sign of our cousin. More than an hour passed, we had gone through customs, our passports had been stamped and still no sign of Harold. As we were coming out to the street, we saw a little man standing in the wind, holding his felt hat with one hand; he looked anxious. Somehow I had the feeling it was him. We started walking toward each other at the same moment.

"I've been looking for you everywhere," he said. "Where were you? As I saw you coming out I recognized a family air. Anit, you resemble your mother."

We embraced and I introduced him to Charlie. The family lived on Twentieth Street very near Gramercy Park. As we sped across Manhattan, Charlie and I were dazed by the spectacle. Sidewalks black with people, dark buildings, cars by the thousands in a cloud of appalling noise. Through the glass window I tried to find a piece of sky, but couldn't, it was out of reach, too high above those immense skyscrapers.

Harold had booked a hotel for us, the Gramercy, facing the park. The hotel had probably seen better days in the nineteenth century, but it was only for a week. Suddenly we felt so tired, nothing mattered anymore. We just had to sleep. Later on that afternoon, Harold came back for us to take us to dinner at his parents'.

I had met both my great aunt and uncle, their oldest son Edmond, and their youngest daughter Gloria when I was five years old. They were visiting from the United States and staying at my grandparents' palace in Nice. In those days, before the crash and the war, the whole family was immensely rich. I really did not remember much about them, except for a tantrum my then seventeen-year-old cousin Gloria had thrown. I had looked at her thinking she had very bad manners and was horrified by her screams. All this horrible show because her father had said no to one of her extravagances.

Tonight was a reacquaintance. I believed they were as curious about us as we were about them. As soon as we entered the plush apartment, they plied us with questions. Why had we come to the United States? Did we have a job lined up? Who gave us the affidavit to enter the States?

I thought this was a strange way to greet us. Were they suspicious? Did they think we might ask them for money? We were not used to direct questions of the sort. In Morocco sticky personal questions were always coated with sugar. I also felt that we were looked upon like exotic animals. To them, Morocco was so remote and wild. They were astonished at how well we spoke English, though with an accent of course. On the other hand, neither Charles nor I could easily understand their American speech. We had to concentrate to follow the conversation. I told Charlie later on, when we were alone, that they all sounded like quacking ducks, especially the women. We had a good laugh at our private little joke.

I had time to observe my American family while sitting at the dinner table. Simita, my great aunt, was still a beauty at her age; tall, very straight, with the most exquisite face and manners. She was the centerpiece of the household and knew it. On the other hand, my great uncle Benjamin was a short, bald, bespectacled, and much older man. He kept squinting at his wife adoringly across the table. I knew from family tales that throughout their married life he had always treated her like a queen. While discreetly looking at each of the hosts, my eyes lingered on the costly lace tablecloth, the china, the silver. But to my surprise there were only crystal tumblers for water. No wine glasses and no wine!

The food was brought to the table with great ceremony by a very old black woman. It was too bland and colorless for our taste; we missed the spices we had been accustomed to at home. I closed my eyes for a minute or so with a vision of the wonderful meals at home that we had so often criticized. There was nothing I could do to change things now. I turned my attention to the old servant Maria. She looked interesting. Her face resembled a raisin in a white kerchief. She welcomed us with a large toothless smile and later told us that she had come from a Portuguese colony in Africa. She had been purchased as a very young girl and brought to Portugal. She had been freed and brought to America, and had been in the service of Simita and Benjamin since the boys were very young, and she felt she was part of the family. I took an instant liking to her and promised myself to befriend her.

As we started eating, I noticed our American family ate with one hand under the table. How strange! At home both hands had to be on the table for good manners. The silver also seemed to be displayed differently on each side of our plates. I kept sending furtive glances to Charlie sitting at the end of the table, to see how he was doing.

Edmond, Harold's older brother, and his wife Beverly were sitting directly in front of me. He looked somber and morose, while on the contrary Beverly looked frivolous, constantly shaking her beautiful strawberry blonde hair. She also was very voluble and talked without stop about her French ancestry in New Orleans with obvious pride. It looked like she was trying to impress us.

Harold, who sat next to me, proved to be the warmest person in the family. He had a crisp sense of humor, was a little bohemian in his dress and manners, and looked carefree and entertaining. Too bad he had a crippled arm and a drooping eye, the result of a childhood accident, I was told. My great uncle and aunt seemed ashamed of him; I could see the way they behaved with him, and I deplored it.

After a long dinner, I felt very tired and wished I were in bed, but we had to endure. Simita was pulling out some old photographs. We gathered around a low table to look at them. Many were of my grandmother Nejma and my grandfather Leopold, whose brother Benjamin was our host tonight. We spoke at length of our family relations. Strangely enough, I was related on both sides. Simita, besides being my great aunt, was Nejma's niece and therefore also a first cousin of mine, once removed.

That night, bobbing on the too-soft mattress, I dreamt that I was floating on enormous waves in the middle of a storm. In the morning I woke up totally groggy. Charles did not seem to have been affected at all by our lumpy bed; as a matter of fact he was still snoring hard at nine o'clock.

"Hey, Charlie, wake up! Do you realize we're in New York?" His eyes barely opened, and I repeated, "Yes, in New York."

He sprung out of bed like a jack-in-the-box and said,

"What time is it? Oh my God, I'll get dressed in a jiffy, I am starving."

New York; to us the name itself sounded like a whirlwind. So much to see, to do, and where to start? We had a map, but when one knows nothing of a city, it is still a gamble. So we walked and walked and walked, street after street, bewildered by the crowds bumping each other on the sidewalks. Why was everybody in such a hurry? Why was steam billowing from holes in the ground? What was underground? We soon found out. Going down a flight of dirty broken stairs, we emerged behind an old decrepit platform. People were standing in line buying tickets for a train, so we watched for a few minutes. Suddenly the whole station rattled; a fierce wind blew my kerchief off. I thought I was hallucinating when a long series of wildly painted cars entered the station full speed. The New York subway. It wasn't pretty!

The next day our goal was to see Fifth Avenue. There I stood under a street sign as Charlie took my picture for our families in Morocco, to show them we were really in the United States. By now my poor feet were already full of blisters, but we continued on, after eating a hot dog for the first time at a corner stand. To us the name hot dog was ridiculously funny. Later, we found ourselves in front of the Metropolitan Museum. Impressive. Inside we both collapsed on a bench, but then we were curious to visit and started walking again. Meandering through halls of statues, paintings and more paintings, we could barely stand on our feet when I suddenly stopped in front of two enormous 17th century tapestries.

"Charlie look, I can't believe it."

"What's so extraordinary?" he asked.

"Read what it says: 'From the Benguiat collection'. That's Grandfather Leopold and his brothers! These tapestries must be worth a fortune. Can you imagine? I could have inherited all this if it weren't for the 1929 crash. And here we are with almost no money to our names."

Charlie was silent while digesting that. The week in New York went very fast, running from the East River to the Hudson and from the Statue of Liberty to Harlem and beyond. It had been strange and exciting, as if we had been uplifted each day, transported by eddies of wind, dust, and noise all twisted together through countless streets and spiraling up and down skyscrapers.

One event I'll never forget was when we stopped, in front of Macy's store windows. Row upon row of small boxes showed images of people and things moving like in the cinema. We stood there, two idiots, open mouthed, not understanding. We were seeing television for the first time.

We spent he day before our departure for California saying goodbyes to the family, packing suitcases and getting a last glimpse of the fabulous city. Harold, whom we had seen many times during our stay, took us to Grand Central station where we boarded a train to Chicago and from there to Los Angeles on the Yellow Chief.

It was difficult to describe the feelings we both had at the mention of names like New York, Chicago, California. Names that had nourished our youth, that in our minds were almost unattainable, and yet here we were, in the very places we had dreamed of for so long. Unfortunately, we had no time to visit Chicago, only two hours between trains. This was too little time to venture out of the station, in a city we knew nothing of but the name and the fame.

The trip from Chicago on to the west was tiring, for it lasted three days and nights. We also had very little money to spend in the dining room car, only enough for one meal a day, keeping the bread for the rest of the day or evening. On the other hand, the scenery was grandiose. Our eyes, glued to the window during all our waking hours, drank in the rolling cornfields of Iowa, the Mississippi, where I felt the excitement of an explorer, then the Platte river and Nebraska's vast plains, where we were surprised by the amount of snow on the ground, the last week of April.

The train stopped in other cities with strange names: Omaha and Cheyenne, Indian names that evoked cowboy movies, John Wayne and the like. Our eyes were tired, our bodies cramped, but still we looked at the passing scenery every day from sun up until the skies and the earth faded into a blue mist. One morning we woke up high in the Rocky Mountains; a passenger mentioned that we had just gone over the Continental Divide. I had no idea what it meant and was ashamed to ask, silly me. Later on that day the train whistled past Salt Lake City; from a distance we could see the mighty Temple. It impressed us, but we had no idea who the Mormons were. We had occasionally seen pairs of young missionaries in the streets of Casablanca, giving away little books, without thinking much of it.

After a glimpse at the southern tip of the Great Salt Lake, I was amazed at the sudden change of scenery. The green slopes of the Wasatch mountains had given way to an arid high plateau, the Great Basin. Almost no trees, reddish cliffs as far as the eyes could see, the ground covered with a wild silver gray plant I had never seen before. Sage, somebody next to me said. We did not see Las Vegas when the train stopped there late at night. It would take a few more years before we discovered this totally artificial city that sparkled like a multi-faceted diamond in the middle of nowhere.

The excitement mounted that morning, the last day of our trip, as we traveled through the incredible Mohave desert with its mirages, bald mountains and emptiness. Anticipating our arrival, we were already nervously closing our bags, changing our tired clothes, refreshing our faces with cologne. Again the scenery changed, the forested San Bernardino Mountains and miles upon miles of orange groves left us speechless. What riches, what beauty. This was California. I could not believe we had crossed a whole continent. The train slowed while it went through the worst portion of Los Angeles. Factories, ramshackle houses, beaten up roads. My God, what had we gotten into? I did not know what to think. I was even afraid to look at Charlie. What a horrible place. Could this really be Los Angeles?

We entered the station. After stepping out, looking around, it did not seem so bad after all. The great hall was in the Spanish style of architecture, and a big yellow sun was pouring through large arched windows. Outside, huge palm trees swayed in the warm breeze, and I was reassured. Both Charlie and I started looking for Gloria, Harold's sister. She was coming to get us, as was arranged in New York before our departure. A dark blue limousine slowly came to a stop along the curb. Out came a uniformed chauffeur; I saw him look around once, then he came toward us and said,

"Are you miss Anit?" and nodding at Charlie, "The gentleman must be your husband, then. I am here to drive you to your cousin's mansion."

I looked at him in disbelief. Was this really for us? What luxury! My whole idea of Los Angeles rotated a hundred and eighty degrees. I had been so scared of the city's ugliness when the train was pulling in.

We drove miles upon miles, going west through what seemed to be several towns and neighborhoods, some horrendous and some very decent. At last we came to the plush, exclusive and manicured streets of Beverly Hills and pulled into a driveway leading to an enormous Normandy-style manor. The driveway was almost blocked by several other cars: a convertible Jaguar, a black Cadillac and a utility car perhaps belonging to the gardener who was coming out of the fenced garden as we pulled in.

Charlie rang the bell; we did not know what to expect, so both of us were somewhat nervous. The door opened, framing a tall woman elegantly dressed in flapping creamy silk pants and matching top. It was Gloria. I recognized her at once, even though she was much older than when I had seen her last. She had her mother's lovely face, but her eyes were hard and haughty. She mumbled something like,

"Welcome. I didn't expect you so soon. Make yourselves comfortable. If you're hungry look in the fridge, you'll find things to make sandwiches," she said, and abruptly left the living room where we were standing.

We stood silent in that huge room for a few minutes, not knowing what to do or where to turn next. What a reception! To us it was outrageous. Here we were arriving from so far away, expecting family style hugs and kisses or at least warm greetings, but nothing, not even a smile. Gloria should have at least shown us how to get around in the house; we certainly did not know where the kitchen was, for one thing. Anyhow, we were not brought up to raid refrigerators.

Charlie was not in a good mood, and I did not know how to make heads or tails of such a reception. We looked around at the overstuffed sofas and armchairs, covered in bold flowery chintz, mounds of cushions everywhere, high vaulted ceilings and cathedral windows. On the walls were a few paintings of doubtful origin, and lots of knick-knacks and ashtrays on top of glass and mahogany tables. I suggested we might as well walk around and visit the house on our own; nobody else seemed to be around.

After going upstairs, looking into a few nondescript rooms, we found a bathroom, which we needed badly, then down again and into what looked like an office. There we sat on leather chairs staring at walls covered with copper plaques and two gold records. I had vaguely heard that Paul, Gloria's husband, had something to do with movies, but had no idea in what capacity.

Childrens voices caught our attention. They were coming from behind the curtained windows. Pushing them aside, we looked into a lush garden and a vast blue pool, where two boys around eight to ten years old were fighting in the water with loud screams. I looked at my watch. Almost six in the afternoon. We were starving.

The door opened suddenly. Gloria stepped in.

"You're still there? Oh my God! I had completely forgotten about you. Did you eat something? No? But why not? Let me go and make you some sandwiches, follow me to the kitchen."

Gloria had no idea where we really came from. In Morocco, guests and especially family would be welcomed with loud good wishes to start, then fed a banquet that had taken a week to prepare, and to finish would be offered beautiful presents. Here everything was so foreign, so cold, so impersonal, it made us very uncomfortable.

In the kitchen Gloria slapped together slices of a cottony white bread, smeared with mayonnaise from a jar, something I had never seen, then she stuffed the whole thing with pale slices of ham.

"Here you are, this will keep you for a few hours. Paul and I are invited for dinner tonight, so we will not see you. By the way, you are not sleeping here. I'm giving you the keys to my mother-in-law's apartment. She is traveling. The place is only a few blocks from here. You'll come tomorrow for dinner, but anyhow feel free to use the pool anytime. Let's go outside, I want you to meet the boys."

The garden was lush with exotic pacific flower bushes we had never seen before. Tall trees made a natural fence against curious neighbors, a pool house at the other end was open, inviting guests to a luxurious setting. Here were the two sons Gloria had mentioned, splashing furiously in that enormous pool. Charlie and I, holding hands, were speechless. This was really the Hollywood we had seen in the movies, the place we had dreamed about for so long. My feelings were mixed. I was part of all this now, but was I really? I longed to be alone with Charlie to discuss all we had seen that first day. It seemed enormous.

Guy and Roger came out of the pool at their mother's command to say hello, but they both looked uninterested by our arrival and went right back into the water. The sun was going down behind the pool house, splashing pink and orange tints into the fading blue sky. A cool breeze running through the palm fronds made me shiver. I was tired and wished for a good bed. Gloria called the chauffeur to drive us to our new residence. As we were leaving, I got a glimpse of Paul, Gloria's husband. Tall, gray haired, slightly stooped. He waved at us with a tired hand. Strange people, I thought.

I noticed that the streets were perfectly clean, not a piece of paper flying around. The mansions we passed looked like toys in an expensive store that spoke of riches beyond imagination. Not a soul walked the wide tree lined streets. It all looked like theater decor.

It had been a very long and eventful day; still, we were not sleepy when we entered the plush modern apartment. We talked deep into the night about the day's happenings. How foreign we felt in this new country, particularly here in this part of California, even though the climate and specifically the light was the same as the part of Morocco we came from. Would we adapt? How long would it take? After all, we had played all our cards on this venture; we could not afford to be losers.

The succeeding days were full of surprises, some bad and some good. Finding how expensive a cup of coffee was in a Beverly Hills drug store, or paying five dollars for a lousy shoe brush was appalling. How could such simple things be so expensive? Before going out every morning we counted our little money with concern. On the other hand, had I not stayed in this fancy neighborhood, I would have never collided with the actress Greer Garson at the corner of Roxbury Drive and Wilshire Avenue. I gaped in disbelief as she apologized for having stepped on my foot.

The crowning moment of it all came a few days later while shopping at Ralph's market. I was slowly pushing a cart through the aisles wondering at all the unknown items on the shelves when I stopped short. Who was next to me but Bogey! Yes, Humphrey Bogart in person, carrying a basket. I was dazed, thinking, I am really in the land of dreams, I wish they could all see me now, my sister, Mother, Father, my friends. I was surely going to write them about it, but I knew they would never believe me.

A week passed in the utter luxury of our borrowed apartment. We slept and made love on satin sheets. A maid in a dainty uniform came every morning to serve us breakfast on the finest English china, then silently cleaned the rooms and left. What a difference with our noisy Moroccan maids who banged into everything as they passed.

Our days passed idly exploring the neighborhood, peeking inside elegant stores and hotels, staring at fabulous cars and people, but also trying to find the least expensive places to eat every day. We never once had the idea to go beyond Beverly Hills after my cousin Gloria declared early on that there was nothing worth seeing outside of that community, and she had added, "It is even dangerous!"

Timidly we took advantage of Gloria's pool and garden, but seldom ventured inside the mansion. We finally met Paul Francis Webster, Gloria's husband. Indeed he was famous as a lyricist; his songs were played everywhere. "Secret Love," sung by Doris Day, would be released later that year, and win him the first of his three Academy Awards (he was nominated for sixteen Oscars over his career). He was presently finishing the lyrics for

"Seven Lonely Days" with Alden and Earl Shuman. Marshal Brown was also coming to the house to work on the song. From the garden I could hear the piano and their endless discussions.

"Anit, Charles, you're invited to…" The rest of the sentence was swallowed by Gloria coming out of the kitchen with her mouth full of a sandwich she was carrying on a paper napkin. "Sorry!" she said, wiping her mouth. "I am giving a reception this coming Thursday for the debut of Paul's new song. Of course you'll be there; guests will be arriving at seven PM. Enjoy the pool, I have to run, see you then."

My first thought was what we were going to wear for that evening? I had no idea what the dress code was here in California for such an occasion. I had not brought any evening gowns and Charlie's dressiest attire was a dark suit, not very appropriate for the climate here. Our meager finances definitely did not allow for spending on such items as evening clothes.

Oh, well.

Seven-thirty Thursday evening, we were standing in front of Gloria and Paul's mansion. The driveway and sidewalk were full of expensive cars, glinting in the light of a glorious sunset. The doors to the house were open; from inside came the sounds of loud voices, laughter and the clinking of glasses. I looked at Charles; he looked at me and together we said, "Let's go."

The place looked grand tonight, huge exotic flower bouquets had been placed strategically under superb lamps for maximum effect. Other lights came down from the cathedral ceiling, enveloping the whole room in a pinkish glow, but the most interesting thing here was the people. I was mesmerized! Doris Day, Gloria's neighbor, was running across the room holding a full glass, almost tripping on her long flowered skirt; my God she looked like a kid with almost no makeup on.

"Charles, look at her tiny waist," I said.

"Lovely," he said, his eyes not missing a thing.

Gloria was coming toward us with two glasses full.

"Let me introduce you to my friend Rosemary Clooney," she said. At this point I felt a little lost, all these famous people, it was too much at once. Timidly at first we went around and introduced ourselves to such icons as Louis Jourdan, the French actor, who was also one of Gloria's neighbors, and to other actors, songwriters and composers. Oscar Levant was sitting at the piano hitting some notes with two fingers; he looked pensive, almost sad.

I said, "May I?" and sat next to him, not too close. "I would love to hear something you wrote."

"Do you know that playing some of my work could ruin me in a crowd like this one?" he said. "The critics are ferocious."

So there was fear among all that glitter. Now I noticed how the women were looking at each other. Envy for a glittering diamond necklace, mean looks towards a beautiful silk gown or a young wrinkle-free face. The men were more discreet toward each other, drowning their feelings in glasses and glasses of Scotch and other liquor, plunging their half-drowned eyes into the outrageous décolletage the women wore. Strange crowd, I thought, another world altogether to us. We were transplanted from an archaic land, to this whirlwind of fast money, this superficial unreal spot in the world. Toward the end of the evening, the noise became appalling. The music, the drunken voices yelling across the room, the uncontrollable loud laughter. We had had our fill and decided to sneak out unnoticed.

One morning toward the end of the month Gloria called.

"I am inviting you both for lunch. Here is the address of the restaurant, I am sure you'll like it. Twelve noon."

She hung up. She never had invited us to a restaurant before. What could she possibly want from us? We had finished lunch and were enjoying a lush dessert of fancy ice cream when Gloria said abruptly,

"You'll have to leave the apartment this coming week, my mother-in-law is coming back from her cruise. I thought I would tell you today to give you time to look for something else."

I could not swallow the piece of cookie I had in my mouth and made a horrible noise with my throat. Charles, who was facing me, suddenly looked like a melting wax figure. It was awful news, but in a few moments we composed ourselves and I said with a forced smile,

"We're not worried, I'm sure we'll find an apartment in a few days; we are grateful for all you have done for us, thank you."

What Gloria did not know was that we had spent ninety eight percent of our money and did not know where to go or what to do. She had never once asked if we had come with enough money to survive or counseled us how to go about finding a job. As with many other very rich people, she never thought of how the other half lived.

Sleepless nights followed that fateful day. We plunged into piles of newspaper want ads from morning to night, looking for jobs. The American jargon was difficult to understand; a puzzle we had to decipher that complicated matters.

For my part, I had really never had a serious job before, except perhaps for a very brief time in that toy factory with the nasty owner and his crazy dog, and that short time at the clothing factory in Sweden. That was a long time ago. I had no idea what to do and wasn't skilled in anything except painting and sewing. Charles was not much better. Before our wedding, he had briefly worked as a clerk for a notion wholesaler, as a teller in a Casablanca bank, in father's real estate business, and finally at the army base, but nothing concrete or long term.

Finally, Charlie called a friend from Morocco who had settled in Los Angeles the year before. He was managing a ribbon factory and reluctantly agreed to employ Charlie, who of course knew nothing about ribbon making. At the interview with the manufacturer's big boss, Charlie had to lie, saying he had majored in chemistry when asked if he was skilled in mixing colors for the ribbon dyes.

I, on the other hand, found a job in one of my specialties, sewing. The factory was located in East LA, at the corner of an ugly, run-down street, the same type of street we had passed a month ago when arriving by train; the kind of place that back then had sunken my hopes.

Inside the factory was not much better, with its cavernous, badly lit rooms. Women of all ages bent to their work with only one thing in mind; making as many pieces as they could, whether it be sleeves, collars or any other part of the garment they had been assigned. Sewing machines were going full speed, filling the air with the roar of a hundred engines. I was taken around by an employee, who explained to me the various stations. We finished the tour in a hot and steamy area were they pressed the finished dresses. The whole thing was scary. I could not picture myself there with these poor miserable people. My job would be to hand-sew snaps on piles of dresses heaped on a table. My wage would be one cent per snap!

I started that same day. By five o'clock I had not made fifty cents. How these women could sew so fast was beyond me. What was I going to tell Charlie when I got home? Home now, by the way, was a joke; we had found a grayish room with a kitchenette for rent in a not-so-good section of Hollywood.

I cried all the way back from the factory, but when I saw Charlie, I burst out laughing. A real clown. He was standing there in the middle of that miserable room covered in a multitude of colored dyes and sparkles, from his hair to his shoes. My laughter was not appreciated at all. He looked at me furiously and banged the door as he entered the bathroom to take a much-needed shower. Later, all cleaned up, we sat with a bowl of canned soup and told each other the miseries we had endured that day.

By the end of May I was out of a job and so was Charlie. I could not sew snaps fast enough. In Morocco I had been taught refined sewing. Here it was a different story altogether. At the factory, the Mexican women were making fun of me and my fine couture ways.

"We sew snaps with one lousy thread in each hole and who cares if it doesn't hold," they told me. As for Charlie, he had had several fights with his friend the manager, who was a little runt wanting to play big boss. This did not sit well at all with him.

One of our nightmares was not to be able to pay the rent at the end of the month. The days passed, once again peeling through newspapers in search of jobs, a boring but necessary pastime. Every day, food was another problem we had to face. At the supermarket we always looked for the cheapest items. Once I came home with a can of cheap ground meat, heated it, ate it and found it tasted pretty good, and so did Charlie, only to find out the next day that we had eaten dog food!

But we also made love a lot; it was wonderful and did not cost a penny. Both of us had come a long way together; we remembered the hard times in Sweden and how we had succeeded. There was no reason we could not make it here, but beautiful California could be cruel too.

The next jobs we landed were going to be the good ones, we thought. Charles knew it was going to be hard work, but the pay was adequate. I was employed in a large factory as a cutter and I considered it an upgrade.

The way we came back home every night is almost impossible to describe; 'Dead meat' is the phrase that comes closest to the way we felt. How terrible was the fate of the manual workers in this country, no better than in third world countries. Charles was lifting fifty pound cans of Dutch Boy paint all day long, with half an hour for lunch and two ten minute breaks in eight hours of slavery. I had to stand up walking around a twenty foot table, machine-cutting thirty or forty layers of cloth following a pattern, and deadly afraid to make one mistake. At night my poor swollen feet made me cry in pain and my handsomely built young husband was broken up and moaned till morning.

My cousins seemed to have totally forgotten about us; not even a phone call. This meant that we had very little social life; Gloria and Paul were at that time the only people we knew in Los Angeles. But life has its bizarre ways of doing things. Looking through the papers one Sunday, Charles saw an ad for a Bastille Day celebration at the French Consulate. It was to be a costume party; how exciting. We absolutely had to go.

By this time we were both on our third jobs, I as a sample maker at a sportswear manufacturer, and Charles working in a sawmill. It was a half step up from the horrible places we had worked before. We had found a wonderful house for rent between Sunset Boulevard and Fountain Street. The owner was an old Chinese man who lived next-door and practiced Tai Chi Chuan every morning in his narrow garden.

To us the house was almost paradise compared to the cheap flimsy apartment we had first rented. It had hardwood floors on which we danced Flamenco every night, hitting the floor hard with our heels. It was wonderful; we could make all the noise we wanted, and we did. Behind the kitchen window was a small yard, all overgrown with flowering bushes and a very tall palm tree. Inside, the house had almost no furniture; a bed, a couch in the living room, a table with four chairs in the dining area and that was all. But the rooms were large, with lots of windows. The bizarre thing about that place was the old streetcar that came by several times a day, passing almost flush with our back garden fence, each time making all the plates and cups rattle on the shelves.

We were actively preparing for the Bastille Day bash, deciding to wear our beautiful Moroccan costumes for the occasion. The French Consulate was pretty far from where we lived and public transportation was very bad in LA at the time. It was time to look into buying a car, and we soon found one to our liking and within our budget: A light blue Buick sedan. We had the down payment, but when the dealer asked if we had any credit and we said no, he would not sell us the car. That way of doing business was totally foreign to us. In Morocco you had to pay cash and that's what we had intended to do.

The next day Charles broke his eyeglasses. We found an optometrist somewhere on Fairfax Avenue who told us to pay a deposit, giving us credit for the rest of the amount to be paid when retrieving the merchandise.

It was that simple; for a lousy twenty five dollars we now had a credit history with which to buy a car.

Bastille Day, or rather night, was going to be full of surprises. At the Consulate the reception rooms were already full of noisy guests in their various costumes. Champagne was free and so were the delicious foods artistically displayed on long tables. It all looked superb, but we did not know a single person in that crowd. I was a little jealous of the several joyous groups around us. In the beginning we were not aware of the stares and the comments about us, but soon people came to compliment us on the beauty and the authenticity of our costumes, asking all kinds of questions about Morocco. At the time our country was a remote place on the map for Americans. As we were walking about, chatting with our new acquaintances, a woman walked up to me.

"I have been looking for you everywhere. You are Dina's daughter, are you not?"

I had stopped, letting Charles and the others continue.

"No, I am sorry, I am not who you are looking for," I replied.

She had a puzzled look on her face.

"Funny," she said. "I could have sworn you were her. Let me introduce myself. I'm Beulah Roth. You have an accent – could I ask you where you are from?"

"I come from Morocco. That is why I thought of wearing this costume."

"Magnificent. Would you mind if I walk with you for a bit? You have such a charming accent."

She was a strange person, probably in her fifties, very intense. Her way of dressing was somewhat extravagant but at the same time chic.

"I am looking for my husband, I lost him in the crowd. Let's find him together. He is Sanford Roth. You know, the photographer."

No, I did not know him, I told her; she looked surprised. By this time we had joined with Charlie, whom I introduced to her. She seemed fascinated by his good looks and his manner, especially when he kissed her hand.

"What a charming couple," she kept repeating. "I am sure Sanford will be as excited as I am."

At this time we heard a man's voice through the loudspeaker.

"Messieurs, Mesdames, et Mesdemoiselles. Ladies and Gentlemen, we are now announcing the prizes for best costumes. Premier prix, First prize. Mr. and Mrs. Charles Bohbot, for the beauty and authenticity of their costumes. Please come forward."

Did I hear it right, did we really win first prize? As we pushed our way through the crowd, I kept repeating, "We are coming, we are coming." They marched us solemnly around the main ballroom while the guests applauded with frenzy.

Beulah and her husband, who had rejoined her, came to congratulate us, and she said,

"Would you like to come to our home for a glass of champagne?"

"We would be delighted," Charlie replied. Off we went to the discovery of another stratum of Los Angeles society.

Beulah and Sanford lived in West Hollywood, in a big white two-storied house nestled among high trees and lush flower bushes. Inside, every object upon each piece of furniture was there to catch the eye and to complement one another. Obviously these people had traveled a lot and were discriminating in their tastes. They seemed to carry a sort of snobbishness in everything they did and said, and boasted about spending six months out of the year in Europe. As we were sipping their good Champagne that evening, they thought to impress us with the names of renowned French people they had met in Paris.

"Sanford photographs so many famous people," she said in her approximate French, "Jean Cocteau is one of our friends, you know, and just before coming back this spring we met Jean Paul Sartre and Simone de Beauvoir. Marvelous people," she continued, reverting to English.

It was all very interesting, but neither Charles nor I were truly impressed. We also had seen these two bigger than life writers in 1949 in Paris. The only difference was that we had not spoken to them. Despite their apparent snobbishness, Sanford and Beulah were really good people. We became good friends, but with a twist: to them we were more like the children they had never had. They invited us to join them at galas, fabulous concerts, charity balls, and even séances conducted by the renowned writer Aldous Huxley.

The trouble was, I had no wardrobe to go to places like these. I had to wear Beulah's silk dresses that she insisted on giving me, and those were definitely not to my taste. In Morocco I was always elegantly dressed, but here I had no money for such extravagances. It made me feel insecure, but when I saw what interest these fancy people showed while we were talking, I forgot all about the dresses and shoes that were not mine.

It was now Christmastime. While driving in Hollywood Charlie made a stupid left turn and ran into a streetcar. The door on his side was torn apart by the impact. Miraculously he was not hurt, but both of us were really shaken up. On top of all the bad luck that day we had to deal with the cops and a stiff fine. The door was tied with a heavy rope for quite a while; the price of repair was beyond our means. Beulah and Sanford had invited us to a big birthday gala in Brentwood. We had to park our mutilated car at least ten blocks from the mansion for fear the guests would see us arrive in such unstylish transportation.

That evening was also memorable for other details. The place was in the Hollywood grand style. The house, a mixture of Rococo and Spanish with Greek columns, was painted all white like a huge illuminated meringue cake. Sanford and Beulah were waiting for us; we spotted them among a crowd of guests milling in the garden. It was actually more a park than a simple garden. I could see huge trees and many flowered alleys in the darkening distance.

Women looked like royal peacocks, wearing sumptuous long gowns, their priceless jewels glittering under the hanging Chinese lanterns. More subdued men wore tuxedos in dark blues and blacks. I walked through a lush dream-like garden and almost expected to encounter a fairy around a grass knoll.

Beulah was pulling my arm.

"Darling, I have to introduce you to so and so, they are divine and they are dying to meet you and your so-handsome half."

All this was going on while we were snatching delicate hors-d'oeuvres off dainty trays, the best Caviar, the smoothest foie gras. I stopped in front of a table reserved only for smoked salmon. What attracted me there was a huge ice carving of a siren maiden playing in the waves. I had never seen ice carvings like this before, and there was even more to discover. Looking around for the bar, I came upon a marble fountain where cherubs and nymphs were pouring champagne, blowing the bubbly wine through their pursed lips. Turning around, I found myself alone. Where was Charlie? We had been separated somehow, being channeled here and there by various guests. I entered the big house looking for him, went up the grand staircase. There he was, surrounded by a handful of people.

"Charlie!" I called waving my hand. "I am here."

Silently he made a gesture, inviting me to join. I had no idea what I was in for. Those elegant guests pushed us against the wall, trapping us as if they were hunters cornering a quarry. They came closer and closer asking the weirdest questions. I was wondering what was going on when Charlie whispered in my ear.

"I told them we came from Morocco."

So that was it. We were really looked upon as some exotic creatures.

"Let's play their game," I whispered back.

"Are you married?" a gentleman asked Charlie.

"Oh yes I am, I have several wives and this is my favorite," he said taking me tenderly by the waist.

"You do not mind your husband having many wives?" a lady asked me, opening big round eyes. "I would be so jealous, I couldn't stand it." She recoiled in horror.

"Is Morocco in Africa?" asked another man. When Charlie answered it was, he got all excited.

"Do you have monkeys in your town?"

"We even have lions," I said jokingly.

"Did you hear that darling," he said, turning to his wife, "they have lions!"

I was ready to burst out laughing. We finally escaped that strange group and found ourselves in the garden once more. There was a crowd toasting the hostess, a very old lady dressed like a queen in gold lace, her neck and white hair sparkling with diamonds. Champagne glasses were raised. A gentleman spoke.

"We are commemorating my good friend Ursula's ninetieth birthday tonight. For this occasion she is giving one million dollars to her favorite charity, to build a cemetery for cats and dogs."

I almost fell to the ground. This was a fortune. Coming from a country where there were few pets, and most animals either worked or were raised for food, I thought this was the craziest thing I had heard so far. I thought about all the poor people that would have been so happy with a fraction of a fraction of that sum. The enormity of it all stayed with me for days. People here were freer to do as they pleased. Finally, they were better than us to their pets.

We were now at the very end of 1953. So many things had happened in this past year, it seemed like more than ten years had elapsed. From our ardent wish to leave Morocco for the glitter of America, to the long days of travel, the discovery of new lands, and the meeting of strange people.

One of the gentlemen we had met the night of that big party was a producer. He had been attracted by Charlie's good looks, foreign accent, and suave manner, and had asked him to come to his studio for a screen test. Charlie never made it big in the movies, but he did appear in a couple of pictures, and continued to act in and direct live theater.

As for me, what did the future hold? So many opportunities were open to me now. Sewing professionally, becoming a fine artist, a chef, a yogini, having children. All of these and more would be in my future. I knew that my insistence to come to America had been the right thing to do. My life would continue to be very exciting, I knew it, I felt it very strongly. This was the country of adventure I had dreamt of for so long, that all my experiences and wanderings had led me to, and this would be my home.

THE END

Made in the USA
San Bernardino, CA
16 August 2017